Heart AND Steel

Heart AND Steel

BILL COWHER

WITH MICHAEL HOLLEY

ATRIA BOOKS

New York London Toronto Sydney New Delhi

ATRIA
BOOKS

An Imprint of Simon & Schuster, Inc.
1230 Avenue of the Americas
New York, NY 10020

First Atria Books hardcover edition June 2021

ATRIA BOOKS and colophon are trademarks of Simon & Schuster, Inc.

For information about special discounts for bulk purchases, please contact Simon &
Schuster Special Sales at 1-866-506-1949 or business@simonandschuster.com.

The Simon & Schuster Speakers Bureau can bring authors to your live event. For
more information, or to book an event, contact the Simon & Schuster Speakers
Bureau at 1-866-248-3049 or visit our website at www.simonspeakers.com.

Interior design by Silverglass

Manufactured in the United States of America

1 3 5 7 9 10 8 6 4 2

Library of Congress Control Number: 2021933992

ISBN 978-1-9821-7579-5
ISBN 978-1-9821-7581-8 (ebook)

To my parents, Laird and Dorothy Cowher: Thank you for showing me the true values of life: work, appreciation, and love.

To Kaye, Meagan, Lauren, and Lindsay: I'm fortunate that I experienced so much of this journey with all of you. You're the backbone of all I've done, and your collective support—and presence—allowed me to experience professional success and growth. I love you more than words can express.

To Marty Schottenheimer and Dan Rooney, my mentors in football and life: Your principles gave me things to aspire to, and helped me become the man I am today.

To my wife, Veronica: Thank you for your unwavering support, love, and inspiration. With you, I can always see what's important in life. I look forward to the next phase that we travel together.

Contents

FOREWORD

Bill Cowher stood out to me, even before we met the first time. After the 1991 NFL season, with the retirement of Chuck Noll, my father and I began the task of finding the next head coach of the Pittsburgh Steelers. There were several names on the list of coaches we wanted to interview, but Bill's relative youth caught my eye.

At thirty-four years old, he was the youngest candidate. Initially, I wondered if we'd even bring him in for an interview. When we eventually did, he stood out for different reasons. His passion for and love of football quickly filled the room. There was never a doubt about his ability to stand before a group of young men and hold their interest and attention. That was true on the first day we hired him, in January 1992, and that tireless drive remained for each of his fifteen seasons as the Steelers' head coach.

As a member of the Steelers' Hall of Honor and the Pro Football Hall of Fame, Bill is obviously an exceptional coach, teacher, and leader. He's also an incredible family man. I saw up close how he successfully managed the demands of coaching while maintaining his family-first perspective. There are many reasons Bill and my father, Dan Rooney, shared a special relationship. I believe that their emphasis on family was a major one, and it gave them a connection that was far deeper than the game they both loved.

I can vividly remember my childhood when my father and my grandfather, known affectionately as The Chief, worked hard to make pro football into the year-round popular sport it is today. Back then, they were determined to transform a humble league (the Steelers' equipment was stored in my grandfather's basement in the offseason) into one that became part of a city's and nation's traditions. It was a big assignment, but even with that, I saw how my dad balanced marriage and parenting nine kids with work. His work with the Steelers and the league was important, but so was family time. He never changed, even when the Steelers became an iconic organization in pro sports.

That type of stability is important to Bill, too. I saw him at work and admired him there, just like the rest of Pittsburgh did. He was our representative: a regular Pittsburgh guy from a regular Pittsburgh neighborhood. Like many of us, he and his family made time for all Steelers games during football season. His dad was in Crafton, listening to Myron Cope on the radio, and my dad did the same thing on the North Side. Even Bill's last name plays perfectly with the Pittsburgh accent. Bill Khour. We knew he was one of us, and he cared as much as we did. He poured a lot of time—and himself—into coaching the Steelers. The team's history and legacy mattered to him.

I also saw him with his wife and daughters, and how they brought out another side of him. He has three daughters, and so do I (along with a son). Our kids are all around the same ages, so Bill and I watched our kids grow up together. And we saw each other grow as men. I realized that, as thrilling as Steelers games were for him, he was even happier when he watched Meagan, Lauren, and Lindsay compete in their sports. It was nice to see him go to NFL meetings and have his family on the trips with him.

One of the things you can say about Bill is that, simply, he's a winner. His teams made the playoffs the first six seasons of his career, and after his fourth season, he became the youngest coach to lead his team to a Super Bowl. We played in some of the league's biggest games during his fifteen seasons, including Super Bowl XL, when we won the fifth of our six Lombardi trophies. Clearly, Bill was the right coach at the right time for the Steelers.

As you'll see in the pages that follow, Bill is a winner away from football as well. His story's path is not typical nor smooth. He was a good athlete who played college and pro football, but not without adversity. He coached his hometown team and won a championship, but there were some sobering lessons learned along the way. And just a few years after the end of his coaching career, he and his family leaned on faith and one another after receiving sudden heartbreaking news. Bill has been through a lot, and through it all he has continually shown strength, compassion, and love. I'm glad I got the chance to work with Bill with the Steelers, and developed a friendship that has lasted long after his time on the sideline. There are so many things I could say about him. After reading his memoir, you'll see what I mean.

—Art Rooney II, President, Pittsburgh Steelers

Author's Note

I grew up fifteen minutes from old Three Rivers Stadium, and for fifteen seasons I had the privilege of being the head coach of my hometown team. Pittsburgh Steelers fans likely remember me as the excitable and emotional man on the sideline. They saw me run up to players, practically nose to nose, and make some point—either with joy or disappointment—and do it with *emphasis*. The more animated I was, the more jut there was to my jaw. It became a bit of a hallmark. Many times, older ladies approached me in Greater Pittsburgh grocery stores to deliver a message: They liked it when the TV cameras caught me yelling.

I *was* that passionate coach who wasn't afraid to raise his voice. But I also had other gears. Those layers were critical for someone who wanted to coach young men and be trusted enough to lead them. I also needed different dimensions at home with my wife and daughters. The four of them understood that every new season meant that I'd give a lot of myself to the job—but they didn't expect me to give all of myself to pro football. I was constantly balancing who I was as an aspiring championship coach and who I was and wanted to be as an engaged husband and father.

In the following pages, I'll take you inside both of those journeys, in football and life. I'll share who I am and the surprising paths I took to get here. I'll tell you about the mountaintop moments, the humbling valleys, and everything in between. I'm hopeful that you'll come away with a deeper appreciation for all the people who do contribute and have contributed to football and family over the years. Their stories are a lot more than meet the eye.

All in all, I coached the Steelers for 261 games. Fifteen years in the public eye. I did a reasonable job of keeping my private life, well, private. Until now.

1

Billy from Crafton

As far back as I can remember, I was always surrounded by people who were passionate about one of two things: work or sports. For me, as early as nine years old, it was both. I embraced work so I'd be free to play all the games I found irresistible.

I didn't think there was anything unusual about the lives and routines of the families around me, because that was life for kids in the 1960s and '70s of my Pittsburgh neighborhood. We were tireless grade-schoolers in the working-class area of Crafton, and we treated our games like our full-time jobs.

My family lived in a brick Victorian on Hawthorne Avenue. It was a street where PAT buses—public city buses in Pittsburgh— would sometimes wait until the end of a play before driving through our pickup football games. Even then, several years before high school, I saw myself as a linebacker. I shared a bedroom with my two brothers, Dale and Doug, and the posters on our wall told part of my story: One showed the Chicago Bears' Dick Butkus, intense and athletic, in action, and the other was of his equally strong divisional rival, the Green Bay Packers' Ray Nitschke. Both of them, in those pictures and in reality, always seemed to be ready for what was next. The next play. The next quarter. The next game.

That was me.

No matter what I had to do away from sports, I could always see a path back to the games, whether playing them or discussing them. For example, I can still remember delivering the old *Pittsburgh Press* on Sunday mornings in the fall. I had about thirty customers during the week and even more on Sundays. I'd race to finish my route, then sit with my father, Laird Cowher, as he watched Notre Dame football highlights on TV (he always loved Notre Dame), then get ready for church. He followed all sports, but I wouldn't say he was athletic. He was a tall man, about six-four, and lean. He had dark hair and a strong jawline. While Laird was his given name, everyone called him Bill. Which made me "Billy" to my family and friends. My father was our Sunday school teacher. We attended Hawthorne Avenue Presbyterian Church, about four doors down from our house. Dad's hour-long lesson plan was structured the same way every week: If we paid attention and did what we were supposed to in the first forty-five minutes, we could spend the remaining time talking about sports.

In a lot of ways, that arrangement was a glimpse of how my father operated. He was an accountant who had a meticulous approach to his work. In his office area in the house, you could always find five sharpened No. 2 pencils along with an orderly assortment of staples, erasers, sheets of paper, and paper clips—all in a designated area. He put his thoughts on paper, whether it was to-do lists or his feelings about a particular topic. If any of us went to his desk for any reason, he'd loudly remind us, "Leave it the way you found it." If one thing was slightly out of place, he could always spot it. Business, and details, were important to him, but so were sports.

Baseball was his first love. I remember how he'd spend hours with me in the cinder alley behind our house, trying to teach me how to throw a curveball.

"Snap your wrist, Billy!" he'd say in exasperation. "Snap it." He'd show me the motion and then execute it flawlessly. When I tried, I'd either skip the ball well short of him, causing the cinders to fly in the air, or I'd leave the ball too high. (I continued to play baseball, but I could never throw the curve. Or hit it.)

Dad was no-nonsense about baseball, both as a coach and an umpire—he'd let you know if you weren't playing the right way. One of my best friends growing up was a kid named John Lynch. John lived one street over from us, on South Linwood. He spent so much time at my house playing Foto-Electric football and table hockey that Dad was comfortable speaking with him the same way he spoke with us, his sons. Dad was the umpire for one of John's baseball games and sensed that a frustrated John, not having a good day on the mound, was hitting batters on purpose. Dad called time and approached the hill.

"John, I know what you're doing. Don't be a punk. If you hit one more kid, I'm going to throw you out of this game."

Even better, after that game, Dad saw John walking home. Dad slowed the car and offered him a ride. John tried to give Dad the *No thank you, Mr. Cowher* treatment, but Dad insisted that he get in. Of course, John knew that another lecture was coming. Dad used that brief drive as another opportunity for more coaching on the right way to do things. That was a consistent theme with my parents. They wanted us to play well, and they wanted to see evidence that we were improving, too.

I couldn't get enough of sports. I played baseball, basketball, football, and tennis. I was on the run from the moment I opened my eyes in the morning until the end of the day. I excitedly went with my dad around the city, whether it was to the Civic Arena to see Duquesne University basketball, to walk up steep Lothrop Street (also known as Cardiac Hill) for University of Pittsburgh football games, or to Three Rivers Stadium to see the Steelers play.

I was endlessly active, and tall but reed thin, so my mother, Dorothy—everyone called her Dot or J.D.—tried her creative best to help me gain weight. She did all she could to get some pounds to stick. Every night before bed, she'd have a milkshake for me to drink, and she'd blend in a little of everything. When she made steak for dinner, I always got an extra one. She loved making brownies, and it made her smile when I filled up on them. If I went to Wendy's, I'd order the triples. For breakfast, strangely, it was the smell of burnt toast that lured me to the kitchen. We had a toaster that wouldn't pop on its own, so the bread would often burn—and I grew to love the smell and the burnt toast itself. I'd eat everything Mom made and then either walk out the door if I saw the school bus coming down Hawthorne or run if it had passed the house because, fortunately, I could catch up to it when it turned on Linwood.

It was a blessing to grow up where I did, and how I did. I never consciously thought at the time, *My parents are a great team*, but they were. They were both inspiring, with different styles. My mother was a stay-at-home mom. She was personable and warm, with a knack for making fast friends. She'd played basketball growing up, so she held her own in a house full of athletic boys. Everyone in the neighborhood knew how friendly she was. She could be seen walking everywhere because she didn't drive. My father tried to teach her many times, and it led to some naturally funny exchanges between the two:

"Your father said that when you're making a turn, you don't have to turn the wheel back after that," Mom would say.

"But, Dot," Dad would reply, "I didn't say to take your hands off the wheel!"

They pushed all of us boys to reach our potential as athletes. My brothers and I were constantly going off to some sports camp. We lived less than one hundred miles from West Virginia University, so I attended overnight football camp there multiple times. The first time I went there at eight years old, I was probably the youngest kid there. Jim Carlen was the head coach, and I was there when the one and only Bobby Bowden took over for him. My parents put in the investment for my brothers and me, and they always wanted to know the same things when we returned: How did you get better? What did you learn?

By the time I entered Carlynton High School in the fall of 1971, a few things had become clear to me. One was, I shared the same love and mastery of numbers that my father did. All aspects of math came easily to me. I looked forward to any math course, whether it was algebra, trigonometry, or, eventually, calculus.

Our football team definitely had a math problem. That is, most of the time we had between twenty-two and twenty-four players on the entire roster. Everyone on the team played offense and defense. I started out as a center and linebacker, then switched to a tight end / linebacker combination. At center, I expected to make every block. At linebacker, I expected to make every tackle. My thoughts on the field were straightforward: I was overjoyed to play, and I wanted to find every way possible to help my team win. There was nothing intricate about our playbook: We had six plays, three passing and three running; our six became twelve when we flipped the formation and ran the same plays.

Our not having a lot of players led to our becoming an incredibly close team. I loved those guys, and I knew that it was mutual. By high school, I had long been hooked on the strategy and competition that football provided. But what playing on our team really taught me was the importance of unity and getting something—even the smallest contribution—out of every person on the roster.

In my sophomore year I became the best player on our team, being selected as one of our captains. It felt good to be the person everyone felt he could connect with, and the guy the others looked to for leadership and playmaking. What felt even better, though, was watching everyone on our team have a role that was uniquely his. That's the beauty of football: You don't have to be a great player or great athlete to be a part of it. It's a sport that destroys divided teams and rewards those who rely on one another. At its best, football is a unifier and a confidence builder for young boys.

In football-crazed western Pennsylvania, we were a Class A (or small division) team. We had success on the field, but the memories I'll never forget were, simply, the hangouts. John Lynch was still one of my best friends, along with Tom Hennessy, Bill Clay, and many other guys from the team, including my younger brother, whom we called Dougie. There didn't need to be a special occasion for us to do something. We just liked getting together.

My desire to socialize got the attention of my father. In a way that only he could, he forced me to change the sequence of what I wanted to do. I'd tell my parents that I was going out with the guys, and my dad would respond, "Okay, Billy. Go out. I'm sure your competition is lifting weights or doing something to get better. But it's all right. Go out."

I knew what he was doing, and I didn't like it. But his words resonated; I'd often lift weights first, then head out with my friends. He was pushing me, and sometimes my mother felt that he was pushing too much. "Don't worry about it, Billy," she'd say with assurance. "You know how your father can be sometimes."

What I didn't realize until many years later, well into my thirties, was that my father was not only clipping every article written about me, he was also keeping his own scouting report of how I played. He needled aggressively, but his pride was obvious when he spoke with other people about me or let them see his writings. He'd meet a total stranger, and if I was there, he'd say, "And this is my son Billy. He had twenty tackles in his game last week. He's the best player in his conference." I'd just shake my head. I was a confident and passionate player, but my father had more confidence in me than I did in myself.

"Any attempt to evaluate Bill's performance on a game-to-game basis would be asinine," he wrote in 1973. "If he had a bad game, I can't recall which it would have been. . . . Some of his efforts were of superstar proportions."

As a sophomore, I was named an all-star player in our league, the Black Hills Conference. I got stronger and more confident the next season, and I repeated as an all-star. I was six-two and about 190 pounds. I'd stopped playing baseball by then, but I'd replaced it with track and field throwing the shot put. I also kept playing basketball, as the center on our team. My love for basketball and my love for football were equal. Even though I was supposed to be our option in the post, I liked going to the corner and scoring from there. I played basketball with an edge, and my toughness from the football field didn't always go over well on the basketball court. At least once I fouled out of a game in the first half.

I loved basketball. But I was a realist. Despite the occasional letters I got from college basketball coaches, I knew that I wasn't a college basketball player. There was no future in it for me. Football? That was a different story. I thought I'd play college football. What I didn't know was where it would be.

||||||||||||

Butkus and Nitschke had retired from the NFL by the end of my junior year in 1974, so I began to focus my attention on a couple of other linebackers: Hacksaw Reynolds of the Los Angeles Rams, and a Steelers rookie, Jack Lambert. They were both thin linebackers, like me, but they made up for the perceived deficiency with pure energy. Their obvious love of the game seemed to prevent them from ever getting tired. One of Lambert's teammates, Jack Ham, was also a smart and instinctive player. I liked watching Ham where he was, with the Steelers. But I desperately wanted to be where he'd been in college, at Penn State.

Penn State was *the* place for young linebackers to thrive. I'd picture myself suiting up in the iconic navy and white and running into Beaver Stadium. But I got a letter from Penn State that dashed that dream; I was told I was too thin and too slow to play there. A similar letter came from Indiana University and Lee Corso, their head coach. I was heartbroken and knew there were doubts about me and my league's level of competition, but that rejection just made me hungrier.

I became even more obsessed with the game. I was sure not many people in the country wanted to be on the field as much as I wanted to. I often felt that I *needed* to be out there, and it was my responsibility to help myself and others exhaust all resources in order to win. I was better than most college coaches thought, and a big part of the reason was that I never got tired of playing football.

By the summer of '74, the summer before my senior year, I was focused. I went to another football camp, this one at Indiana University of Pennsylvania (IUP), about an hour from home. I stayed there and got a taste of what life would be as a college player. A few of my teammates from Carlynton also went to the camp, and so did kids from one of our conference rivals, Fort Cherry. (One of their best players was Marvin Lewis, who attended the camp, and he was a player who had college visions just as I did.)

I got better at IUP. I became more of a leader and strategist than a football player. It allowed me to see some of my teammates in a different environment, and it reminded me that they were willing to make a sacrifice in the middle of July just as I was. I began to understand that it was another way to bond and build trust as a team.

During the season, if we were in a tough situation, I knew I could look at those players and know that they were just as committed as I was. We could always recall the hard work we'd put in during the summer, on the field, and how we'd strengthened our friendships and respect for one another off it.

We lost just two games my senior year, and I had another all-star season. However, college recruiters weren't impressed. I got used to a pattern: I'd visit schools all over the country, from all the top conferences. I'd walk in and they'd look at me as if they'd seen a ghost. They knew from the film that I was tall and thin, but I guess the difference in seeing a 195-pound linebacker on film and in person was drastic. The college coaches already knew I wasn't the fastest player, so when they combined that with my size, the visits ended with, essentially, thanks for coming.

By early 1975, the only scholarship offer I received was from William & Mary, a Virginia school about a six-hour drive from Pittsburgh. I liked that it had a strong academic reputation, and the head coach, Jim Root, genuinely seemed to want me. Root's assistants began their recruitment my junior year and kept in consistent contact. As far as I was concerned, I was headed there in the fall.

Still, one of my final college visits was to the University of Maryland. The program had become one of the best in the nation with the arrival of head coach Jerry Claiborne. They played my style of ball, too. The year before, they had five shutouts. They had an amazing hybrid defensive lineman / linebacker, Randy White, who became a second overall pick in the NFL draft. The program finished in the Top 15 nationally. Who wouldn't want to go there? If I walked off that campus with a scholarship offer, I'd have a lot to think about.

Well, I walked off the campus. And once again, there was no offer. I headed to the airport for the short flight from DC to Pittsburgh.

As I took my seat waiting for the plane to depart, a man came to my row and sat down. I don't remember wearing a jacket or a hat that identified me as an athlete, but the man talked to me as if he knew who I was.

"Hey, big guy, where are ya headed?"

I could tell he was talkative and friendly. I told him that I was from Pittsburgh and that I'd just taken a college visit to Maryland.

He smiled. "If you're good enough to play at Maryland, then you're good enough to play for us!"

His name was Larry Beightol. The "us" he talked about was North Carolina State. He was an assistant coach there, and he spoke with authority. He talked as if he knew that the head coach, Lou Holtz, would agree with his scholarship recommendation. He casually mentioned that Holtz would likely visit me on Hawthorne Avenue. We chatted the rest of the flight.

I didn't have time to think if Beightol was serious about what he'd said because he followed up about two weeks later. He'd watched film of my games and confirmed what he'd said on the plane. Sure enough, to the delight of my parents, Holtz scheduled a trip to Crafton to see us.

Things were moving quickly and I was conflicted. William & Mary pursued me as if they wanted me. I couldn't shake the feeling that North Carolina State came after me because they had a scholarship to give. They were late recruiting me. Did I really want to go there?

Those were some of the thoughts I had as I sat in our living room in the spring of 1975, with my parents, as Holtz made his case for North Carolina State. My parents were thrilled that day, but very much themselves. Mom told the coach to have a seat, then she went off to get him something to drink.

Dad listened a little and bragged a lot: "You're getting one heck of a football player. A lot of schools would be as glad as you are to have him."

I sat there thinking, *Dad, a lot of schools?* I had two: William & Mary and this one.

Holtz said all the right things about taking care of me and helping me grow from boyhood to manhood. He'd built a powerful, nationally respected program in Raleigh after he'd arrived there from . . . William & Mary.

Everything was pointing to State. My parents wanted me to do it. My friends were not used to seeing kids from small-team, small-conference schools such as ours play in the Atlantic Coast Conference. They wanted me to go. And a glance at Coach Holtz's résumé seemed to be a push toward the South as well: Here was a man who'd said goodbye to William & Mary for an opportunity at NC State, and it worked out for him. The message seemed to be clear that the same would work out for me.

The decision was made. I planned to spend the next four years in Raleigh, North Carolina. This decision elevated my game and changed the course of my life.

2

Connecting in Raleigh

August 1975

As soon as I put my bags down in Raleigh, I felt that I was home. I may have been looking at North Carolina's beautiful rolling hills, but I never felt far from Pittsburgh. One immediate reason was my new roommate and teammate, Russ Matt, the first person I ran into after the eight-hour drive to campus. I remember shaking his hand and giving him a knowing smile.

Russ was a sophomore. I remembered him from when he showed me around during my NC State recruiting trip. He was a defensive end from Jeannette, Pennsylvania, about thirty miles from Crafton. Since he was from my area, I didn't need to explain the confidence I had as an eighteen-year-old freshman. A football player from Pittsburgh—that simple description said a lot at the time.

The Steelers had won their first Super Bowl previously that year, beating the Minnesota Vikings, 16–6. The Steelers did it with a style that reflected their city. It was fierce football, built upon an unstoppable running game and a bruising, punishing defense. *My* linebacker, the rookie Jack Lambert, was in the middle of that defense, known as the Steel Curtain. It was hard to run or pass on them, and when opponents did anything positive—such as catch the ball—aggressive players swarmed in an instant. That's what a team representing Pittsburgh was supposed to be: fast, smart, and tough. You could tell some teams were made uncomfortable just by the sight of the Steelers. I loved that. Even though I wasn't close to playing at that level, the Steelers allowed me to swell with pride because I saw myself in them.

Russ felt the same way, and so did several of our other players. We had the spirit of a Midwestern or Northeastern team, even though we were from the South. Coach Holtz recruited extensively in New Jersey, Ohio, and of course Pennsylvania. I had teammates from familiar western-Pennsylvania cities and towns such as Beaver Falls, Greensburg, Apollo, and Monroeville. We all had that passionate, ready-for-anything attitude. I didn't realize just how soon I'd need to use it.

I never allowed myself to think the team needed me. For one, I still was edgy because so many schools had passed on offering me a scholarship. No one had handed me anything, and I approached every practice and game as an opportunity to prove myself. One of my so-called shortcomings—I was too light—had lessened. A little. I lived at the College Inn, which was a multilevel apartment building for State athletes. At a cafeteria there, I ate three of my four daily meals. The fourth was usually a midnight snack at Wendy's, continuing my Crafton tradition of eating triple burgers. Still, I had 210 pounds on a six-foot-three frame. I was able to keep some weight on but remained thinner than I wanted to be.

I began on the freshman team, which was no surprise to me. Our team had been among the best in the country the year before, so it wasn't as if I were going to walk in as a freshman and take an upperclassman's position. However, after a short time on the freshman team, that's exactly what happened. The varsity had been hit by a number of injuries on defense, and suddenly it was my turn to be on that roster. As a starter at inside linebacker.

I knew I could play major-college football. I just didn't think it would happen a month and a half into my freshman year. Less than a year earlier, I was going sideline to sideline in the Black Hills Conference, playing mostly at "fields" rather than in stadiums. We had devoted fans in high school, but the crowds weren't in the thousands. But here I was at Carter Stadium, with nearly fifty thousand people watching, clad in State's red-and-white colors, with their cheers and the Power Sound of the South, State's talented marching band, with us at all times.

One of our early games that season was against Indiana. It was one of the places where I'd been told I wasn't good enough for major-college football. At home, we beat them, 27–0. I was motivated by people who said I couldn't do something. I always remembered. Beating Indiana like that was like winning a bowl game. I wish I could tell you that all of our games were that easy. About a month after the Indiana shut-out, we took on South Carolina. Our defensive alignment was a 3-4, meaning that there were three linemen and four linebackers in our front seven. I was one of the inside linebackers, and my job was to go through a guard named Steve Courson to get to the South Carolina quarterback.

Or maybe I should say my ambition was to bypass Courson on the way to the quarterback. At six-one and whatever his listed weight was (260? 270?), Courson was the strongest player I'd ever played against. I remember early in the game when he broke the huddle and put his left arm down in his stance. *You've got to be kidding me*, I thought. That arm was bigger than one of my legs! I continued to attack him, but I wasn't sure if he felt any of my hits.

I was sore for nearly a week after playing against him (we won that game, too), but I learned a couple of things from the experience.

Our league, the Atlantic Coast Conference, had dozens of players who were on their way to the NFL, so it was wise to expect the strongest, the fastest, the smartest . . . every week. I also realized that my mind was one of my best assets.

At my size, it wasn't realistic to think that all of my success would come by overpowering an opponent. Did that happen sometimes? Sure. But I also impressed my coaches by quickly picking up the schemes they wanted the defense to play. Within that 3-4 defense, I had the ability to play multiple positions. I loved studying football, so I found a lot of joy in diagnosing plays by figuring out a team's patterns, remembering what plays were run out of certain formations, while paying attention to a lineman's body position to know if a pass or a run was next.

I don't know if that came from my love of math and analytics instilled by my dad or if it was instincts. Maybe both. Maybe it was just a will to win, because I went into every game exploring every way we could win it. I didn't care how we did it and who got the credit for it. All I wanted was the victory.

My parents made the drive from Crafton to Raleigh for every home game. They'd make the trip with my younger brother, Doug, and, sometimes, my girlfriend, Donna (a high school senior). My parents would watch the game, then take us all out to dinner. My parents would stay overnight in a nearby hotel and had just one rule for whoever made the trip with them: *Don't be late.* No matter if he had everyone with him or not, Dad was leaving for home at 5:00 a.m. Sunday. He drove a gas-guzzling Chevy Biscayne, and he timed out his gas stops for the trip as well. His mission was to get settled in the living room and in front of the TV so he'd be ready for the Steelers' game. He was serious about it. If you weren't ready to go by five, he'd either leave you or wear you out verbally so you'd wish that he had. I got left behind during my freshman year, too, but in two very different ways.

Our team won seven games and earned a trip to the Peach Bowl, where we lost to West Virginia. I'd gotten more playing time than I'd expected and done it from various linebacker spots. I enjoyed our scheme and playing for Coach Holtz. But three weeks after the '75 Super Bowl, which the Steelers won again (this time defeating Roger Staubach and the Dallas Cowboys), more pro football news soon followed: The New York Jets had hired a new head coach—Lou Holtz. He sent a letter to all his NC State players' parents—I still have it—and promised to remain a part of his players' lives, even though he was going to New York. Coach Holtz, at thirty-nine, was considered one of the younger coaches in college football. He was replaced by one of his former assistants, Bo Rein, who looked like one of us. At thirty, he became the youngest head coach in the country.

When I got back to Crafton in the spring, I arrived with a different look. I'd cut my hair. Actually, I cut *some* of my hair. When Donna first saw the Mohawk, her face told me what I needed to know. She was not a fan. Maybe the relationship couldn't have survived another year of long distance with any style, but the Mohawk apparently helped her take the mystery out of it: I suddenly became her ex-boyfriend.

Some of the music I listened to at the time provided the perfect soundtrack for where I was in my life. One of my favorites was Earth, Wind & Fire's album *That's the Way of the World*. The title speaks for itself. As I progressed as a football player, I realized that people might judge who I was solely based on the sport I played and how I looked when I played it.

By my junior year, I had a reputation on campus as "the crazy football player." That was only half true. I played the game with a crazed look. I'd grown into one of our best players and leaders. I was a team captain, and everyone on my team—and the other side—understood what I was willing to do for a win. Compared to the future pros I played against, I wasn't fast. My 40-yard dash time was nearly 4.9 seconds, a tick slower than most pro teams wanted at my position. I was muscular with low body fat, so I looked more like a lean basketball player than a football player. But I used my mind, and mouth, on the field. I knew I could get inside a player's head and make him uncomfortable. I felt that I was always in better condition than my opponents. I had more energy. I needed to win more than they did, or I thought I did. So, I'd be intense out there. *I'm gonna be here all day. I'm not backing down. Be ready.* My opponents weren't sure what I was going to do, but I did. I played with intensity, never doing anything to cost our team field position or games, but always on the edge.

Sometimes, on a night out, a few of my teammates and I would shoot pool for money. We were pretty good at it. We didn't get into fights, but from afar people would look at us and conclude that we were just looking for a confrontation.

I understood why people who didn't know me thought I was unhinged. If you just watched our games to figure out who I was, the logical conclusion was I was nuts. But I didn't live at the stadium or the pool hall. My enthusiasm for math led me to first major in accounting. It didn't hurt that by testing out of some intro math courses I'd earned four credits. I switched to education, though, and was excited to be on that track, too.

⁕

One of the classes I most looked forward to was psychology. Yes, it was part of my degree requirements, but that's not why the course kept my interest. A player from the women's basketball team was a classmate, and I found myself paying attention to her even when we weren't in class. I used to see her in the College Inn cafeteria, and I'd look, maybe even smile, but I didn't say anything.

Part of the reason I didn't talk to her was because I didn't know what to say. And I wasn't confident I'd call her by the right name. She and her identical-twin sister were stars of State's team. They were both blonde, with feathered Farrah Fawcett hair. They were both just over six feet tall. They'd begun their college careers at Peace, which was in Raleigh, before transferring to State. They were the Young twins from Bunn, North Carolina. They were Kaye and Faye. But what if I approached Faye and called her Kaye? Or the opposite?

One night after a home football game, I went out with a couple of my teammates. We went to a popular bar called the Square. One of the twins was there. I told one of my teammates, Tom Prongay, how I felt about this striking young woman, and before I knew it, Tom was off to approach her and tell her the news.

"Do you see that guy over there?" Tom said. "His name is Bill Cowher and he's got a crush on you."

"Well," she said, "if he feels that way, I think he should come over and tell me himself."

Now I had no choice. I introduced myself, and we talked for the rest of the night. I walked her back to her apartment and told her that I'd call the next day. But in the morning, I panicked.

Which name did she say? Kaye or Faye?

When I called, one of her roommates picked up.

"Is Aye there?" I said on purpose. I knew I'd get close enough with a rhyme.

"Who?"

"Is Aye there? You know, the twin basketball player. This is Bill Cowher."

"Oh . . . Kaye, it's for you."

Got it. Kaye.

It was a name I'd never forget.

I asked Kaye what her plans were for the day, and she said she was going to the library. What a coincidence, I told her. I was headed there, too. I was already doing what I could to be where she was. As we talked more, I understood the odds she'd overcome and the opportunities she was working hard to create for herself.

She'd grown up in Bunn, a small farming town about thirty-five minutes from Raleigh. The population was just a few hundred people, surrounded by tobacco fields.

Kaye and Faye were the babies of the family, barefooted towheads running around in rural North Carolina. Their parents, Claude and Irene Young, were good people. They worked hard to provide a simple life for their five children, but the twins always held a curiosity about a life bigger than the one they knew.

Before she graduated from high school, Kaye's boyfriend at the time asked her to marry him. Her father encouraged her to do it; her mother said she shouldn't. The twins were talented basketball players, and Title IX meant young girls could also dream about the same scholarship opportunities as boys did. That's what led Kaye and Faye to Peace and then State, where they led one of the Top 10 teams in the country.

Kaye was one year ahead of me in school, so we knew that our on-campus time together was limited. Who knew where she'd be after graduation? We spent a lot of time together when we could. I went to her games and she went to mine. She even watched the intramural basketball games I'd play. I met her parents in Bunn. She met my parents when they came to Raleigh, and they expected her to join us for dinner when they were in town.

We were clearly made for each other, but not everyone understood it. People would see me in those games. Maybe they didn't understand why I got so excited when our team held South Carolina to just a field goal the entire afternoon in a 7–3 win. Or why I was so emotional in a home loss to a school, Penn State, that made me grind my teeth as soon as I saw their helmets. *Not good enough, huh? I'll show you I belong.* There was also this: I wasn't the only one who wanted to date Kaye. Some were jealous she'd chosen to spend so much time with me.

"He's not crazy," she'd tell her friends. "You don't know him."

Kaye was smart and understood me on many levels. As an athlete herself, she could relate to my competitiveness. As a student, she'd look at my papers and make suggestions that would straighten them out and provide clarity. In the spring of 1978, after my junior year, we were headed to jobs in different parts of the country.

She and Faye had been drafted by the New York Stars, of the newly formed Women's Basketball League. The team played their home games at Madison Square Garden, usually before Knicks games. I knew how hard Kaye worked and how good she was, but it still was incredible to say, "My girlfriend is a professional athlete." I was so happy for her when she bought her first car, a Mazda RX-7, for $7,000.

I had some work to do, too, before my final season of college football. I was always drawn to jobs where I could get my hands dirty. As a kid, that meant the newspaper and all of its leaking newsprint. As I got older, I worked in a nursery, digging and planting. I worked at UPS, loading and unloading trucks. I worked in a steel mill, and I worked as a boilermaker. I could do these jobs for a month to six weeks, make enough money to take care of college expenses, and still have time to work out.

All of that was fine for college, but, like Kaye, I needed to have a plan for the pros. I had one more year to show scouts what I could do, but in my opinion I'd proven I could thrive as a Division I athlete. In the fall of '78, NFL scouts viewed one of our players as a first-round talent, our sensational star running back, Ted Brown. As someone who practiced against him, I knew he was as good as the scouting reports said. And as someone who practiced against him, I knew I could play in the league if the players were at his caliber.

Our team that year was the best one of my college career. We won five of our first six, and it was the first time that we were equally balanced on offense and defense. I was happy to come away with victories against all the teams in the "the Triangle"—North Carolina, Duke, and Wake Forest. We also beat West Virginia, the school that beat us in my first-ever bowl game. A trend I didn't like was that every time we played a ranked team, we lost. Our games against Maryland and Clemson weren't close. While we held our own against the second-ranked team in the country, Penn State, it was still a 9-point loss in Happy Valley. In more ways than one, that loss was a little too close to home.

We finished our regular season with eight wins, which earned us a trip to the Tangerine Bowl in Orlando. This was going to be my last college game, and my teammates knew me well enough to know how I'd approach it. But they didn't know everything. They didn't know that I could go even deeper—and more crazed—than normal to prepare for this game, and they didn't know why I could do it.

I didn't want to hold back anything, so I respectfully asked all the coaches to leave the room so I could speak candidly to the team. When I saw the last coach walk out, I stood in front of my brothers and spoke from the heart.

We were playing the University of Pittsburgh, who were ranked. And it was a bus ride away from where I grew up. I could feel my voice rising as I made this story personal, as I wanted them to feel that Pitt had disrespected me and them. I told my teammates that I'd gone to watch Pitt games as a kid, how I'd supported them, and they didn't even think enough of me to look my way down the street when I was trying to play college football. I scanned the room and could see that almost everyone hung on each word—raw and profane—I spoke. I wanted them to put themselves in my shoes and feel the rage that I did.

I was emotional. My eyes narrowed and my teeth clenched. "We are not going to lose to that team. I don't want to be in that city, my city, knowing that I lost my last college game to that team."

Most of the guys were roaring and pushing me to keep going. I could see Tim Gillespie, one of our guards, in the back of the room with his hands over his ears. Tim was a devout Christian, and I sensed that he didn't like some of the colorful language I used. In the flow of the speech I said, "Gillespie, focus on the theme of the message and not the words I'm using."

After it was over, he came up to me and said, "Great talk, Cowher. But, man, if you had used the f-word one more time . . ."

He smiled.

We beat Pitt 30–17 and finished the year ranked eighteenth in the country. I learned a lot about playing college football in my four years at State. Before my last game, I learned that getting yourself ready to play is not all that's required of a leader. At times you've got to personalize a message, get the whole group to believe it, and push everyone toward an untapped level of excellence.

I'd have to do that if I wanted to keep playing after college. No one had made it easy for me before I came to North Carolina State, and I didn't expect it to be easy on the way out.

3

Dream Chaser

A month after that final college game against Pitt, another Pittsburgh story bolstered my confidence. The Steelers had no idea how much they inspired me and how their historic victories gave me strength. But that's what happened in January 1979, when the team from my city once again proved to be the NFL's best.

This Super Bowl win, another victory over the Dallas Cowboys, was their third Lombardi Trophy in five years. No team had won three Super Bowls before, and no team played quite like the black-and-gold. Their greatness pushed me to think I was obligated to be great at something. They belonged to the city in many ways, big and small, and one that stood out after that third Super Bowl was this: They were a team capable of delivering whatever the situation called for.

That was Pittsburgh.

That was me.

For the Steelers, it meant they wanted to overwhelm opponents with a ferocious running game. That's what they wanted to do. But it's not all that they *could* do. When the Cowboys appeared to be ready for the Steelers' running game in the Super Bowl, Pittsburgh quarterback Terry Bradshaw threw for 318 yards and 4 touchdowns. Bradshaw had been a pro for nine years, and he'd never had a game like that—in the regular season or playoffs—in his career. *Now that's a champion,* I thought. Doing more and going further than anyone expects.

For me, it meant it was time to watch pro players in a different way. I loved football to my core, so I'd always be a fan of the game. But now it was time to be a fan and a professional. I'd enjoyed playing college football and doing it as a captain on a nationally ranked team. My getting a scholarship to a school such as NC State was my parents' dream. We weren't rich; every camp they sent us to was a financial sacrifice. It was a relief, and a blessing, for them to know that my pursuit of football and a degree wouldn't come at a huge cost.

The NFL draft was scheduled a few days before my twenty-second birthday, and I was eager to learn my new city. I wasn't picky. I was ready to play for any team, located anywhere. I was realistic, too. Pro scouts visited Raleigh to see Ted Brown. Anyone who followed college football at the time could understand why. Ted finished his Wolfpack career as the most productive runner in the history of our conference. If you include his numbers from our three bowl appearances, he rushed for over 5,000 yards in 49 games. He was on his way to being someone's first-round pick.

And I . . . was not. I'd made a lot of big plays for our team, many of which were due to anticipation and instincts. As I said, I knew how to play every linebacker position in the 3-4 defense. I didn't miss tackles. I was passionate enough to prepare myself, and my teammates, to win games. However, the perceived drawback remained: I wasn't as big and fast as pro teams wanted. I wasn't going to suddenly gain speed, but I did everything I could to get around my lack of bulk.

And I mean everything.

A few times, when I knew scouts were coming to measure and weigh me, I'd either slip a two- or five-pound plate from the weight room into my shorts. So, when I stepped on a scale, my numbers might read 228 or 231, depending on which plate I used that day. I wanted to play in the NFL. If something as superficial as a few pounds would help my cause, I'd do it.

I didn't know what to expect from the two days of the twelve-round draft. Well over three hundred players would be selected, and I helped myself relax with reminders.

Are there one hundred college players better than me?

Might be.

Are there two hundred?

Maybe.

How about three hundred?

No way.

The draft days, Thursday and Friday, finally arrived the first week of May 1979. Six rounds in, no one had called my name. I was in Raleigh for the draft, waiting by the phone. I'd told a few of my wisecracking teammates to not play any games, pretending to be NFL teams. This was the career I had in mind. I didn't want to joke on draft day. As expected, Ted had been drafted in the first round by the Minnesota Vikings with the sixteenth overall pick. A couple of other players from our conference, Jerry Butler and Steve Fuller of Clemson, had been taken in the first round as well.

I waited two days for a call that never came. More than 300 players had been drafted—actually 330—and I hadn't been among them. I couldn't believe it. How could the league have missed like this? Every team had gotten it wrong, and I was excited to prove it.

As an undrafted free agent, I had one offer, and it was to attend a training camp in Chester, Pennsylvania, with the Philadelphia Eagles. This was about pride and betting on myself. It surely wasn't about money. The Eagles, coached by Dick Vermeil, had a playoff team. As I looked at them closer, they'd also invested in my position. One of their Pro Bowlers, Bill Bergey, was a linebacker, and they'd also drafted two linebackers—Jerry Robinson in the first and Al Chesley in the eleventh—before signing me.

I've always been comfortable with statistics and probability, so I knew how to problem-solve this camp: I had to make the roster as a special teamer, and I had to beat out Chesley to do it. Since he was drafted, he already had a built-in advantage. I thought of ways that I could shine enough to get the coaches' attention. I was in great shape, with about 6 percent body fat, and that was a huge help in the competition Coach Vermeil created. I'm not sure if it was more physically or mentally grueling, but it was clearly designed to test all aspects of desire and stamina. A typical day began with a two-and-a-half-hour morning practice. Then lunch. Then *another* two-and-a-half-hour afternoon practice. Meetings, for another couple hours, were the nightcap.

It was demanding, but purposefully so. No one who is uncertain about football will put up with that schedule. The commitment weeded some people out before the coaches had to do it themselves. In that atmosphere, between the schedule and the summer humidity, you deserve credit just for making it week to week.

We played our first two preseason games against Baltimore and Kansas City, and I remained on the team. Two more games, Baltimore at Veterans Stadium and Miami on the road, and I got through those. I thought I'd played well for the coaches and answered a big question for myself. I belonged there. I thought I did after college and during and after the draft. After a summer in eastern Pennsylvania, I knew I did. But that's all it was: a summer of pro football. The Eagles kept Chesley and cut me. I was a free agent without a team and, if I believed the messaging, without a league.

There was good news in pro sports, though, and it was practically in my family. Kaye and I had grown even closer since she'd left NC State, even if we were in different parts of the country. She was getting ready for her second season with the New York Stars, and she—and the league—began to get even more publicity. A player from UCLA, Ann Meyers, had just won the national championship and tried out for the Indiana Pacers. She didn't make the Pacers, but she signed a six-figure contract with the New Jersey Gems. Meanwhile, the famous yogurt company Dannon approached Kaye and Faye about doing a commercial together. Female athletes were getting more attention than they ever had.

I was thrilled to see it all, and so happy for Kaye. I wasn't sure what my career held for me, but I knew I'd support Kaye in hers. It was nearly fall, which meant football season, and it was strange not to have a game to play for the first time in fourteen years. I'd been on a field, somewhere, in pads since I was eight years old. It was impossible for me to just cut that off. I decided to go back to school and finish my vocational-education degree.

My roommate was Randy Hall, a former State receiver. We lived in Cary, North Carolina, which was a fifteen-minute drive from Raleigh and thirty minutes from Chapel Hill. That mattered because I had work to do in both places. I did some teaching at Chapel Hill High School, and I enjoyed sharing my enthusiasm for math with teenagers and helping them figure it out when they got stuck. There, my teaching occurred in the classroom. In Raleigh, it took place on the field.

My head coach for three seasons, Bo Rein, hired me as a graduate assistant. My job was to study film, highlight key points, and help coach the linebackers. I often surprised myself as an apprentice on the coaching staff. I knew how I felt about the game and my hunger to win. What I didn't realize was how satisfying it was to share my knowledge with a player, watch him absorb it, then see him apply it on the field and get results. I'd helped players get a little better, and I thought that was cool. I still wanted to play, but that experience with coaching opened my eyes to that as a possibility. One day.

But with another college and pro football season over in January 1980, it was time for me to go back to Crafton. My hometown really was the City of Champions, now in two sports. My father was over-joyed that his first-love team, the Pirates, won a dramatic World Series over the Baltimore Orioles. When the Steelers won their record fourth Super Bowl, a takedown of the Los Angeles Rams, it was hard to tell someone from Pittsburgh anything about winning.

That's why it must have been awkward for some people I grew up with to see and hear me in the neighborhood. I'd made them all proud with my career at NC State. But they knew I didn't get drafted, and they knew I'd been cut by the Eagles. In other words, hey, maybe it was time for me to think about doing something else. I'll never forget jogging around the neighborhood, trying to keep myself in shape so I'd be ready for my NFL call. I was running on South Linwood, one street over from my parents' house on Haw-thorne. I noticed a car slowing, then the window came down. It was John Lynch, who'd been one of my best friends since grade school. He asked what I was up to.

"John, I'm going to play in the NFL. I know I can play at that level."

We exchanged small talk for a little while, then he drove off and I kept running. I could see that he thought my athletic career had ended. He didn't say it then, but he told me later exactly what he was thinking: *Bill Cowher, that poor guy is just chasing a dream.*

Yes, I believed in myself, but John had brought up a good point. What was my plan? In case I didn't make it as a pro football player, what was I going to do? I didn't know the answer definitively, and it made me uncomfortable. I always wanted to have two plans, a pri-mary and a backup, available at all times.

It had been nearly a year since I was passed over on draft day, and the league had kept going. In late April 1980, there'd be another two-day draft and another class of free agents looking for work. I believed there was something out there for me, and I was right. The Cleveland Browns had signed me as a free agent in January and invited me to attend their training camp. I was given a $1,000 signing bonus, $713.70 after taxes.

Still, this time, I felt as if I had a couple of advantages over the draft picks and free agents I was competing against. I heard the Browns were switching from a 4-3 defense to a 3-4. The 3-4 was the alignment of my college career. I knew what coaches wanted from it, and I knew all the linebackers' responsibilities from that look. I was also excited by the Cleveland coaching staff. The Browns had hired a defensive coordinator, Marty Schottenheimer, who'd spent the previous two seasons with the Detroit Lions.

I liked my chances. A new coordinator looks at film like everyone else, but his decisions tend to be based on what he sees, not what he expects someone to do. I felt it was the best opportunity I had to make a fresh impression, based solely on what I could bring to a team. I felt that way even before I began to learn just how much Marty and I had in common.

We're both from Pittsburgh, and his high school—Fort Cherry— was one of Carlynton's conference rivals. He was also a tall (six-three) and thin linebacker, and he played collegiately at Pitt. He played in the American Football League before getting into coaching at thirty years old.

Marty talked the way I imagined an English professor would—if he was told he could only talk about football from now on. He was thoughtful and thorough. Every now and then, he'd drop a word that you'd have to look up to know exactly what he meant. Most of the time, his message was some version of this: Be prepared for everything; at all times know the game situation and what you're supposed to be doing.

I worked as hard as I could and quickly picked up Marty's defensive scheme. Some of our veterans had difficulty with the switch, so they sometimes paused a beat before making a play. I felt strong and instinctive. It was the best I'd felt since my last year of college.

I played in all four preseason games, and in the fourth game I played on special teams. Knowing how Marty valued special teams, I felt that I had a real chance to make it. I remember checking in with Kaye and letting her know about my progress. She was still in the WBL, but now her team was the New Jersey Gems. It was more and more likely that both of us would make our living from professional sports.

The Browns were scheduled to play the Patriots on the first Sunday of September, and the final cuts would be at least a week earlier. I was a bubble player, always one or two moves from being pushed off the roster. I'd observed and heard about the routine when a player is about to get cut. First, a coach or someone from the staff will call you in the evening and let you know to bring your playbook with you in the morning. Then, when you get to the facility, usually someone is waiting for you by the door. The person has a blank expression on his face because he's been picked to deliver the worst sentence any bubble player can hear:

"Get your things. Coach wants to see you in his office."

Or something like that. It was awful.

I'll never forget walking toward the front door of the facility on the day that we learned about final cuts. An assistant coach was near the door, holding a clipboard. I braced myself as I thought about my future. In the next couple of seconds, I'd either think of traveling to New England to play in a game or prepare a résumé for my next job teaching math in a high school classroom.

"Hey, Bill," he said.

My heart sunk. *He's talking to me. This can't be good. What does he want?*

"How's it going?" He smiled.

And that was it.

He hadn't said anything about handing in my playbook or going to see the head coach, Sam Rutigliano, or Marty in an office. I found myself walking fast, just in case he changed his mind. I made it all the way to the locker room without being called or stopped, then I sat and finally smiled, then laughed, to myself.

Orange, white, and brown pants and jerseys and hats were everywhere. I had a jersey, number 53, hanging in a locker with my name on the back. There was that familiar Cleveland helmet—pumpkin orange, no logo, a solid brown-and-white stripe down the middle—by my side. Growing up in Pittsburgh, we had no love for the Cleveland Browns. They were just "the team a couple of hours away." We didn't like them and they didn't like us. But this was *my* team now. I'd rooted all those years for the Steelers, but now I was in their division and my job was to beat them twice a year. I'd rooted against some longtime Browns such as Doug Dieken and Charlie Hall, but now they were brothers and teammates.

When I worked out and studied, I was no longer doing it to get to the NFL; I was doing it to stay. I'd done it.

I'd made it to the NFL.

4

"Someday I'm Gonna Hire You"

Despite being lifelong Steelers fans, my parents were jubilant. Just as he had bragged about me in high school, Dad was at it again when he told people we knew—and those we didn't—Billy was now playing for the Cleveland Browns. He may have been surrounded by black and gold on Hawthorne Avenue and all over Crafton, but it didn't stop him: He placed a Browns bumper sticker on the family car.

After some hard-core Steeler fans secretly bent the car's aerial into a *P*, Dad was furious. He promised to stay up all night so he could catch the vandals in action.

"Dad, just take the bumper sticker off," I pleaded. "It's probably some kids being silly. It's all right."

"Nope. I'm gonna get those SOBs, and they'll be sorry."

I couldn't have asked for more supportive parents. They'd attended every home game of my college career, and now they were ready to do the unthinkable for me: They were going to switch their allegiance from the Steelers to the Browns.

They chose the family road and the tougher one, too. The Browns hadn't beaten the Steelers since 1976, my sophomore year in college.

They hadn't made the playoffs since 1972, my sophomore year in high school. Northeast Ohio had an underdog spirit, and some of it came from having to watch all the Steelers' success. I had now lived on both sides of the rivalry, and I was grateful this side allowed me to play out a childhood dream.

I was halfway through my rookie year the first time we played the Steelers. The game was in Cleveland, with eighty thousand fans packed into Municipal Stadium, on the shores of Lake Erie. I'd already been through my home-game routines a few times during the season. I knew to build in extra time on game day, going from my high-rise apartment in Berea to the stadium, normally a twenty-minute drive. I knew how excited all the tailgaters would be. I'd made the run from the locker room, through a tunnel, and onto the playing field several times. But to run through that tunnel at the end of October, hearing the Browns fans' excitement and anticipation, and to look across the field to see the Pittsburgh Steelers—*my* Pittsburgh Steelers—on the opposing sideline was incredible.

Our teams had the same 4-3 record, and it didn't matter to me that so many Steelers such as Terry Bradshaw, Lynn Swann, John Stallworth, Franco Harris, and Jack Lambert were all inactive for the game. I didn't care. I wanted to win. I knew I'd be on the field as a starter. (I wasn't technically listed as one of our starting players. But that's how I viewed my role as a core special teamer and backup linebacker.)

I was on the kickoff coverage, kickoff return, punt coverage, and punt return teams. All of them. It meant whether we began on offense or defense, I was on the field first to help set the tone for the game. When it was time to punt or receive on fourth down, I felt it was my time; fourth down was my time to shine. I *loved* playing special teams.

Back in college, as one of our best players, I asked the coaching staff to put me on kickoff coverage. As a defensive player, I'd rather have the offense start at their own 20-yard line than their 40. I always believed that the real defense started on the kickoff. It was a big part of the game that wasn't talked about enough, and I wanted to have a say and be a part of it.

We trailed the Steelers by 12 points in the fourth quarter that October day, but in what quickly became the identity of our team, we rallied in the final few minutes—a Brian Sipe touchdown pass to Ozzie Newsome—to win, 27–26.

The next week brought an even bigger crowd—eighty-four thousand!—as we played the Chicago Bears on *Monday Night Football*. One of our inside linebackers, Robert L. Jackson, was hurt, so I became the starter. I played the entire game. I knew Coach Rutigliano saw my value, and that was one of the reasons I made the team.

But it became clear to me Marty Schottenheimer was my real advocate. He trusted I knew what I was supposed to do, so in turn I wanted to reward that trust by being a smart and dependable player. We held Walter Payton to 30 yards that night, and I led our team in tackles. We beat the Bears, 27–21. We also won our next game, against the Colts, 28–27.

We were 7-3 when we saw the Steelers again, this time in Pittsburgh. Bradshaw was back at quarterback, and he stung us in the last ten seconds of the game with a winning touchdown pass. A win would have made the weekend perfect. The day before the game, I brought a few teammates with me to my parents' house for dinner. My roommate on the road was Doug Dieken, an offensive tackle. I used to spend a lot of time with him, other linemen such as Robert E. Jackson and Joel Patten, and one of the best athletes on our team, wide receiver Dave Logan.

I was at ease with players on our team but also mindful of my place on the roster. I knew who I was. A star player could afford to be five minutes late to a meeting or a practice, but I was the opposite; I'd be the one getting there earlier than everyone else.

At practice, after I'd gotten my own reps in, I'd stand behind one of our starting linebackers—regardless of position—and try to see what he was seeing. I was around so many great players, so I wanted to observe and listen to them. How'd they read plays as fast as they did? What were they looking at? When they looked at their triangle, or their three-pointed frame of how they viewed a play, what did they see? For a linebacker, the triangle might be looking at a guard, center, and fullback. It makes it easier to see what's happening out there.

Some of the best information I got was after practice, picking the brains of those great players. I was always there late. I didn't want anyone to outwork me at practice. There was always something for me to work on. Besides, I'd had it drilled into me that the more you can do, the better chance you have of sticking around.

That's not to say we didn't have fun.

When I wasn't asking Clay Matthews football questions, I was competing against him in Intellivision baseball. A bunch of us would hang out at bars and clubs around Cleveland, having drinks and listening to music. I couldn't let them know everything, so I had to show some restraint when certain songs came on. My teammates knew that I appreciated music. What they didn't know was how much I enjoyed dancing, especially to disco. It just wasn't cool for a football player to be into disco as much as I was, but I couldn't get enough of it.

You couldn't tell me that Michael McDonald wasn't a god. I played the Doobie Brothers' song "Minute by Minute" constantly. I was crazy about the *Saturday Night Fever* soundtrack. If music was playing, it was likely in my range. I was in my element with Michael Jackson's *Off the Wall*, Fleetwood Mac, Motown, the Rolling Stones, America, and Supertramp. If music was on and I was alone, I'd dance to it. Around the guys, sometimes I had to dance in my seat.

The hit song that all of Cleveland sang, though, was about us. Twelve days before Christmas in 1980, we had a division-leading 10-4 record. After one of our road wins, we were greeted by thousands of fans at Hopkins Airport. Our team had a nickname, the Kardiac Kids, based on our close games and dramatic last-minute wins. The city was wild about us, so I shouldn't have been surprised when "The Twelve Days of Cleveland Browns Christmas" became a number one hit on local radio and a top seller throughout the region. It was in the style of "The Twelve Days of Christmas," but with Browns-centered lyrics. For example:

> ON THE FIRST DAY OF CHRISTMAS
> [OWNER] ART MODELL GAVE TO ME
> A RUTIGLIANO SUPER BOWL TEAM. . . .

Unlike Pittsburgh, Cleveland had never seen a Super Bowl team. The fans believed that we were it, and I agreed with them.

That enthusiasm slowed a bit in our next-to-last regular-season game, when the Vikings did to us what we usually did to other teams. We led Minnesota 23–22 with fourteen seconds left at Metropolitan Stadium. If we held on to win, we'd make the playoffs. The Vikings had the ball at their own 20, and they didn't have any time-outs left. Eighty yards in fourteen seconds with no time-outs? How likely were they to pull a win out of that?

Marty put me in the game, and he told me my specific assignment: cover the star of my college team, running back Ted Brown. I was to stay back and make sure Ted didn't get behind me. At the snap to Vikings quarterback Tommy Kramer, I pedaled back several yards. He threw a quick pass to the tight end, and I noticed that the defensive back on the coverage was playing loose. As soon as I went toward the tight end to make the tackle—flip—the ball was out. He'd flipped it to . . . Ted.

My guy.

This was trouble.

It was a hook and ladder, and I was way out of position to do anything about it. I should have known better. The tight end wasn't going 80 yards on the play I'd pursued. I should have stayed with Ted, who took the lateral and ran 36 yards to our 46 before running out of bounds. Now with four seconds left, there was time for one last play. It was a heave toward the end zone, a Hail Mary that was tipped at the 2-yard line and then miraculously into the waiting hands of Ahmad Rashad for the winning touchdown.

Everyone talked about and was stunned by the ending. But I thought about the play before. If I had done my job, the final play wouldn't have happened. I was crushed, but I'd learned a lesson in that loss: Be aware of the situation, and do the *assigned* job accordingly.

We weren't down for long. The final game was against the Bengals, and we beat them and won the division with an 11-5 record. We took on the Raiders in a divisional playoff game in Cleveland. It was the coldest I've been on a football field. The official temperature was zero, with a windchill of thirty below. When I sat on the bench, I could feel my feet getting stuck to the ground.

The coldest game was also one of the most heartbreaking. We were driving in the final two minutes as we trailed, 14–12. We were in field goal range, but kicking the ball that day was an adventure. There had been missed extra points and field goals due to the stone-like football. Brian Sipe tried to hit Ozzie Newsome in the end zone—the play call was Red Right 88—but his pass was intercepted. End of season.

iiiiiiiiiiii

My next task, as with a lot of my teammates, was to go to work. I'm not talking about off-season workouts; I mean, we actually had to get jobs. My rookie salary in 1980 was $20,000. I didn't have enough money to focus solely on football. Even after the loss, the excitement for the Kardiac Kids remained. People in Cleveland were drawn to the personalities on the team, so there were postseason Browns events. Many of them were basketball games, around Cleveland and the entire state of Ohio. Browns players could be paid as much as $300 to $400 per game—three or four times a week—to play exhibitions against other teams.

I remember playing with Doug Dieken, Robert E. Jackson, and Dave Logan, who'd played Division I college basketball. People paid to see us. Some teams played hard so they could say they'd beat us. We were good, and that $900 to $1,200 per week was more than I made as a pro football player!

My other off-season job was teaching. I was a substitute teacher in the Berea school system, so I was able to put my vocational-education degree to work. There were no secrets; the students knew that I played for the Browns. I found myself teaching split lessons, modeled after the ones I'd learned from my father. As Dad had when I was a kid, I told my students that if they mastered their math lessons in the first part of class, I'd allow them to ask me Browns and other football questions in the final fifteen minutes. They loved it and I did, too.

The end of my off-season, late summer 1981, should have signaled the beginning of training for Kaye's basketball season. She'd been an established pro for three years and was ready for her fourth season in the Women's Basketball League. But there were hints of trouble when some players on her old team, the New York Stars, didn't get paid for work that they'd done. There was no formal announcement from the Stars or Kaye's team, the New Jersey Gems. The league just went under, and that was it. There was no other professional league in the country for talented women such as Kaye to play in.

With the league now defunct, Kaye moved from New York to Cleveland. We shared the apartment in Berea, then decided to buy a condo in North Olmsted, about fifteen minutes away. Clearly, we knew we loved each other. What we didn't know was what it was like to spend extended time together. In the span of our relationship we had been away from each other, in different cities. Being together was the unknown for us personally and professionally.

I didn't take it for granted that I'd just make the Browns again in '81. I was on the fringe of the roster, so I viewed each day as a fight for my job. I made the team and gained a new friend as well, a six-foot-six lineman named Matt Miller. Matt was fun to be around, so it didn't surprise me that when I introduced him to Kaye's twin sister, Faye, they began dating. The four of us hung out together several times, and when we did, it felt like family.

As an offensive lineman, Matt was part of the position group I already socialized with the most. Our center was Tom DeLeone, one of the rare Browns who were actually from the area. He grew up about forty miles from Cleveland, so it wasn't unusual for him to introduce us to his buddies. One friend of his who spent a lot of time with us was John DeMaine, a business owner from Akron. John played golf and racquetball, and he played well. I felt that I did, too. We often played each other and did it with a lot of energy, competitiveness, and words. The winner of whatever game we played always had a lot to say about the accomplishment.

There were fun moments off the field, but I felt no joy from football during the season and neither did my team. I hurt my knee in one of our preseason games and missed the entire regular season. It didn't help our team that 1981 was a reversal of the Kardiac Kids. When we played close games, we lost more than we won. When the games weren't close, we usually lost those, too. We'd finished first in our division in '80, and we were last in '81 at 5-11. I couldn't wait to take the field in 1982. I'd been assured that my injury wouldn't affect my ability to play at the same level.

I was confident I'd continue to play pro football, but I hadn't forgotten the feeling of uncertainty. That *What am I going to do now?* I'd experienced after college and before the NFL. I didn't have a backup plan, and I never wanted to be in that position again. I'd occasionally talk with one of our defensive coaches, Dave Adolph, about coaching. Dave coached in college for more than a decade before going to the pros. I asked him if I needed my master's to coach in college. We talked casually about the process and what I'd need to do to enter that world. Just in case.

I'm not sure if Dave ever shared our conversations with Marty or any of the other Browns assistants. Maybe he did, or maybe an exchange I had with Marty one day was just coincidental. We'd had a joint scrimmage with the Buffalo Bills one evening, and during the action, I broke my right hand. I didn't want to draw attention to it, but it throbbed constantly. Any touch of it sent pain shooting through my hand and entire arm. The next afternoon, I was on the field in full pads, ready to go. I didn't think I could afford to be injured.

"Hey, Cowher," Marty shouted. "How's the hand?" He'd definitely noticed I'd created some do-it-yourself contraption to protect it.

"I'm fine. I'm ready."

He looked at me and nodded. "Cowher, you're pretty tough. I like that about you." What he said next stuck with me: "You're not only tough, you're smart. Someday I'm gonna hire you."

My '82 season wasn't interrupted by an injury. Instead, it was a players' strike. We played our first two games of the season and then that was it. Every player in the league didn't show up at their respective facilities for fifty-seven days. Numerous issues were on the table such as revenue sharing, retirement benefits, a new wage scale, and a path toward true free agency. By the time the strike ended, our sixteen-game schedule had been reduced to nine.

I was amazed by how much the new wage scale changed my life. I was in my third year and my salary was about $25,000. The new scale called for *rookies* to make, at minimum, $40,000. I was no rookie, so my new salary meant that I'd easily make more money playing nine games than I would have in sixteen under the previous collective bargaining agreement. My days of needing other jobs in the off-season were over.

It was such a weird season that our '82 record, 4-5, was good enough to qualify for the playoffs. We went to Los Angeles, and this time our game with the Raiders wasn't close. They beat us, 27–10, and I hurt my knee in the fourth quarter. On the plane back to Cleveland, my teammates talked about their off-season plans while I thought about the surgery and rehab I'd need.

The league was changing, and so was our team. The strike had taken attention away from our new high-profile teammates. They were Chip Banks and Tom Cousineau, and they were both . . . linebackers. Players such as me, affected by the slightest roster turn or tweak, noticed these things. The new linebackers' arrival meant an eventual squeeze-out for other linebackers. It was common sense and basic economics. A team is willing to tie up only so much money in one position group.

I could have dwelled on that, or my surgery, in early 1983. But something far more meaningful and exciting happened in my life. I'd known Kaye for nearly five years and lived with her for two. Back in Raleigh, before I ever spoke to her, I thought there was something special about her. Now I knew what it was: She was smart, friendly, athletic, independent, beautiful. Really, everything I needed and wanted, and she felt the same way about me. It was time.

On April 9 in Kaye's hometown of Bunn, North Carolina, we got married. My best man was Matt Miller. The celebration began in that small town, moved down the road to Raleigh, and continued when Kaye and I went to Jamaica for our honeymoon.

One month away from my twenty-sixth birthday, I felt great about all aspects of my life. I approached our '83 training camp with a lot of optimism. For the first time in my life, I was able to keep some weight on, so I was able to stay between 235 and 240. I knew what to expect from the physical demands of camp, and since we had the same coaching staff in place, I instinctively knew our defensive concepts. I was ready for my fourth season of pro football, even if it wouldn't happen in Cleveland.

To my surprise, I was traded halfway through the preseason. I was pleased with how I'd played, and apparently the Philadelphia Eagles were as well. The Browns traded me to the Eagles in exchange for an eleventh-round draft pick, and I couldn't have been happier about that. It was the first time in my football career that a team had placed value on what I'd done and decided that they wanted me. I'd enjoyed my time in Cleveland, but I was thrilled to go to the Eagles as a player that they'd gone after.

I don't think there's any coincidence that 1983 is what I consider my finest football season. I played well, and I played with a lot of confidence. There's no substitute for confidence in pro sports; I'm a believer in it because I've seen it and personally experienced it.

My first season in Philly was also the first there for the special teams coach, Frank Gansz. He taught and talked about special teams in an unconventional way. He'd been an air force pilot and coached at Navy, so he made military analogies to what we were doing. One of his big messages: Stay alert at all times and keep your head on a swivel. I remember sitting in the locker room one day, either reading or talking with someone. Suddenly there was a clap in my ear.

"Got you, Cowher!"

It was a gleeful Frank Gansz. He walked away with a coaching-point reminder: "Keep your head up."

He was creative, and we all loved playing for him. He had a point system, and it kept everyone competitive and involved. Various points were earned for good blocks, tackles, and coverage. He never missed an opportunity to teach or motivate, and sometimes he'd quote Napoléon or Genghis Khan to drive home the message.

After the 1983 season—Philly went 5-11—Kaye and I went back to Cleveland. We'd kept our place there, and in those days, it wasn't unusual for a player from one team to work out with a team he didn't play for. A lot of my friends were with the Browns, and I'd left the organization on good terms. I was able to train there and glean insight from the coaching staff, which still included Marty and Dave Adolph.

While I wanted to coach one day, in 1984 it still seemed so far off. I'd signed a multiyear contract with the Eagles, and my salary for the season was $130,000. I was also a special teams captain. I was beyond wondering if I could play pro football. Five years in, I had a niche on special teams, with the ability to understand and fill in at multiple defensive positions. I wasn't a player any team should count on to be a star, but I could be counted on for the two things that Marty always emphasized in Cleveland: preparation and dependability.

Halfway through our fourth game of the season, I felt it in my knee. I was hit by one of my teammates, and then I was down. In a blur, I went from feeling good and confident about the season to taking a spot on injured reserve. My season was over.

A few weeks later, I could see that I wasn't the only pro player having tough times. Back in Cleveland, many of my old teammates were in a rut. They lost their first three games of the season, got a win, and then lost four more in a row. At 1-7, there was a coaching change: Sam Rutigliano was fired and replaced by Marty Schottenheimer.

I felt for my buddies, but I had to focus on Philly. Our team wasn't playing so well, either. Even though I was out for the year, I still attended Frank Gansz's meetings to learn and to get mental reps. I couldn't be out there with my guys, but I could think along with them and maybe help with something I picked up on film.

Those were my thoughts late in 1984. I was not thinking about Marty. But he forced me to reconsider my priorities when he called me at home in December:

"Hey, Cowher, I want you to know that I'm going to be the Browns' head coach next year, too."

"That's great, Marty."

"Well, I'm putting together my coaching staff now. And I want you to think about being my special teams coach."

I was shocked. He knew I wanted to coach one day. He'd said he'd hire me someday. I didn't expect it to be now, when I was twenty-seven years old. I didn't imagine I'd be a professional coach until much later, if ever.

"Cowher, how much money are you making right now?"

I told him it was $130,000 and it was going to be $140,000 in '85.

"As a coach, you're going to work three times as much as you do now, and you're going to get a pay cut. I can pay you fifty thousand dollars."

Marty was always clear and direct, so that was the selling point: retire as a player, work more as a coach, earn less money.

"Think it over," he said. "I think it'll be a good move for you. I'll need an answer in a couple of weeks."

We hung up and I just stood there for a while. It was a lot to take in and think about.

Five seasons into my career, I'd already picked up several lessons that had taught me the essence of the game. I'd learned how a coach should relate to his players. I'd watched and listened to the best ways to communicate. I could relate to players who had been benched, cut, or traded because all those things had happened to me. Playing at the highest levels can bring out a player's deepest fears and insecurities, and coaches will never get the most out of their players if they don't view them as people first.

These were all good things to know, because each hour brought me closer to my answer for Marty. I talked with Kaye about it, and she totally understood where I was. The more the two of us talked, the easier the decision was to make. No one wants to take a 65 percent pay cut, but even that wasn't a factor in the big picture. How many years, realistically, were left in my career? I'd had three knee surgeries already, and with most of 1985's games on artificial turf—including all of them at home—that wasn't going to help the knee feel any better. Besides, I believed in Marty as a head coach. And I believed in myself to do everything necessary to succeed in this new career.

Yes, a new career. "Someday" had arrived. I called Marty and accepted the offer, with the terms that he had presented. He told me he was happy for me and to keep our deal quiet until after the season. I didn't tell anyone, but I wonder if Frank Gansz could tell how extra-attentive I was in his special teams meetings at the end of the season. I took a lot of notes. I asked questions. I paid attention to the way he addressed the room. I had a lot to learn about coaching.

There'd been a reason Kaye and I had kept our place in North Olmsted. We were headed back to Cleveland, and I was returning to the Browns—this time as Coach Cowher.

5

Learning to Think like a Coach

Before I left Philadelphia, our head coach, Marion Campbell, had a message for Kaye and me. I didn't know the coaching life and its demands, but Marion did. He'd coached in the pros since the early 1960s.

"Can I talk to your wife about this?" he asked.

"Sure."

"Loosen the reins on him during the season," he told Kaye. "And when it's over, pull him back in."

He smiled, knowing I didn't fully grasp what lay ahead for me in the 1985 season. I listened to Marion, Frank Gansz, and many others tell me about long hours, increased responsibilities, and the importance of preparation. I listened. I didn't quite get it, though, until I started doing the job.

Cleveland was already home, so these were familiar streets and sights. The people were familiar, too. I'd been teammates with several players that were still on the Browns' roster. Now, as a twenty-eight-year-old member of "management" on Marty's staff, I was one of the bosses rather than one of the guys. It was a transition for sure, and it was awkward for a while.

"You think you're better than us."

"You've changed."

"Oh, you can't hang out with us anymore?"

I heard it all.

The players were right that some things had to change in the relationships I'd had with my teammates. It was the first time I began to realize that the more responsibility you get, the lonelier you get. It doesn't mean that you're bigger or better than anyone else. It means that since you're held to a higher standard, you can't do certain things anymore. For example, it was going to be difficult—or impossible—to socialize with a player one night and then objectively hold him accountable the next day in a special teams meeting. I'd vacationed with some of these guys. Those days were over.

I had a lot of work and introspection to do on the coaching mentality itself. I could get advice on that, but ultimately the advice was to figure out what worked best for me. No one had a stock answer on the way to do it, because it didn't exist. The thing I had to be mindful of was leadership. How close can leaders get to the people they're leading while still maintaining control and earning respect? It isn't a peer relationship; it's a power relationship, with the coach holding the power.

In my first days of coaching, I also realized how much I didn't know about planning and organization. Marty told me that special teams had ten minutes on the practice field daily. That was ten minutes Wednesday through Friday.

"How do you want to spend that time?" he asked. "What do you want to do with the kickoff return team, punt coverage, and the hands team?"

The hands team? *Oh my.*

I'm the special teams coach; of course I've got to cover the hands team, the group of players you send on the field to recover an onside kick. The hands team is usually out there to finish a game that your team is winning.

I'd honestly forgotten about it.

As I look back on it now, my first thirty-minute special teams meeting was an unintentional comedy. Before the meeting, I thought I had a sensible plan for each topic. I planned to spend ten minutes each on kickoff return, kickoff coverage, and the drills we'd do the next day. Got it. No problem.

When the meeting started, I found myself enjoying it. Then I looked at my watch. I'd spent twenty-five minutes talking about kickoff coverage without ever getting to the other two phases. There was a lesson in that experience as well: Thoughtful messaging (and sometimes carefully timed messaging) is part of coaching, too.

Fortunately, I worked for the perfect boss. Marty knew how much I had to learn. A glance around our coaches' meetings told part of the story. I was the youngest one in the room, seven to ten years younger than some and fifteen to twenty years younger than others. They had experience that I didn't, and nothing could change that. But Marty trusted I'd put in the time to improve, and that's exactly what I did. He'd put his faith in me, that rare pro coach with no previous coaching experience, and I wanted to show him that it wasn't a mistake. Marty couldn't have been more supportive; he was even encouraging when, in my first game as a coach, against the Chicago Bears, the opening kickoff was returned for a touchdown.

The time spent at work was unlike anything else I'd experienced. The cliché is that there are only so many hours in a day—and it seemed that all of mine were spent at the office. An eighty-hour week was not unusual. I suddenly became a writer; anything that I observed or learned, I wrote it down somewhere. I spent hours studying, reading, interviewing, learning. I'd always loved the game and was comfortable with my knowledge of it. But my introduction to coaching was a reeducation.

One thing I didn't have to learn or change was passion. My players knew that I'd always have that, and in my first few months of coaching, my enthusiasm made up for the experience that I lacked. They knew I was genuinely excited when I described how ten to twelve plays on special teams could turn a game around and win it for our team. A punt downed at the 2-yard line; a blocked punt; a big return. All of those things could awaken a sleeping team and lead to a win. It helped my credibility that I'd made my living on special teams for five years and literally had the scars to prove it.

I still acted like a player on the sideline for most of the season. When players came off the field, I'd pound their backs and slap their helmets, trying to set the tempo. At times I'd be on the sideline lined up with the kickoff team. Then I'd run the field with them. Sometimes I'd bump into the officials and knock them over. I'd be so into the game that I wouldn't even notice. Marty warned me to cut it out and said the officials might throw a penalty flag on me one day. I'd nod, apologize, and inevitably do it again.

In '85, we became the first team in NFL history to win a division without a winning record. We were 8-8 and earned a trip to Miami for a divisional playoff game with the Dolphins. No one expected much from us, with Dan Marino and the Dolphins installed as 10-point favorites. We jumped out to a 21–3 lead, but Marino led a comeback and Miami won, 24–21.

My first season as a coach had been successful. Marty was happy with the work I'd done, and my players told me that they appreciated how I'd made them better. A few months into 1986, I had a lot more to learn as I became a rookie again.

This was an incomparable first: I was a father now. On March 3,

Kaye gave birth to our daughter, Meagan. I was grateful to be a dad and thankful that I could be fully present for the first few months of her life. With our family growing, we decided to move from our condo and into our first house. It was in Strongsville, about twenty minutes from the stadium. Buying a house is always risky in such a fragile profession, but I felt good about the direction of our team.

A big reason for that was Marty. He was incredibly organized, and the questions he asked made me a better coach. It was simple: He wanted to know what you were doing and why you were doing it. Process was big for him. His approach forced me to think more thoroughly, because the last thing I wanted was to meet with him and have no answers for why I wanted to do something.

Another reason for optimism? Bernie Kosar, or simply "Bernie" to people in Cleveland.

Bernie had been a national championship quarterback at the University of Miami, and he grew up in northeast Ohio. He planned his college graduation and draft status in such a way that the Browns would be in position to select him. Cleveland fans weren't used to pro athletes working that hard to come to the city, so they loved Bernie before he even put on a Browns uniform. He'd been good as a rookie, but he appeared to be stronger and more confident in 1986. Marty had hired a new offensive coordinator, Lindy Infante, to work with Bernie, and they hit it off immediately.

Watching Marty manage in '86 told me a lot about his range and intelligence. In '85, we'd been a run-oriented team that leaned heavily on our defense. We'd had two 1,000-yard rushers in Kevin Mack and Earnest Byner. In '86, looking at the improvement of Bernie and the personnel around him, Marty shifted and accepted we'd be more of a passing team. He assessed our strengths and weaknesses and then decided how to proceed. He didn't make the decision based on what he wanted. If he'd done that, we'd have looked a lot like we did in '85. He did it with our greatest winning percentage in mind. He was doing math, which was always going to win with me. And what he was doing was the essence of strategy.

Nearly at the halfway point of the season, we were 4-3. In our eighth game, at Minnesota, we trailed 17–3 at the beginning of the third quarter. Bernie and the offense had struggled. The Vikings got the ball first in the third quarter, and any kind of score by them would have put us in big trouble. But the defense held, and the Vikings' Wade Wilson came out to punt. As a coach, you can point out the potential soft spots in an opponent's punt protection unit, but to see your team apply those coaching points is gratifying. It sends the message to the players that spending all that time on studying pays off.

Wilson took a couple of steps and began to punt, we blocked it, and Felix Wright ran it in for a 30-yard touchdown. One play and we were back in the game. It's the beauty and suddenness of special teams. Later in the game, Wilson was able to get off a punt, but we downed it at their 2-yard line. Pressured another time, Wilson was forced into an 18-yard kick.

Before long, I was like a preacher at a revival when discussing special teams. I believed in them, and I believed in the players who performed on them. We'd gotten ourselves out of a hole in Minnesota and tied the score at 20. Then, remarkably, special teams struck again. With four minutes to play, we kicked off to the Vikings. They fumbled the kickoff, and Wright—there he was again—recovered. That led to the winning field goal.

I was content to step back that day and watch our special teams get tremendous praise within the locker room and in the media throughout the week. It was the perfect illustration of what we talked about; a half dozen special teams plays were a huge part of a win on the road.

Our fans found a lot to be excited about in '86. Having played in

Cleveland, I knew what happened when the community fell in love with a team: Everyone broke out in song. This time the song, set to the classic tempo of "Louie Louie," was "Bernie Bernie (Super Bowl)." The opening lyrics were complimentary and hopeful:

BERNIE BERNIE, OH YEAH, HOW YOU CAN THROW . . .
BERNIE BERNIE, OH YEAH, SUPER BOWL.

Everywhere you went in Cleveland—or Strongsville—all you saw was orange and brown. More than a few people gifted Kaye and me an orange-and-brown onesie for ten-month-old Meagan. The Browns were 12-4 and the number one seed in the conference. We were strong everywhere—offense, defense . . . and special teams.

When Bernie threw for an NFL record 489 yards in a playoff win over the New York Jets, his song was blasted all over the city. It was the first Browns playoff win in seventeen years, and it set up a championship game at home against the Denver Broncos. We were one win away from the Super Bowl.

I couldn't have felt better with six minutes to play in the game. Bernie threw a 48-yard touchdown pass to Brian Brennan to put us up 20–13. Then, on the kickoff, the Broncos were unsure what to do with the football, which began bouncing inside the 10. Did it have enough momentum to get into the end zone and allow them to begin their drive at the 20? Or should they pick it up and run with it? Neither happened. They smothered the football at their own 2, and that's where their drive began.

Or, I should say, that's where "The Drive" began.

In one of the most dramatic and impressive drives I've ever seen, John Elway and the Broncos marched 98 yards to force overtime. Elway ran when he had to; checked down when he had to; and, as a former baseball player, threw fastballs into the stiff Cleveland wind when he had to. The Broncos won the game in overtime. After a loss like that, no one stands in appreciation at what the other team accomplished. But the more I look back on it, I can see how special it was.

There was no coaching lesson to take from that loss. We were talented, well prepared, and hungry. We were good enough to win it and we didn't. I couldn't grumble about the loss for long because Marty had a new assignment for me in 1987. After two years as a special teams coach, he promoted me to the secondary.

I was in my third year of coaching, but in some ways this was harder than being a rookie coach. I didn't have a plan then, but I had the experience of playing special teams. Now I understood that I needed a plan, but I had no experience with the secondary. Beyond that, the two stars of our secondary—Pro Bowlers Hanford Dixon and Frank Minnifield—knew exactly what I didn't know. I'd played with Hanford, a cornerback, and he remembered me as the slow linebacker. I was now a slow linebacker coaching him and others about cornerback and safety play, two positions I'd never played.

I had a lot of work to do. Ironically, this was the time when I learned the most as a coach. A lot of coaches weren't teaching from the perspective of having played a position as a pro. They were relying on their teaching, study, and communication skills to help players get better. My mission, from the end of the season in January to the beginning of the season in July, was to become a scholar on the secondary.

Marty, as usual, had meaningful advice that I never forgot: "Be prepared for every question they can possibly ask you. This is important: If you don't have the answer, don't guess. Tell them you're not sure but you'll find out. Don't try to be someone you're not. You're not going to know the answer to every question. The most important thing is getting it right, not *when* you get it right."

When I played, I respected coaches who could tell me something I didn't know and who would communicate it to me with no filter.

Could I teach a Pro Bowl player how to play his position? No. But, through detailed film study, I could show him how to play it better. I made myself an expert on technique.

A defensive back doesn't have the luxury of making a misstep. Every step matters. Every half step matters. I wanted to show players such as Hanford, Minnifield, and Ray Ellis that by paying closer attention to anticipation and angles, they could appear even faster than they already were.

By this time, I knew exactly what I wanted to say in meetings and to do in practice. Over that season, I devoted hours to fundamentals. Sometimes the instruction was as exact as practicing the angle the lead foot should be pointing before making a turn and taking a first step. The difference between a pass breakup and a completed pass is sometimes one step.

Once again, I was in charge of a group that performed well. Although we won fewer games—ten—than we had the year before, we were a better team. We ranked in the top three in offense and defense, and Bernie, who was just twenty-four, became a Pro Bowl quarterback.

Away from the field, it was a great time for the Cowhers. Our daughter, Meagan, was nearly two years old, and she was talking, walking, and running all over the place. In early November, she got a playmate. Our second daughter, Lauren, was born. Thankfully, we had a two-game home stand, so I didn't miss the big moment.

I knew the biggest difference between our '86 and '87 teams was experience. We had more of it, especially with our offense, so I felt we had as much of a chance as anyone to win a championship. In the playoffs, we found ourselves eye to eye with the Broncos again. This time, in the middle of the game, there didn't appear to be a drama in the works. After Elway threw an 80-yard touchdown pass to Mark Jackson—the secondary coach wasn't happy about it—we trailed, 28–10.

But Bernie was having one of those games, and he brought us all the way back to tie, 31 apiece, in the fourth quarter. Elway threw another touchdown pass to put them up (I saw our missed tackles in the secondary), but then Bernie had the offense on the move again. We were a few yards away from potentially tying the score when Earnest Byner raced toward the end zone. The Broncos forced a fumble before Byner could get there, which they recovered, earning another trip to the Super Bowl—instead of us.

As a player, you're told a single play doesn't win or lose the game for you. As a coach, you realize the depth of that truth. We spend hours and hours studying and dissecting film, teaching and practicing, trying to find the best action to take in a game. Then during the game, there's the reaction to what an opponent does. Sometimes the other player is faster than you thought, so a play you expected to work won't that day. Or someone is a little bit stronger in person. Or there's an injury. Good coaching happens when you're able to diagnose issues on the fly, then come up with an alternative in a few seconds in front of thousands of screaming people, then communicate your ideas to players so they collectively understand it.

There's nothing easy about it. It's chess, but chess in three-second bursts when you're hitting someone or being hit every play. And being yelled at. It's fascinating, and no one ever figures it out completely. There's always something about the job that you didn't plan for but have to adjust to.

I found that out up close in 1988, and it affected my family's decision-making in 1989.

The first change happened in the off-season, with our altered coaching staff. Lindy Infante had built a strong offense and good rapport with Bernie, and the Green Bay Packers were impressed. They hired him as their new head coach. That left us without an offensive coordinator. Marty decided to do the job himself.

Not only did our offensive numbers go down, but so did our quarterbacks. I mean, all of them. Injuries led to four quarterbacks getting starts for us in '88: Bernie, Mike Pagel, Don Strock, and Gary Danielson. Lindy's departure, and the decline of the offense, was a story line all year. We won ten games again and made the playoffs. Pagel started our playoff game against the Oilers, which we lost, 24–23.

Given all the challenges he had during the season, Marty did a great job holding the team together. That's why I was floored when he approached me and gave me the news:

"I just want you to know that I'm no longer going to be the head coach of the Cleveland Browns. But you should know that Art Modell wants to talk with you. He's very interested in you staying on the coaching staff in some capacity."

Wait, Marty had been *fired*?

Marty had taken the team to the playoffs each full season he had the job. Marty had taken the team to back-to-back conference championships. And he'd been fired?

My education as a coach was ongoing.

I talked with Art Modell and listened to what he had to say. He wanted me to stay in Cleveland, even though he didn't know whom he wanted the new head coach to be. And he also said he loved the way I coached special teams and wanted me to return to that role.

While I was flattered that he wanted me to stay, I didn't want to force my way onto anyone's staff. I also thought I could add more to my coaching résumé. I thanked him for the consideration and politely declined.

It was just before New Year's Day, 1989. Marty, my mentor, was unemployed.

So was I.

6

Revelations While Rising

Kaye and I sat in our Strongsville living room in January 1989 knowing we had a quick decision to make. In the NFL, everything happens fast.

Just one month earlier, I'd been a Browns assistant coach, preparing for the playoffs. Then a few days after our Christmas Eve game, Marty was fired, and I didn't want to stay on the staff without him. It meant I needed to find a job. By the third week of January, I had two offers from two of the best coaches in the league.

The head coach of the New York Giants, Bill Parcells, wanted me to coach his secondary. I was humbled. Coach Parcells had already led the Giants to the 1986 Super Bowl title, and his current team was talented enough to win another. He also had an incredible coaching staff, which included a smart, innovative, up-and-coming defensive coordinator named Bill Belichick.

One day after Parcells made his offer, I got a call from Marty. He'd been hired as the head coach of the Kansas City Chiefs. He also asked me to join him as his secondary coach.

Kaye and I agreed: I couldn't make a bad decision. I knew firsthand how prepared and thoughtful Marty was, and while I didn't know Parcells, his quick wit and ability to motivate had already made him an NFL legend. Kaye and I went back and forth on the offers, then I called Parcells to let him know my decision:

"Thank you for considering me. But I'm going to take the job in Kansas City with Marty."

"Well, how much is Marty paying you there?"

"Ninety thousand."

"Ninety thousand? I'm offering you one hundred and thirty thousand!"

It didn't occur to me how strange this may have looked to people. For the second time in five years, I'd decided that my best option was to walk away from a six-figure salary and instead join Marty's staff.

I told Parcells that the cost of living in Kansas City, for a young family such as mine, was better than what it would be in New York. Besides, the decision wasn't as much about money as it was loyalty. I'd played for Marty and he'd given me a chance to be a coach. I wanted to be there for him with the Chiefs. Parcells said he understood and wished me well.

There's no question I'd picked the tougher job. The Chiefs had won a combined eight games in the previous two years. Almost every position group needed a boost. The secondary, however, was the exception. With Albert Lewis, Kevin Ross, and Deron Cherry, the Chiefs had three players who could have excelled for any team. My immediate focus went to helping them improve. But my attention shifted when Marty shared some news.

Dave Adolph was Marty's choice for defensive coordinator in Kansas City, just as he had been in Cleveland. But there was a family issue, and Dave suddenly said he couldn't join the staff. Now there was an unexpected vacancy for the top job on defense, and with four years' coaching experience, I thought I was ready to do it.

While Kaye and the girls remained in Ohio, I lived in the Adam's Mark Hotel, less than a mile away from Arrowhead Stadium. Marty stayed there, too, and I talked with him daily about our plans for the '89 season. I also lobbied him every chance I got. Every time he mentioned a coordinating candidate, I'd remind him that I could do it. He'd watched me grow as a coach, and he'd been pleased with the results. The two years I coached special teams in Cleveland, we were the top special teams group in the NFL. I'd helped our secondary become a reliable and high-achieving unit the two years I coached them. Marty had seen me in front of the team several times, presenting information in a way that engaged the players.

"Come on, Marty," I'd persist. "I can do this."

Marty was hesitant. He'd added Tony Dungy to the defensive staff, and Marty thought of making him the coordinator. Tony was just two years older than I was, but he'd been a defensive coordinator with the Steelers. His experience there appealed to Marty.

"Tony's done it before and you haven't," he said.

"You were in the same position once. You'd never done the job until someone decided to give the young guy a chance."

By February, the time of the scouting combine in Indianapolis, the defensive coordinator position still hadn't been filled. After I'd scouted all the cornerbacks and safeties at the combine, I prepared to leave Indy. On the morning of my flight, I got a call in my room.

"Bill Cowher . . ."

Marty always called me that—or Billy Cowher—when he wanted to emphasize a point. He said it as if it were one word. *BillCowher.*

"When's your flight back to Kansas City?"

I told him it was in a few hours.

"I need you to push that flight back a couple of days and stay here to scout the linebackers. As the defensive coordinator and linebackers coach, you need to see everybody."

It took a second for it to sink in. He'd done it; he'd made me the defensive coordinator. I couldn't thank him enough, and then I couldn't end our conversation quickly enough so I could call home and share the news with Kaye. I was thirty-one, and now the youngest coordinator in the NFL, but I was ready. This was Marty putting his faith in me as a coach, leader, and manager. He was the head coach, but he had taken this same route to that position. He'd built his reputation on defense, and I knew the two of us would meet often to make sure I understood the scope of my role.

I quickly learned there was another reason, beyond general coaching, that Marty wanted me to study the linebackers. We held the fourth pick in the draft and had an opportunity to select a great player there. Troy Aikman, the UCLA quarterback, was expected to go first to the Cowboys. A handful of franchise players would be available after Aikman, and just one of them was a linebacker. Long after his playing days were over, Marty still thought like a linebacker and so did I. The player we wanted, naturally, was Derrick Thomas, a game-changing linebacker from the University of Alabama.

Our general manager, Carl Peterson, was frustrated Thomas showed up at the combine, ran the 40-yard dash, then decided not to perform other drills. "Who are these guys?" Peterson said to Marty and me. "We fly all the way here and they think they're prima donnas?"

Many players who were assured of being top picks took the same approach as Thomas. If teams wanted to see them in thorough workouts, they'd have to take a trip to the player's home campus. While Peterson was annoyed Thomas didn't give him much to see in Indy, he was still intrigued by Thomas's undeniable talent. At six-three and about 250 pounds, Thomas was as strong and fast as any player in the draft.

Just before we worked out Thomas—and four other players—in Tuscaloosa, Peterson pulled me aside and whispered, "I want you to work him out so hard that he'll regret not working out in Indianapolis. Do whatever you need to do. Just pretend this is a guy who missed your meeting the night before a game."

No problem. I'd done and given plenty of linebacker drills in my life. After a few minutes of nonstop drills, one of the four players dropped out. He was too winded and needed a break. Thomas, though, smiled his way through the drills and didn't appear to be breathing hard. *All right*, I thought. *I'll go faster.* Another player dropped out, but Thomas was still smiling and eager. I'd gone through all of my linebacker drills. I checked in with Peterson.

"How about some defensive back drills," he said.

I told the players I wanted to see how they looked in coverage. As they ran up and down the field, Thomas was the first one down and first one back. *There's no way Peterson is frustrated now*, I thought. If we were able to draft Thomas, he'd make all of our jobs easier. He was as tireless as he was talented.

When I finally told Thomas the workout was over, he looked at me and flashed an easy smile. "That's it, Coach? You haven't got any more drills for me?"

The truth was, I knew more about playing linebacker than coaching the position. I took a similar coaching approach with this position as I did in Cleveland with the secondary. But this time I traveled for a deeper education. I'd become friendly with Bill Belichick, the Giants' defensive coordinator. When I didn't take the secondary job that Bill Parcells offered in New York, Parcells told Belichick to fold coaching the secondary into his responsibilities. What it meant was that we were both coordinators who were also in charge of position groups that we'd never coached. We decided to have an information exchange.

So, I flew to New York in March 1989 and spent a long day with Belichick at Giants Stadium. In the morning, I taught him everything I'd learned about coaching defensive backs, and in the afternoon he taught me all he knew about coaching linebackers. He was privileged enough to coach Lawrence Taylor, arguably the greatest outside linebacker ever. When we drafted Thomas in April, I could see that he had similar traits.

In my first season as defensive coordinator, I was grateful that Marty allowed me the space to grow as a leader, while not letting me get too far away from our defensive principles. I knew that he liked unpredictable game plans in which we'd throw a variety of coverages at an opponent. He'd emphasize what he wanted during our last coaches' meeting of the week: "Bill Cowher, I want to see some zone in the game tomorrow."

The great thing about Marty was that he'd listen to any new ideas, as long as you'd thought them through and had good answers to his questions. And he always had questions. I knew he'd have plenty for a defense I wanted to incorporate into our attack, called the blitz zone.

The concept of the blitz zone is to manufacture a rush with a fifth rusher—that's technically a blitz—and still play zone behind that blitz. At its best, it can create havoc for a quarterback. Most quarterbacks see a blitz look and automatically think it's man-to-man coverage. They then decide that they're going to throw to a "hot" receiver, or someone who knows the ball is coming to him quickly in situations such as this. But the blitz zone often forces quarterbacks to pause for a second. Instead of seeing six guys turning their backs to him and running down the field, he sees six guys looking at him as they play their zones.

Marty had two big questions about the concept. What happens if the rush doesn't achieve its desired effect and every eligible receiver is able to get into his route? In that case, he said, somebody wouldn't be accounted for. He was right. His question forced me to tinker and have a defensive lineman as a "spy," for the situations Marty described. His other question spoke to our personnel: How often did we need to use it?

I mentioned that the concept is there to manufacture a rush. But we often got there organically with the superb play of Derrick Thomas. From the moment he stepped on an NFL field, Thomas clearly was one of the league's top pass rushers. He was a linebacker and defensive end, and he made an impact whether he rushed the passer or dropped into coverage. I was in my fifth year of coaching, and I'd never coached anyone with such rare skill.

When our defensive staff reviewed postgame film, we got used to just marveling at something unexpected Thomas did. For example, there were times he was supposed to drop into coverage and he'd rush the quarterback instead. That would be a problem for most players, because that rush would lead to a hole in the defense where they were supposed to be. But Derrick was so fast that he'd get a pressure or sack even when that wasn't the call.

I'd tell him, "If you sack the quarterback, even if you were supposed to be in coverage, you're not wrong. But if he completes a pass in the area you were supposed to be, you are wrong." He wasn't wrong much. He had the fastest first step of anyone I've seen; he'd take that step and his opponent would immediately be in distress. I didn't have to push him to get to the quarterback. He already knew how to do that. He told me he wanted to be Lawrence Taylor, so I'd challenge him on the few occasions he wanted to coast.

"LT isn't just great on third down," I'd say. "He's great on first and second, too."

I used to give out written tests to make sure players knew their assignments and the opponent's strengths and weaknesses. I'd get on Thomas when he didn't pass his. But he was so charismatic he didn't miss a beat.

"That's all right, Coach. I guarantee you I'll pass the test on Sunday."

Thomas finished with 10 sacks as a rookie, made the Pro Bowl, and was named Defensive Rookie of the Year. Our team doubled its win total from the previous season, and although we didn't make the playoffs, everyone associated with the Chiefs could sense we were headed in the right direction.

In 1990, I realized I still had a lot to learn about management. I understood all of the technical aspects of the game, but coaching is so much more than that. In my second year as a defensive coordinator, I began to understand how necessary it is to blend technical mastery with an ability to lead diverse personalities. I was still teaching. Instead of a classroom full of high school math students, it was a meeting room full of adult men. They were treated like superhuman celebrities outside the stadium, but they were as normal as anyone else doing a job. Just as there isn't a single approach to dealing with all employees, the same goes with professional football players.

I learned that lesson in a vivid way with our first-round pick in '90, a linebacker named Percy Snow. I'd drilled it into our defense that we always needed to run to the football. I wanted to see my players run to the ball on every play in practice. If they did it in practices, they'd do it in the games. I probably preached that point more than any other.

Snow didn't always do that in his rookie season. In one film session, in front of the entire defense, I showed a clip of him lagging and eventually giving up on a play. He was sitting in the front row, just a few feet away from me.

"Percy, this isn't good enough," I told him. "We run to the football here in Kansas City. There's no exceptions. I don't care who you are, you run to the football."

He had his head down, not even looking at me. I reran some film, and I started to get agitated that he didn't bother to lift his head and see the coaching points that I made. Finally, I stopped the film, turned the lights on, and said, "Percy, I'm asking you to run to the football. Do you have a problem with that?"

He lifted his head for the first time and I saw him glaring. The veins in his neck were bulging. "I ain't got a fucking problem. Do you have a fucking problem?"

I'd embarrassed him in front of his peers. He was angry for sure, but being called out in that way likely irritated him more than anything else.

"No problem here," I said. "I just want to make sure we were all on the same page. We're good, right?"

"We're good."

He felt that I'd challenged his manhood and backed him into a corner. No, I didn't like the way he approached the play. But there's a way to correct the issue without humiliating a player—no matter how unintentionally—in front of the group. Everyone deserves respect. From that moment on, when I had pointed criticism for a player, I'd call him into my office for a one-on-one conversation.

During that 1990 season, we had a six-game stretch in which we went 5-1. I started to feel confident about who we were and what we were capable of. It turned out to be too much confidence. We were 9-4, and our next game was at Arrowhead against the Houston Oilers.

Houston played a wide-open offense called the run-and-shoot. The Oilers were a Top 3 scoring team in the league, and they'd just scored 58 points against the Browns the previous week. They had four good receivers, but I decided I could take away their two best ones, Drew Hill and Ernest Givins. I'd put my Pro Bowl corners, Lewis and Ross, on them. Then I'd blitz their quarterback, Warren Moon, all day.

Honestly, I loved the game plan. I hadn't seen other teams try it, and I was convinced we'd discovered something. It turned out to be one of my worst days as a coach. Moon threw for 527 yards and

3 touchdowns, and the Oilers beat us, 27–10. The performance was bad enough, but my approach to it was even worse. I was stubborn. I watched it unfold, and I refused to make any adjustments. It was as if I thought my scheme were suddenly going to click and we'd shut the Oilers down.

Marty's hallmark was preparation, and the Oilers had exposed my lack of it. I didn't have a backup plan in case things broke down. I'd been too inflexible for that. I walked off that field with the worst feeling I've ever had as a coach. I knew I'd let the team down, and my confidence was so low I felt I'd let my family down, too.

It was mid-December and Kaye was pregnant with our third child. I couldn't help thinking that here I was, the father of a young family, coaching in a way that could lead to my firing. My fear intensified the day after the game when Marty asked one of *his* mentors, Joe Collier, to sit in on my defensive meetings.

I was screwed.

Collier was an innovator. He was the reason Marty ran a 3-4 defense because Collier had done it first in Denver, with the famed Orange Crush defense. I was thirty-three years old, and Collier had been a coach as long as I'd been alive. My mind was racing. Was Marty losing confidence in me?

I tried to run my normal meetings during the week, even though I saw Collier sitting in the back of the room taking notes. I spent the beginning of the week wondering what he had to say, and then in the middle of the week my thoughts went elsewhere. Kaye went into labor three days before our next game, at San Diego.

I remember sitting in the hospital waiting room, writing notes for the next day's practice. A nurse interrupted me: "Sir, if you want to be there for the birth of the baby, now is the time to do it." I was there for the arrival of Lindsay, on December 20, 1990.

I'll never forget the drive home that night. I felt an overwhelming sense of pressure and responsibility, probably the most I'd ever felt. The realization of where I was, and what I was doing, began to hit me. I knew I needed to provide for the family, and if I was going to continue to do that, I needed to get better at my job. I needed to be sure I was doing all that I could, as well as I could, to be successful in this business. I wasn't a player; I was a coach. This was my life.

When I got to work the next morning, a handwritten note was on my desk from Joe Collier:

Bill, you're a good football coach. I've watched you interact with players, I watched how you dealt with this last loss. I want you to understand that if you stay in this business, you're going to have days like that. The most important thing is that you learn from it and you don't let it happen again. Don't ever doubt yourself or your abilities. You know what you're doing, you have the pulse of your team, your players believe in you. You're a damn good football coach.

Joe

I must have reread Joe's note three or four times. It was such a meaningful and timely note in my career. I had no professional confidence that week, and he picked me up. Lesson learned. Never again would I be so committed to a game plan that I'd be unable and unwilling to change it.

We won our last two games of the regular season to finish 11-5 and qualify for the playoffs. For the second time in three years, a team I was on lost a wild card game by one point. This time it was a 17–16 loss to the Miami Dolphins. The first time it happened, in 1988, Browns owner Art Modell wanted to talk with me about staying on another coach's staff as an assistant coach. Now, in 1990, Modell wanted to interview me for the head coaching job in Cleveland. Marty's replacement, Bud Carson, didn't last two full seasons with the Browns. The team was in decline, and Modell wanted to start over.

Just going through the interview process was eye-opening to me. I was asked how I would lead the organization; what my philosophy was; what I thought of the roster; and how I could relate to other parts of the organization, such as business and marketing. I thought I interviewed well in Cleveland, but I wasn't surprised when I didn't get the job and a friend of mine did. The position went to Belichick, who'd just helped the Giants win Super Bowl XXV over the Bills, 20–19.

I didn't know when I'd get another opportunity to interview for a head coaching job, but the experience changed the way I looked at and listened to Marty. I paid extra attention to how he dealt with the media. I had deeper appreciation for how he'd get the players' attention by personalizing Raiders Week. The Chiefs-Raiders rivalry was deep, and Marty made sure each player understood how much the game meant to him. He seemed to believe a good-versus-evil narrative existed between Kansas City and Oakland, and he played it up before each of those games.

I found myself studying Marty throughout 1991, never imagining that it would be my last year in Kansas City. There was no hurry to leave. I had the opportunity to coach good players, our defense was consistently ranked in the Top 10, and the coach I worked for—and the coaches I worked with—made the atmosphere great. I used to joke with Tony Dungy that he was the calm voice in my head. Whenever a team completed a couple of passes in a row, Tony knew that I'd want to respond with a blitz or something to get their attention. My philosophy was that you shouldn't wait for the storm; why not create it?

Tony knew this, and he'd calmly say into the headsets, "Let's not overreact to what they're doing here, Bill. We'll settle down and play Cover 2." He understood Marty, too. When I talked with Tony about different defenses to bring to Marty, Tony would say the same things I did: We'd better get it right, we'd better have answers for Marty's questions, and we'd better not screw it up in practice.

In December 1991, the Chiefs finally won a playoff game. It was the first time in two decades that had happened, and what made it sweeter was the opponent: the Raiders, whom we beat 10–6. I was fortunate to work for a coach such as Marty, who'd taken teams to the postseason six of the last seven years. He knew how to set up a winning culture, and we all benefited from being around him.

Maybe that was a reason everyone in the organization looked at me when our '91 season ended with a 37–14 loss in Buffalo. A few head coaching jobs were open, and since I'd interviewed for one last year, there was a thought that it was my turn. There was one particular job opening that the whole league watched.

The Pittsburgh Steelers, my beloved hometown team, were looking for a head coach. They hadn't done that since I was play-ing pickup football on Hawthorne Avenue in the late 1960s. Chuck Noll had the job for twenty-three years and won four Super Bowl titles in the 1970s. In the '80s, the team never made it back to the Super Bowl, with several seasons of missing the playoffs. Noll, who began coaching the Steelers when he was thirty-seven, said it was time to step away.

Every day, someone asked me if the Steelers had contacted me. Every day, the answer was the same: "No."

"Why haven't they called?" Kaye asked. "I'd think that you'd be on their list."

"I don't know. Maybe they're looking elsewhere."

After a few days, I accepted that they weren't going to call. And that's when they did. Each time Dan Rooney called, Kaye would sit nearby and be confused by my answers. That's because she didn't realize what the team's owner and president was asking me. All she heard was answers such as:

"Yes."

"She's great."

"Oh, I took them to the park. They love it there."

"Yes, they're doing well. I see them whenever I can."

I'd hang up and Kaye would shrug. "What did he ask you?"

I told her that he asked if I was going to the combine; he wanted to know how Kaye was doing; he'd asked what I'd done with the girls that day; and he wanted to know about my parents. That's how our first couple of conversations, ten to fifteen minutes apiece, went. He'd sneak in a football question or two, but what he really wanted to know was how I was doing with my family.

Finally, he called and talked about getting me to Pittsburgh for an interview. Everything about his approach was meticulous and family oriented. It was obvious to me that something about the Steelers job and the Steelers hierarchy was different.

I tried to hide how much I wanted the job. Everything I valued about work, family, and football was tied to Pittsburgh. The city had inspired, taught, and shaped me. No matter where I'd been, whether it was Raleigh or Cleveland or Philadelphia or Kansas City, Pittsburgh was in me.

Many nights, I tried to block out all of my emotions. I didn't want to be obsessed with getting the job. But after going to Pittsburgh for an interview and being invited back there for a second one, I couldn't help myself.

During that second trip to Pittsburgh, I could feel how serious my candidacy was. I was asked more specific questions about my philosophy, the roster, and coaching in Pittsburgh. There were fewer and fewer *If you were to be hired* . . . questions. There was momentum, a shift, and suddenly I felt like I was a world away from Kansas City.

At one point in our conversation, Mr. Rooney stood up and closed his office door.

"Do you want to be the next head coach of the Pittsburgh Steelers?" he asked.

"Yes! Yes. Thank you."

"Don't you want to know how much you're making?"

Oh, yeah. I wasn't even thinking about it. The contract offer was for four years and more money than I'd ever made in my life. Accepted. I was a husband and father who could more than provide for his young family.

I immediately called my parents and told them the news. I was the youngest head coach in the NFL, and unquestionably the happiest one. I had a new job in my old city. Pittsburgh, the place that was already in my heart.

7

Head Coaching Hits and Misses

I'd been a head coach for just a few hours, and it was already clear my new job went far beyond its description. As I thought about all the items on my to-do list, I knew I'd also need a strong understanding of business, time management, psychology, and communications to be successful.

On day one, I barely had time to think about one thing because I felt as if I were chasing everything. I didn't have a coaching staff, so I needed to set up interviews with candidates. I didn't have a secretary. I wanted to introduce myself to the players, who were scattered all over the country. I wanted to be looped in on our free agency and draft plans. Dozens of people were in the building—doctors, accountants, public relations specialists—whom I hadn't met but needed to.

I don't know if Chuck Noll was intentional with his exit plan after twenty-three seasons as Steelers head coach, but by the time I accepted the job in January 1992, Chuck's office was cleared out. There was no sign he had ever been there. There wasn't a master handbook—*How to Be a Steelers Head Coach*—to page through, and as scary and uncomfortable as that was, it was also the best thing for me. I was thirty-four, and I had my own opinions and tons to learn.

I had to figure out how the building worked, what the dynamics were with the front office, the personnel and PR departments, and ownership. I needed to ask questions and get my own answers, not begin with any preconceived thoughts.

When I was offered the job, I was humbled and nostalgic. My thought was, if I could manage to make it three years without getting fired, then I'd be able to attend my twentieth Carlynton High School reunion as the proud coach of the Pittsburgh Steelers. I was still in awe at the end of that first day. I'd met with the media at large and in one-on-one settings. Then I was told my final interview of the day was with Myron Cope. I couldn't believe it. I still viewed him as the unique Pittsburgh legend whose distinct, nasally voice blared out of our kitchen radio back on Hawthorne Avenue in the early 1970s. My father would crack open a beer, listen to Myron's popular show on WTAE, and confirm many of Myron's opinions.

"You tell 'em, Myron," Dad would say in approval.

And now Myron Cope, the creator of the iconic Terrible Towel, was asking me questions about my plans for the Steelers. As much as a part of me wanted to lean back and appreciate it all, I didn't have that luxury.

I'd never before been in control of any large organization in my life. But during my playing career and as an assistant I'd begun to develop my own philosophy. What I didn't know how to do was implement it. I knew that my first decisions as head coach would set the tone for our structure, our system, and ultimately our expectations. None of the people working for the Steelers knew what to expect from me. As every leader should have the opportunity to do, I was starting from scratch.

Kaye and the girls were back in Kansas City in those first few weeks, so my headquarters was the William Penn Hotel downtown. It felt as if my days were packed with interviews and briefings, and I'd reach the end of each day totally exhausted. I projected certainty and calm as the new head coach of the Steelers, but I shared my true thoughts with Kaye.

"I think I may be in over my head," I told her one night on the phone.

She listened to my concerns about all the unknowns that I suddenly faced and said, "Give it some time. One day at a time."

I knew I had a clear vision for the Steelers' identity. I wanted to build a team that played the type of hard-nosed Pittsburgh football I'd grown up watching. We were going to be tough, disciplined, and physical. We were going to run the ball with power and precision. I thought we had the best center in the NFL, Dermontti Dawson, and he was the ideal anchor for the bruising offensive line I wanted. Our defense would swarm to the ball, have swagger, and impose its will on opponents. The secondary had two versatile pieces in Rod Woodson and Carnell Lake, and I was confident they'd feel liberated playing in the scheme that I'd been waiting three years to fully unleash. I'd begun my playing and coaching career on special teams, so they had to be a major part of who we were, too.

If I had to sum it up with a word, it was passion. I was looking for passion. I got the sense there was more passion for the Steelers on the streets of Pittsburgh than there was in the building. I never wanted that to be true, not even for a few minutes, as long as I coached the team.

To bring the vision to life, I needed help. I understood that any good head coach has a talented coaching staff to support him. What I hadn't thought of, until Marty reminded me, was that a good secretary was also essential. He pointed out that the right person would know how to prioritize my time without alienating people who need—or demand—something from the head coach. The right secretary would be able to keep me organized, on schedule, and protected from diversions.

I barely knew how to conduct an interview for that job. When I was looking for a secretary, a nice young woman who had been highly recommended by a friend of our owner applied. Recommended by a friend of the owner? That seemed like all the qualification she would need; I was ready to hire her. We sat there for about twenty minutes talking about what the job entailed. She would have to work long hours, I explained, including some nights and weekends. I reviewed the multiple responsibilities of the position and told her she would be working around men with emotions and warned that it could get difficult at times.

We went through everything I could think of and everything was great until I mentioned she would have to type our weekly game plans.

She interrupted, "Wait, I have to type?"

I had naively assumed every secretary could type. "Well, yeah. Why? Can't you type?"

"No." She cheerfully added, "But I can learn!"

I appreciated her enthusiasm, but I wanted someone who could jump right into the job.

Hiring my first coaching staff wasn't nearly as tricky. The one thing I knew right from the beginning was I didn't want to surround myself with yes-men, people who would tell me whatever they thought I wanted to hear to get the job. At times during interviews, I'd try to catch them. Maybe early in the meeting I'd say something like "You can't be a team that just runs the football, you have to be able to throw it to win in the NFL." Usually the person I was interviewing would agree with that. But then much later I might say "I really believe you can't win games just throwing the football, you have to move the ball on the ground to win a championship." I had people sit there nodding and agreeing with me whatever I said. Those were the people I didn't hire.

My first choice for offensive coordinator was Mike Shanahan, who'd had that role with the Denver Broncos. A free agent, Shanahan had his choice between us and San Francisco. He told me he chose the 49ers because he thought they'd be more successful. Whereas the Steelers had multiple seasons of missing the playoffs, the 49ers were the opposite. Shanahan went with what he knew to be a sure thing in San Francisco over what I hoped to establish in Pittsburgh. Instead, I went with Ron Erhardt, who'd spent nearly a decade working for Bill Parcells with the New York Giants. They'd had a run-heavy offense and we'd be the same way. Perfect fit.

On defense, I wanted to incorporate the 3-4 base alignment and blitz zone into our scheme. I believed that I'd corrected some of the soft spots in the defense, thanks to Marty's persistent questioning. Now, if we taught it correctly, we had the opportunity to take the concept to a new level. I hired two men, Dom Capers and Dick LeBeau, who could be considered coauthors of the novel scheme. I knew they'd be able to expertly coach and explain it. Dom was the defensive coordinator and Dick was defensive backs coach. I was fortunate that Marvin Lewis, whom I played against in high school, was also available to join us. He was an assistant at the University of Pittsburgh, so his new position—Steelers linebackers coach—was a definite promotion.

The only member of Chuck Noll's coaching staff I kept was Dick Hoak, drafted in 1961 by the Steelers as a running back. He was a quality player for ten seasons and then joined the coaching staff in 1971. He'd been a Steelers fixture ever since. Mr. Rooney had suggested that I keep him, but I would've done that anyway. Firing Dick Hoak in Pittsburgh would have been like firing the pope. Maybe even less popular. In addition to being a good coach, Dick represented the values I wanted the team to have. There was nothing fancy about him, and he still lived in the same house he'd bought in 1972.

I thought it was important to set the appropriate tone by hiring a focused strength and conditioning coach. I was reminded of my visits to Penn State, as an assistant coach, and the strength coach there.

His name was Chet Fuhrman, and he and I clicked. I offered him the same position with the Steelers and he took it.

Each time I checked something off my list, it felt as if two new things replaced it. I was so focused on work that I wasn't always aware of things happening right down the street from me. I remember Mr. Rooney telling me one day that it was important for me, as head coach of the Steelers, to attend a civic function downtown. He told me that several influential people would be there, and my attendance would mean a lot to him and the city.

When I arrived, I was greeted by an extremely friendly woman who appeared to be in her midseventies. She talked with me as if she knew me, although I had no idea who she was. "Coach Cowher, my name is Sophie Masloff, and I'm so excited you're here. What a story: You grew up here and now you're back to lead the Steelers. This is great."

I smiled politely. I had no idea who Sophie Masloff was. "Thank you, ma'am. And in what capacity are you here this morning?"

"I'm the mayor of Pittsburgh."

I looked down, red-faced, and shook my head. "Excuse me as I remove my foot from my mouth."

One thing I didn't have to be told was how Steelers fans viewed their team. They were proud of the four Super Bowls the team had won, and they wanted more. And I wanted it for them. After watching film of the '91 Steelers, I knew what kind of talent we had on the '92 roster. It was my responsibility to make sure we—in personnel and in coaching—did all we could to find more good players who could help us.

Just before the draft, Mr. Rooney generously offered the use of the team plane for a scouting trip to Clemson. I wanted to see and work out in person a middle linebacker there, Levon Kirkland. Chuck Noll was going to be on the plane as well, headed to a home he had in Florida. I was ecstatic. Being on the same plane with Chuck, whom I'd never met, was a great opportunity to pick his brain on all things

Steelers football. Fifteen or twenty minutes into the trip, I was clear on the coaching message Chuck wanted me to get.

For example, I asked him about the work atmosphere of the office, and he answered, "It's good." That was it. He didn't explain or elaborate. *It's good.* I asked him how he, as the head coach, navigated the personnel department and ownership. I asked about team doctors and the media, too. He gave all one-word or one-sentence answers. *It's good.* Initially, I was taken aback by his minimalist approach. But the more I thought about it, the more sense it made.

I think Chuck understood the significance of changing coaches after a couple of decades. Especially when the successor is not someone from your staff, and someone you don't know. I was a few weeks away from seeing and hearing for myself: The first year you move into any new situation is tough, and incredibly tough when you're trying to change the existing culture. A number of people who had been with the Steelers organization for several years were set in their ways. They weren't interested in change. Not only did change bring in new concepts, it often brought in new people. It occurred to me, during that plane ride with Chuck, that perhaps Mr. Rooney hired me because he didn't want the status quo anymore.

For years, I'd seen Marty have success with and gain insight from one-on-one meetings with players. Those meetings had a transparency that didn't always exist in group settings. I was determined to do the same thing with the Steelers before training camp began. After just a few meetings, I realized how much work needed to be done to unify a group that was unquestionably fractured.

I met with one of our veteran linebackers, Hardy Nickerson, in a local restaurant to get his thoughts on the season. I was trying to build a relationship and get a good read on the situation. That meeting lasted five minutes. We didn't even get through the appetizer. He didn't want to talk about the Steelers; he just said flatly he didn't want to be there anymore and would appreciate anything I could do to get him out of there. I tried to set up a meeting with our starting free safety, Thomas Everett, who was one of our key players, but he obviously had no plans to report to camp. He wanted to be traded, too. I was getting my read on the situation, and it wasn't good.

Our training camp was in Latrobe, about an hour east of Pittsburgh, and the change of scenery and new season didn't alter things for the team. I learned of a fairly intense offense-versus-defense split a couple of years earlier, and even that had splintered into a confrontation of offensive players versus offensive coaches. The offense had been so against Joe Walton, their offensive coordinator, that they briefly planned to boycott him. Chuck found out about the plan and lashed out, epically, in a meeting. But the "old" problems were still current. It was obvious on and off the field.

The players were not united, everybody went his own way, there wasn't much pride, and there was a barrier between the players and the coaches. It was amazing: The moment a coach walked into a meeting room, all the chatter would stop. The room would immediately go silent and cold. There was no friendly banter between coaches and players; there was barely any dialogue at all. Players would listen, but they wouldn't respond unless they were asked a direct question. We'd bring players into the coaches' room to look at film, but when we did that, other players would walk by the door, look in, and touch their nose. It was their way of letting the player sitting there know they considered him a brownnoser.

We had an outside linebacker who I thought had all the skills to be terrific inside. He didn't want to make the move, and in practice every time he'd make a mistake, he'd throw his helmet and start yelling. We finally gave up on it and moved him back. We had a lot of fights; one afternoon that linebacker who didn't want to be with us got into it with a running back who was angry because he felt he was being underpaid. I've seen a lot of fights on the field, but this was more involved than that. This was personal. They didn't like each other and were happy to take out their frustrations on the other player. Unfortunately, these were two of the best players on the team and we were losing them. Afterward, I tried to talk with each of them in the locker room, but neither of them would look me in the eye.

I'm certainly not one to celebrate a labor dispute, but in that first training camp, I benefited from one. Both Pittsburgh daily newspapers—the *Press*, which I delivered as a kid, and the *Post-Gazette*—were on strike. The dispute had begun in the spring, and it lasted through our entire training camp. So many issues in camp could have caused real problems—and could have caused rifts on the team that would have been difficult to heal—if they had been publicized, but no one ever found out about them. I was lucky I didn't have to answer questions after each practice. There was absolutely no pressure on me from fans. And because there was no public outlet for anyone to vent their frustrations, we had the time and privacy to work through those problems by ourselves.

After camp, we began making small changes when we got back to Pittsburgh. As a way of encouraging players to interact with one another, we moved the lunchroom from the third floor of Three Rivers Stadium to a room just off the locker room. A lot of players had trickled into the third-floor setup, but now with the move to the first floor, we could see that they were going in together and eating together. Eventually we added breakfast so they could come in before the morning meeting and spend even more time together.

I practically demanded that my coaches talk to their players, not just about football but about any subject that opened a dialogue between two people. At first, I think some players were amazed and even suspicious when I asked them questions about their family.

It didn't happen right away, but after a little while players actually came to my office, or into their position coach's office, to talk about their personal problems. These conversations were entirely voluntary, but some players had issues that really bothered them. They felt the need to discuss them, and I got the sense that they were relieved to have the opportunity to talk with someone who cared. I certainly did care about my players—all of them. At times I began to feel like a father who had three daughters at home and fifty-three sons in the locker room. At different times I was a coach, a friend, a therapist, even a marriage counselor. I wanted us to be an organization that cultivated authentic relationships, and I felt that was the best path to make sure it happened.

We all understood that we were in a results-based business. It meant that I could have confidential nonfootball conversations with my players and still, potentially, make football decisions that they didn't agree with. I'd begun to figure out that my system should focus on the three things every player needs: structure, discipline, and accountability. Give us a plan, tell us why we're doing this, and tell us where we're going with what we have. People have to know the rules. If you don't have that structure, how are you going to have any degree of discipline? If you don't have a structure, how are you going to hold anyone accountable?

My expectations weren't extensive or difficult: I wanted people to be on time; punctuality was a big part of what we needed to do. I wanted them to feel free to ask questions; if they weren't exactly sure what was expected of them, then they needed to ask questions, and the responsibility of the coaching staff was to make sure they got a clearly defined answer. I wanted them to practice hard. We weren't going to have long practices, I told them, but I expected them to give me their best every practice. If I didn't get it, that was going to bother me. I understood people were going to make mistakes because that's part of getting better. But when those mistakes were repeated, we'd have to sit down and confront the problem.

One of my biggest coaching challenges happened just before roster cut-down day. I'd emphasized to our team that I didn't care about draft or contract status. I went by what I saw in meetings and practices, then made decisions accordingly. So I didn't know what to expect when I went to Tom Donahoe, our director of player development, and asked, "Can I cut a number one pick?"

I explained to Donahoe that I didn't think linebacker Huey Richardson, the Steelers' first-round pick in 1991, was a good enough player to make our team. I thought moving on from him would also reinforce the message I'd given the entire camp. Donahoe listened and said what I needed to hear: "You just keep the best players." We eventually traded Richardson to Washington for a seventh-round pick.

We hadn't played a game yet, but I felt we'd grown as a team and organization. The next test, for credibility in the city and the locker room, was to stack some wins.

My first game as a head coach was in Houston against my old nemesis Warren Moon. The same Warren Moon who, two years earlier in Kansas City, made me wonder if I was about to get fired. He was a Pro Bowl quarterback, and the Oilers had won our division in 1991. In the '92 opener, they were favored to beat us. They appeared to be well on their way early as they jumped out to a 14–0 lead.

I'd learned my lesson from Kansas City, so I decided I had to shake things up. I knew that the Oilers liked to put pressure on the punter, so I told John Guy, our special teams coach, "First punt we get, if we're inside the fifty, they're going to be coming after us. Let's run a fake punt." Then I added, "But don't make it conspicuous."

With third and 5 on their 42-yard line, our quarterback, Neil O'Donnell, dropped back to pass. He took a 14-yard sack, which put us on our own 44. Since we were no longer inside the 50, the fake punt was obviously off. As our punt team ran onto the field, I was on the phone with Ron Erhardt, verbalizing my complaints.

"Oh my God, Ron, what happened to our protection?"

As I was talking to Erhardt, I looked at John Guy. He had a huge smile on his face and he was motioning a thumbs-up.

Oh, no, I thought. I dropped the phone. "John, tell me you didn't call the fake punt."

"You told me to. You said the first time we punt—"

"I said inside the fifty! But we're not over the fifty-yard line."

He nodded. "Yeah, but I had to tell Mark [Royals, our punter] before the third-down snap so it wouldn't be conspicuous."

I needed a time-out. I turned around to call it, but the ball had been snapped. *Oh, jeez,* I thought. *My first game and we're gonna get killed here.* The Oilers pressured Royals as expected. One of our backup running backs, Warren Williams, went right through their line. We threw a dinky little pass to him, and he caught it and took it all the way to the 2-yard line. Barry Foster ran it in for a touchdown, and the eruption on our sideline energized the entire team. We played with competitiveness and passion all day, picked off Moon five times, and won the game, 29–24.

During and after the game I laughed to myself. *If people only knew the real story of that fake punt . . .* That first win enabled me to begin earning the trust of the team. They began to get some confidence in the process. As a staff, we could feel the players begin to buy in to what we were trying to do.

We won our first three games of the season, and there was excitement about what we were doing and how we were doing it. Foster was our lead back, and it was no secret we wanted to control games on the ground with him. Defensively, we had playmakers, and we weren't afraid to be aggressive and creative with them. As for me, fans and media saw how much energy I had on the sideline, how my jaw would jut when I wanted to make a point—positive or otherwise—and I became an easy caricature. Admittedly, sometimes I got so excited that saliva would spray with my words. I didn't hide my feelings. Signs and headlines around the stadium and city read COWHER POWER with an image of me with a clenched fist or a scowl. I'd have elderly ladies come up to me in grocery stores and tell me that they loved it when I yelled and got emotional.

I know it's hard to believe, but that jaw-jutting image, and the reputation that grew out of it, was probably more a media creation than the real me. Almost all of the time I was in complete control. I understand perception is reality. The cameras loved that scowling guy; football coaches are supposed to look tough on the sidelines. I did scowl, but at least some of the time, rather than complaining, I was giving a player positive reinforcement. I wanted my people to be defiant. "Yeah! Let's go! Don't back down to anybody!"

Cursing? Well, that was different. Off the field, I rarely cursed. On occasion I'd use profanity in a team meeting or during practice to emphasize my point. On the field was another world. I'd use some four-letter words. Other times I'd lose my temper. I didn't throw things—that wasn't me—but my voice inflection was a good indication of my level of frustration, disappointment, and anger. On the field I was almost always able to maintain my composure and stay in control. I had to; it's impossible to manage a football game if you aren't totally focused on the action on the field. Sometimes I'd be that calm in the storm to put everyone at ease. Sometimes, intentionally, I'd create the storm to wake us up and change our tempo.

Another important lesson I learned during year one was figuring out the right balance between publicly calling out my own mistakes and publicly placing blame on the players. After we'd lost our third game of the year, and our record was 6-3, I took responsibility. I told the media that it was on me, that I didn't have the team prepared well enough.

The next day, Mr. Rooney came into my office, shut the door, and warned me, "Be careful how much you criticize yourself. I understand what you're doing, but make the players accountable, too. Make them feel a sense of responsibility. Otherwise they're going to end up walking around here as if it's not their fault. It's a fine line."

Mr. Rooney was good that way. He'd come into the office daily, but never to talk about game plans or calls during the game. Most of the time he'd ask about Kaye and the girls, or my parents. He'd talk about the big picture; truly, he was there to let me know I could lean on him anytime.

Three weeks before Christmas, the first year in Pittsburgh was still a success. We were 10-3. I was no longer living alone in the William Penn. Kaye and I moved into a new house in Fox Chapel, still just a twenty-five-minute drive from my parents' house in Crafton. Kaye was adamant about being a part of a community in which we could blend into a neighborhood, eventually send our girls to the public schools, and raise our family with an expectation of normalcy rather than celebrity. I agreed with her sentiments, even though I gradually began to understand how complex those goals could be for the family of any NFL head coach, especially the coach of the Steelers.

Being the head coach of an NFL team combines the responsibilities of a CEO with the demands of a celebrity. It's all the work with none of the privacy. In a city such as Pittsburgh, with an excitable and knowledgeable fan base, a head coach lives in a fishbowl. When a coach pulls up to a traffic light, he may be stopped next to a doctor who lost a patient that day, or next to a lawyer who lost a big case that day, but if the coach's team lost a game, only one of those three people's bad day is public. The doctor and the lawyer can leave their work at work, but a head coach carries it with him every time he walks into a room.

There weren't many losses to speak of in '92. After a win over Seattle, we were 10-3 and well positioned for the playoffs. That was the good news. The bad news was that Neil O'Donnell, the starting quarterback, was injured during the game. He'd be able to return for the playoffs, but it appeared that he'd miss the rest of the regular season. O'Donnell's backup was Bubby Brister, who had starting experience and was the last Steelers quarterback to start and win a playoff game, during the 1989 season.

If we stayed within our core principles, I was confident that we'd be in good hands with Bubby. Actually, it was a good time to remind myself—and the staff—of Marty's wise words: "Don't try to win a game with your coaching. Let the players determine it. Don't try to be a hero with one call."

That was always in the back of my mind. I never wanted to be the guy who took away any opportunity for the team to win because I rolled the dice. I never wanted a game to come down to winning or losing because I took a risk that was greater than the risk of letting our players determine the outcome. Most of the time late in a game, I'd make the high-percentage move. When I did go against the percentages, I had to be able to justify it to myself, because if it failed, I would have felt as if I'd taken the efforts of my whole team that day and put it on my shoulders by going against the odds. At times I did make the riskier decision because I wanted to make a statement to my team: We're playing to win this.

I got caught in one of those risks in the next-to-last game of the regular season, at home against the Minnesota Vikings. We were on their 40-yard line, and on third and 1 their middle linebacker, Jack Del Rio, stuffed the play. It was a good play by Del Rio, and after he made it, he came near our bench and shouted, "Try that shit again and I'll stuff it again."

I could feel the hairs on my neck stand up. He got me. Really, Jack? I took the whole sequence personally. "Stay out there!" I told the offense. We were going to show Jack Del Rio. We ran the same play again—and he stuffed it again.

For a couple of obvious reasons, I should have known better. We had our backup quarterback leading the offense, and points had been tough to come by the previous two weeks. We'd scored just 6 points in the previous game, and we managed just 3 against the Vikings. Besides, we had a system. This was not backyard football where we ran plays on a whim. Fans might be surprised at just how systematic NFL games can be.

Calling plays, for example, is a skill—both art and science. Generally, my staff and I would plan the first ten plays we wanted to run at the beginning of a game. These would usually be plays we'd run on first and second down. We had another package of plays for third down. We would use those first ten plays to set up the rest of the game; the purpose of some of those ten plays would be to set up a complementary play later in the game. We wanted to let the defense get a look at the base play first. That way when they saw us running what appeared to be the same play later in the game, they would react to it. Then we could run a variation of it, a double move off it, and potentially turn it into a big play.

Among those first ten plays, I always wanted to run at least one gimmick play. I loved gimmick plays. I always wanted to run a reverse early because I knew it would slow down the defense for the rest of the game. I didn't want that defense getting comfortable enough to go flying to the ball. As they saw a play developing, I wanted them to have it in the back of their minds that a reverse might just be coming from the other side. That possibility might force them to be a little more disciplined, make them hold their position an instant longer. I learned that from Dan Reeves, who was especially good at it when he coached the Denver Broncos. A good defense wants to be aggressive, he explained to me once, but when the offense runs reverses and other gimmicks, the defensive players have to be respectful. They have to make sure they handle their basic responsibility in the defense before they can go after the play.

On defense, I'd blitz early in the game because I wanted to see how the other team was going to protect that day. We'd give them a certain look and I'd focus on their center. I always wanted to keep the center uncovered in our defensive scheme, not put anybody on him, because a lot of times seeing what the center does will tell you how they're going to block that day. So if we gave them a certain look and when the ball was snapped the center turned one way, then I knew which way he was going the next time we gave them that look and we could overload the other side.

These were some of the things we began to refine in year one, and the result after the regular season was a division title, a record-setting season for running back Barry Foster (a Steelers-best 1,690 yards rushing), and the second-fewest points allowed in the NFL. Since we won the division and qualified for a first-round bye, we had an extra week of rest to get healthy. I thought the rest would benefit us because it would allow O'Donnell to start the playoff game against the Buffalo Bills.

It was a controversial move that was debated around the city: Can a player lose his job due to injury? Was it a good move to put O'Donnell in a playoff game after he'd been out for a month? At the time, my answer to the first question was a resounding no. O'Donnell was our starter, and I didn't see any reason to have our starter sit for the most important game of the year.

Unfortunately, that game was over quickly. Our scoring troubles continued and O'Donnell looked rusty. We lost to the Bills,

24–3. The consolation from the game, and season, was that we were no longer a franchise that hoped to win. We expected it. We'd become a unified group that not only played for one another, but grew to love one another, too.

With the season finally over, my parents invited all the families—my brothers' and mine—to Crafton for a dinner. The huge gathering had plenty of food, drinks, and conversation. I exhaled, thinking that it was good to be home.

Once I piled a plate high with food, I sat across from my father. He was relaxed and began his normal sports-centered conversation: "And how 'bout those stupid Steelers?" He took a swig of beer. "They have O'Donnell out for a month, and they still put him in a playoff game! Why'd they do that?"

I looked at him. He was so used to these conversations over the years that he didn't realize what he was saying now.

"Wait a second, Dad. You say 'the Steelers.' That's actually me. I made that decision, not 'the Steelers.'"

I was sensitive and ticked off about it because I knew he was right. I probably shouldn't have started O'Donnell in that situation.

"Oh," Dad said, trying to clean it up. "You probably had a good reason for the decision you made."

My family still had to get used to me as a Steelers decision maker. And I still had plenty to learn in the role.

8

In Pursuit of Greatness

I learned so much my first year as a head coach. The Xs and Os are a fraction of a leader's responsibilities. You have to quickly process information; manage your emotions, and sometimes others'; and be skilled at staying in the moment.

It's a job of tremendous focus. In real time, the 160 plays in a game take about five to six seconds apiece. String them together and that's about 15 minutes. But the block of time you're on the field is three hours. The best teams are the ones that can stay energized and disciplined through the time lapses. They can tune out taunts from the crowd and opponents. They can stay composed when the score is lopsided against them, or in their favor.

I learned that the way a group feels and acts is connected to how it thinks. The mind is powerful.

As a kid, I'd witnessed my father's ability to meticulously organize all his accounting materials. I can still see him sitting at his desk, writing out his thoughts. In 1993, entering my second season, I understood the value of my father's routines. I began to write notes daily, and I kept them organized in a five-subject notebook. I wrote longhand, even when a computer was right in front of me. Writing notes by hand reinforced the thought in my mind, which I believed was more important than convenience. (There are a lot of ways to save time, but not all of them are beneficial.)

I wrote *everything* down: the summary of meetings with ownership, pro personnel, and the medical staff; our draft and free agency plans; insights to share with players; assistant coaches' salaries (which I was in charge of); speeches I wanted to make to the team; and things that I wanted us to either incorporate or eliminate.

As a growing leader, I wanted to make sure I was clear on what my job was. And if I literally spelled out the expectations to myself, I knew I could effectively communicate them to others. Basically, I divided the job into three broad areas: first, working with the front office to put together the team and dealing with problems that will inevitably arise; preparing my players and assistant coaches—constantly—to play and coach at least sixteen games and hopefully more; and finally, most visible of all, standing on the sidelines and coaching while being watched by seventy thousand fans.

While each of those aspects of the game has its own challenges, nothing else is as exciting, or difficult, as those three on-field hours on game days and nights. Everything I did, in and out of season, was simply preparation for those three hours. That's when all your hard work translates into the numbers that determine games, contracts, and livelihoods.

It was during this time that I leaned on my faith more than I ever had. I'd gone to church as a kid, but I hadn't been particularly religious since. When I returned to Pittsburgh, I felt the weight of the job. I knew I couldn't handle it all by myself. Kaye and I joined Fox Chapel Presbyterian Church. I decided to turn my life over to Jesus Christ.

I was so thankful for Reverend John Galloway, the pastor of the church, whose messages inspired me. His points were so impactful that I used to hold on to his one-page summaries in the church bulletin and go back to them, days or sometimes years later, for encouragement.

I'd enjoyed our division title in '92, but I knew we couldn't just show up and expect a similar season. Football, the game and the business, is constantly evolving. That was especially true in the spring of '93, which was the first time the NFL had unrestricted free agency. It truly was a liberating time for players. At the end of their contracts, they now had the power to test the open market without any limits from their former teams. The money and movement in the sport would be unprecedented. That meant we'd lose some good starting players, such as inside linebacker Hardy Nickerson, as well as guys who were good in the locker room, such as tackle Tunch Ilkin.

However, free agency also provided an opportunity for us to improve. Statistically, I liked our defense. But I wanted to upgrade and add depth at defensive end and linebacker. I gave our coaches something to think about along the way, too. I thought we'd be at our best if we were all forward-thinking in our processes. I wanted them to be creative. My goal was to create a staff on which innovation was huge. I wanted coaches who wouldn't be afraid to think differently and fail. At times, I'd push the conversation to its tension points.

"Tell me the negatives to this defense," I'd demand. "I see the positives, but tell me the negatives. Shoot holes in it. And tell me why the negative doesn't scare you; I want you to sell it to me."

Like a lot of other things, my approach was inspired by my time with Marty. I'd play devil's advocate, similar to the way he did with me in Kansas City. All these exercises had an endgame: I wanted us to maximize our strengths.

We had several players who were built to execute anything dreamed up from our 3-4 scheme. We had a great outside linebacker, Greg Lloyd, on the right side. He was a bookend, and if we found his complement on the left side, everyone would be happy. But no one like that was on our roster. Dom Capers and I felt that we'd found the answer in Los Angeles Rams free agent Kevin Greene.

Fortunately for us, Greene wasn't touring the league for the biggest contract. He wanted to play for a team that used the 3-4, and he wanted to hear someone convincingly sell him on an opportunity. We were able to do just that. We signed him in March 1993 to a three-year contract for just over $5 million. The most celebrated and expensive signing was in Green Bay, with the Packers giving Reggie White $17 million to play for them. It was the first time that Greene, with his big personality and long blond hair, actually went under the radar. But everyone on our defensive staff believed that he was ideal for the way we wanted to play.

Another opportunity for improvement came in late April, during the NFL draft. For the second year in a row, we found a high-ceiling linebacker in the second round. In '92 it was Levon Kirkland from Clemson. In '93, it was Chad Brown from Colorado. We took a cornerback named Willie Williams in the sixth round, and I could see him quickly contributing, too.

Overall, I didn't feel as rushed as I had in my first season. Sure, there were certain issues, such as trying to find a coaching staff, that I didn't have to worry about; every coach I had from year one returned in year two. The newspaper strike in Pittsburgh was over, and that was great news because there was no longer a team rift for the beat reporters to write about. I could even point out Sophie Masloff and know that she was the mayor of Pittsburgh.

It was good to be back home. If Kaye and I had a date night, we knew we had built-in babysitters close by with my parents in Crafton. We were also fortunate to develop close friendships with a couple of families in Fox Chapel. Kaye would strike up a conversation with anyone, including a woman named Beth Fung. They clicked immediately. A couple of times, they were even mistaken for the other, including during a Steelers game when the broadcasters identified Beth, in a suite with Kaye, as my wife. Beth and her husband, John, also had a young family, so we had a lot in common. John was one of the top transplant surgeons in the country. We were practically the same age—thirty-six—and he was viewed as a prodigy in his field. He had a world-famous mentor, Dr. Thomas Starzl, who performed the first successful human liver transplant back in the 1960s.

John and I got along as well as Kaye and Beth did. We'd have beers, compete in boccie and backgammon (I could never turn off my competitiveness), and share strategic and management insights that we learned in our professions. John was obviously bright, so he quickly pointed out one of the differences in how we navigated our jobs:

"In my field, I'm the strategist and the performer. If there's surgery in the morning, I'm the one planning for it and then doing it. In your field, you're the strategist who has to rely on other people to be the performers."

He was right. Because my success was tied to the performances of several other people, I had to be mindful of their whole selves, not just their athletic performance. I knew I'd always be comfortable with football concepts, but that was only one part of coaching. My players lived in an unusual world, and as someone who pushed to get the best out of them, I needed to understand it.

All day long, they had people looking and talking about them as if they were superheroes, but as soon as they got home, real life was there. Some players would be greeted at the door by their wives, who expected them to change diapers or wash dishes. A player might then share his opinion that linebackers don't wash dishes and defensive tackles don't mow the lawn. After that, the arguments would begin.

I can't count the number of times I was told, "My wife doesn't understand the pressure; she doesn't understand what I go through at practice every day." Or that she didn't understand why her husband insisted that going out in Pittsburgh and socializing with teammates was part of team building. I would point out that many of those wives were working hard themselves at home, making important decisions with the kids as their husbands were at work. It wasn't that they didn't understand the demands of the job; most of the time they did. What they wanted was an acknowledgment of what they were doing, along with some contribution from their husbands at home.

I was able to speak on this with conviction because that was exactly my life. I had more experience at balancing the different worlds than the players did, so I was in position to offer practical advice if they needed it. I knew that the players felt that their job was physically and mentally draining. I also wanted them to know that their spouses at home often felt the same way. These were young people going through exactly the same problems typical of anyone else their age, but they did it knowing they were local and national celebrities in a high-stakes profession. Plus, many of them didn't yet have the tools to master the balance between their professional life and their home life. I know I wouldn't have been great at it at twenty-five.

I was encouraged that players wanted to talk with me about these things. When they'd ask for advice, I'd often have a simple suggestion: "Bring her in here. Let me talk with both of you. I played the game. I'm married with kids. Let's figure out what's going on." Often, that's exactly what we did.

I didn't know how close we were to competing for a Super Bowl, but I was amazed by our collective leadership and intangibles. I could scan the locker room and find several passionate, team-first players: Lloyd, Rod Woodson, Carnell Lake, Darren Perry, Merril Hoge, Duval Love, and our most dominant offensive player, center Dermontti Dawson. They were our top performers and leaders, and I knew I absolutely had to build a relationship with them.

With leaders on the head coach's side, everybody else will follow or get out of the way. But I was also intentional about speaking with everybody, even if it was only a few words.

For example, I was sure to spend an equal amount of meeting time with the offense and the defense. I timed it. Usually at the beginning of practice, during stretching, I'd walk around and talk to everybody, with a special emphasis on those who weren't playing regularly or people I hadn't recently spoken with. I wanted them to know what I did: At some point in the season, we'd have to rely on them and they'd have to be ready. It was friendly banter, with some instructions sprinkled in. *How ya doin'? How ya feelin'? I liked what you did last week. Make sure you know this formation because if so-and-so gets hurt, you're gonna have to play this week. Don't get discouraged; you're doing a good job in your role. We've been watching. Your time's gonna come. . . .*

I know from my own playing career that a few words of personal communication, a little encouragement, can make a huge difference to a player. It had been my experience that it's difficult to inspire people until they believe you care about them. As a player, I gave everything I had for a coach who showed he cared about me as a person. I think that's true in every aspect of life. Whether it's as a parent, executive, coach, or any other type of leader. If you demonstrate to people your concern about them is sincerely personal, they'll eventually give you everything they've got, and what's important to you will become important to them.

Still, as a second-year coach, I couldn't be naive. I recognized I couldn't please everyone, and it was a waste of my time and others' to try. I knew that backup players and benched players might not be crazy about the head coach. Most of them have been stars in high school and college and have never been asked to sit. I was aware that in an organization as large as the Pittsburgh Steelers, some people would be beyond my reach. It was true of every team I played on or coached: At least a couple of players would be out for themselves rather than for what was best for the team. As long as they did their jobs on the field, I accepted them.

I told players that if they were unhappy about something, no matter what it was, to avoid the media and come see me instead. I didn't want to read or hear about team problems in the media. That approach would only hurt the player's cause and our team's. It was also unnecessary. I'd made it clear to my players that they could ask me any question. The only warning was that I insisted on being honest, so they had to be prepared to hear a tough answer. I wouldn't hold back if someone asked, "Why don't I get more playing time?" I'd answer, "The person ahead of you is playing because at this moment I think he's a better player and gives us the best chance to win. You may not like hearing it, but I ask that you respect it."

I'll admit it: I didn't treat everybody equally. Sometimes I enforced the rules subjectively. I believed in dealing with situations based on each individual, what I referred to as "production and tolerance." As long as production was greater than tolerance, I would put up with certain things. (This is an ongoing debate among leaders, and I know some coaches feel differently than I do. But I tried to balance the needs of the team against the actions of an individual.)

A perfect example is how I dealt with Barry Foster, our star running back. He was twenty-four when he began the '93 season, and he was coming off the best rushing year in team history. He was our primary back, and our offense was at its best when he was carrying the ball. But, goodness, he could be a pain.

He didn't like to practice. He consistently showed up last for team meetings. He didn't always listen to what the coaching staff suggested. But in '92, Foster took the ball almost every Sunday and ran for 100 yards. When a player is producing like that, I put up with his attitude. You have to keep your objective in mind: I was hired to win football games. The player's production was so immense in '92 that it affected my tolerance for his behavior.

But '93 was a different story. We lost our first two games of the season, then won four in a row. There was a big difference with Foster: His production had gone from great to good. We had our clashes a few times in the middle of the year. During a shutout win over the Bills, he hurt his ankle and left the game. We were 6-3 and in good playoff position.

Without him, though, we lost the next two games. His absence left a major hole in our offense, so we were eager to have him return. Even with his injury, I believed he could contribute to the team with his presence. One day, I walked through the locker room and saw Foster casually sitting there.

"Do you know there's a team meeting happening now?" I asked.

"I think I should be in the training room," he replied.

I'd seen and heard enough. His maintenance had been too high, his production had been too low, and his team engagement had been too spotty.

"It's not up to you to determine where you should be," I said. "I'll make it easy for you: Why don't you just go home?"

He went home for the day, and we pursued the postseason without him. But I knew that interaction wasn't the end of it. Foster was still a good player who was under contract with us, so I couldn't— and didn't want to—end the relationship. More important, there was an audience—his teammates—with an interest in how this played out. That's the biggest loophole in the production-tolerance ratio: Open that door for one person, and it's not easy to close it behind him. Some people will watch the drama and try to take the same path that their teammate did.

I learned that the best way to deal with people who continually try to take advantage of a situation is to confront them. I found threats and demands weren't as effective as blunt reminders: "You're letting your teammates down and losing their respect." Rather than threaten players, I tried to challenge them. That approach usually grounded a player who got too caught up in himself. I was fortunate to have a team stacked with leaders who'd earned special privileges with their dynamic production but still refused to take advantage of their status. They did things that I couldn't; they were able to articulate to their peers the right message, but in the language that their peers spoke. If I said something to a player, no matter how I said it, it was still the head coach dictating to a player. But hearing that same message from Kevin Greene or Greg Lloyd or Dermontti Dawson made a greater impact. My team leaders had the pulse of the team. When you have strong leadership, you don't need a lot of rules. Those top guys make sure people do their jobs.

I saw a tremendous example of that accountability, savvy, and toughness going into the final game of the '93 season. We were 8-7 and needed to beat the Cleveland Browns for a chance to make the playoffs. The Browns had beaten us earlier in the season, by utilizing an aspect of the game that I valued to my core. They killed us on special teams. They had a player, Eric Metcalf, who'd returned not one but *two* punts for touchdowns. *Long* touchdowns; one went for 91 yards, and the game winner, with about two minutes remaining, was for 75. Even though I was the head coach, I still sat in on special teams meetings, observed, spoke up, and often offered one-on-one constructive criticism to the coach. Special teams was my baby.

I was extremely involved in the defensive and special teams meetings before the final game. But that wasn't my biggest worry. Rod Woodson, our first-team All-Pro, Pro Bowl cornerback, had a bad knee injury. Woodson was a smart and feared player, someone respected by everyone in our locker room and across the league. If he wasn't on the field, the Browns would certainly notice.

I never asked players to play hurt. I didn't want them to do anything that would aggravate their injuries or, even worse, put their careers in jeopardy. It was also true that everyone in the NFL plays in pain. I told Rod that if the Browns knew beforehand he wasn't going to play, Bill Belichick and his staff would devise schemes to take advantage of his absence.

I asked him to consider a safe plan: "If you can go out there for one or two plays, then we'll get you out of there for the rest of the game. Then they'll have to make their adjustments on the sideline."

Woodson nodded. It never crossed my mind that his nod meant that he was planning to play the entire game.

He did just that, and he did it at about 50 percent of his capability. He played within himself and didn't take any chances, yet he still managed to be Rod Woodson. His appearance alone meant the Browns had to honor his presence. They didn't challenge him much all game. That decision by Woodson was huge for our defense, which allowed just three field goals in a 16–9 win. It was as impressive a display of mental toughness as I'd ever seen. Woodson's determination and willpower enabled him to overcome his physical limitations. He believed he could play, so he did.

Another example of our leadership came at halftime of that Browns game. We trailed 9–3. When I began to talk to the team before the start of the second half, I was interrupted by Greg Lloyd.

"Excuse me, Coach," he said. "I got this."

He then went into a halftime speech that grabbed the attention of everyone in the room. He called out the entire team.

"We are not going to lose this game," he said. "That wasn't us out there in the first half. I need to know who's with me right now. If you're not with me, I don't want you out there."

I watched and listened, and it took me back to my last game at NC State. That was me, telling my team that we wouldn't lose to Pitt. Lloyd was a leader. His teammates responded to him and didn't allow a second-half point.

We needed more help to get into the playoffs, hoping for losses by the Dolphins and Jets. Not only did that happen, but we earned a meeting with the head coach and the team I knew best in the league. This was my first matchup against Marty and the Kansas City Chiefs. They were the division champs and favored to beat us, the last team in the playoffs. I loved Marty and owed him my career, but I wasn't the least bit sentimental going into the game. I'd played for him and worked with him. I'd coached many players on his defense. I felt comfortable preparing for them and having a good idea of what they'd do.

So, on a sunny January day in Kansas City, I couldn't have been happier with three minutes remaining. We had the ball and were ahead, 24–17. Three minutes away from my first playoff win, and over Marty, of all people. It couldn't have unfolded more beautifully or perfectly. Marty talked often about the need for fundamental soundness, and that's what this game was coming down to. If we didn't make any mistakes inside those three minutes, we'd win.

Except that's not what happened.

Special teams had hurt us several times in the regular season, and it happened again at the wrong time. Our punter, Mark Royals, had his punt blocked as we were trying to put the game away. That gave the Chiefs the ball at our 9-yard line, and on fourth and goal, Joe Montana threw a touchdown pass to tie it. We went to overtime, and as the Chiefs lined up for a short field goal, I crouched on the sideline. Nothing I hoped for in that moment happened, and as the ball glided through the uprights, I put my head in my hands. Two seasons in, and two tough playoff losses.

But football doesn't allow you to stop and feel sorry for yourself. A lot of work was to be done, and some of it was new to me. I knew changes needed to be made, not just with players but coaches. I made changes with our staff and it was one of the hardest things I had to do.

Coaching is a nomadic profession. Most coaches must make a move every few years, and by the time he's established himself, he may have had five or six jobs everywhere from a small college town to a major city. And with each new job his family has to find a new place to live, with new schools, and a new job if his wife is employed. I knew many coaches who bought a house without ever seeing it. Their wife had picked it out because the coach had no time for house hunting.

When I told the coach my decision, he wanted to talk about it. I sat at my desk and he looked across it and said, "I knew you were going to do this."

And I thought, *Well, if you knew there was a problem, why didn't you do something to correct it?* He was upset about it and defended himself, basically telling me I wasn't justified in firing him. I considered for a second that maybe I shouldn't fire him. Had I not communicated effectively with him? That's when I vowed that I'd never be subtle again. If I had something to say to one of my coaches, I was going to hit him over the head with it, then question him to make sure he knew what hit him.

With that being said, I did fire the coach. The mistake was mine for hiring him in the first place. I gave him the chance he wanted and he blamed me for it. And I accepted it. By definition, the head coach has to take responsibility for everything that happens in the organization. He has to be accountable. Sometimes it requires a variety of acceptances.

In the new NFL world of free agency, I had to prepare for the loss of more good players. With a salary cap on the way, tough decisions had to be made. One of my leaders, fullback Merril Hoge, was a free agent whom I wanted to keep. Dan Ferens, from the business side of the franchise, was negotiating with him. Dan was the first to tell me he didn't think Hoge would come back, as the Chicago Bears had a much more lucrative offer.

I wasn't happy. Hoge was a popular Steeler. He was well liked by the fans for his hustle and relatability. He'd even carved out a bit of a niche for himself with a regular in-studio radio gig with one of the Pittsburgh stations. More than that, I thought he helped us win. I told Dan, "Do you realize how important Merril Hoge is? The guy blocks, he can run, he's great in the locker room. We really need to keep him." Dan said he understood. He also suggested that maybe I didn't know just how much Mr. Rooney abided by principle. Mr. Rooney believed he had a verbal agreement with the agent, so when the agent tried to tweak the agreement ever so slightly, it didn't go well. Dan said I should talk with Mr. Rooney directly for clarification.

It sounded like a good idea. I walked into Mr. Rooney's office and said, "I know we're really close with Merril Hoge. We're not that far away. Why can't we finish that deal? This guy definitely is worth it."

Mr. Rooney got up from his desk, walked past me, and closed the door. He didn't say a word.

Uh-oh, I thought, *this isn't good.*

He walked back to his chair and sat down. He said calmly, "Bill, you're a good football coach. But let me tell you one thing: You don't tell me how to spend my money. He may be a good player, but there are more important things than any one player on any team, I don't care who they are. You coach the players we bring in, and you'll be part of that process. But don't tell me what to do with my money. Do we understand each other?"

"No problem."

I stood in the hallway for a second just so I could process it. I got even closer to Mr. Rooney that day because I had a better understanding of his business values: Your word, your handshake, was powerful to him. His principles were always solid, and I respected and trusted him because of it. I knew we'd never have a problem like that again.

When I walked out of Mr. Rooney's office, I saw Dan Ferens shortly after.

"So, how'd it go?" he asked.

"Let me ask you this, Dan. Who's next on the list of free agent fullbacks?"

We both laughed. We ended up signing John L. Williams and continued figuring out our off-season.

Mr. Rooney was correct: It wasn't one player holding up the infrastructure of the Steelers. I could feel our team getting closer and trusting one another more. I could see that we were more talented than we'd been when I first arrived. I thought we had the best linebackers in football with Lloyd, Greene, and the two young guys, Levon Kirkland and Chad Brown. In the draft, we picked up another promising player, linebacker Jason Gildon. He was one of our third-round picks, while the other third rounder was a running back named Bam Morris. I hadn't given up on any of our runners, but I wanted to make sure we had quality backs just in case we had issues.

|||||||||||||

Before heading into my third training camp with the Steelers, I got a call from my buddy from Ohio, John DeMaine. I'd met John while I played for the Browns in the early 1980s, and we'd been friends ever since. He was one of the smartest businessmen I knew, and I could talk to him about that if I needed to. Most of the time, though, we competed at games. What games? All of them.

My second year in Kansas City, John told me he was coming to town for a visit. When I picked him up at the airport, I handed him a list of games that we'd play while he was there. We referred to it as our own Olympics. Golf. Racquetball. Tennis. Cards. Pool. All in one weekend. We both hated to lose, so we'd have legendary battles that were a test of wills more than anything else.

When John called before my third season in Pittsburgh, he was confirming our family vacation schedule. Why? After my first year of coaching, John had invited me, Kaye, and the girls to a summer place he had in North Carolina. It was called Bald Head Island. Before we went there, I remembered John's description of it—small, remote, laid-back—sounded perfect. At the time, I felt as if I'd been running since becoming a head coach, and with all the physical and mental energy I'd spent on the team, Kaye was the one who kept the house going. She also knew how to put the proper perspective on my job as it related to our lives. She'd tell the girls that their father went to work just like the Fungs and other neighbors did. That my position involved TV time, constant public debate, and recognition all over western Pennsylvania didn't make us special people.

We were grateful that John offered that family vacation because we didn't fully realize just how much we needed it until we got there. Kaye and the girls fell in love immediately. No cars were allowed on the island, so electric golf carts were the way to travel. One day I went to the grocery store with Kaye, and I waited for her outside in the cart.

An older woman saw me and started a conversation: "Hey there, how are you?"

I instinctively clenched. I was convinced that she'd recognized me and was about to bring some Steelers talk into this relaxing family vacation.

"Where are you from?"

I told her I was from Pittsburgh, and she said that she was, too. But then she surprised me: "Isn't it just beautiful here?"

I was rejoicing inside. She was simply a friendly vacationer. She either didn't know who I was or didn't care. And that was perfectly fine with me.

"Yes, it is beautiful, ma'am," I said excitedly. "Yes, it is."

It didn't take us long to figure out that the Cowhers and Bald Head Island were a match. Our first year there we were John's guests. When the entire family seemed at home there, we bought a vacation home. I think John was excited that he'd introduced us to a peaceful place. He was also plotting to wear me down in one of our endless games.

I was ready for our upcoming season. In '93, I wasn't sure if we were ready for a Super Bowl. I knew we were in '94. I looked forward to handing a Lombardi Trophy to Mr. Rooney, and I thought this could be the year.

Heading into November, we were one of the clear Super Bowl favorites. We were 6-3 before a game against Buffalo on *Monday Night Football*. It's one thing to have a team where coaches coach and players play, but your team can achieve greatness when your best players bring a coach's eye for detail to the field. Once again, it was Rod Woodson showing just how attuned to his job he was— even when he wasn't playing.

Rod told me the previous Sunday he'd heard on TV Buffalo quarterback Jim Kelly call an audible. The play was a three-step hitch, which meant that the receiver took three steps, turned, and the ball was right there for him. Rod said that if he heard Kelly call it during our game, he was going to jump it. I knew he could, too. He was so athletic that if he knew what was coming, he could get to the ball a step and a half before Kelly's intended receiver could.

"Make sure Darren's got your back in case it's a hitch and go," I told Rod.

If the receiver stopped and then kept going, we had to be certain that our free safety, Darren Perry, picked him up. Darren was a smart player, so I knew he'd handle it. Then I kept thinking about what Rod told me: *He picked up the audible on TV?* The great ones often push themselves.

Sure enough, Kelly called that audible early in the game. Rod told Darren, "I'm jumping it." No problem. But our other corner, Deon Figures, told Darren the same thing a split second later. Darren didn't have time to correct either corner, and he couldn't cover both receivers by himself. So he did the next-best thing when the ball was snapped. He started backing up as fast as he could.

When Kelly threw that 3-yard hitch, Rod was right there to step in front of it, catch it, and run 37 yards for a touchdown. We won that game, and five more in a row after it. We finished the regular season with 12 wins. For the second time in my three seasons as head coach, we had won the AFC Central Division.

Lloyd and Greene, our bookend linebackers, were named first-team All-Pros. We had a great running game with Barry Foster and rookie Bam Morris, along with John L. Williams, who ran and caught well. We were at the point as a franchise when the star veterans were playing at peak levels, while the young players were flashing just how good they could be.

Our first playoff game was at home against the Browns, whom we'd already beaten twice in the regular season. We did it again in the divisional round, winning easily. It was my first playoff win, and that it came against my first professional team led to some reflection. I was happy that my parents, brothers, neighbors, and friends were at Three Rivers Stadium to see it.

With just one more win, over a San Diego Chargers team that

wasn't as talented as we were, we'd earn a trip to Miami for Super Bowl XXIX. I'm not superstitious, but the Pittsburgh weather for the AFC Championship Game was a bad omen for us. We were in Pittsburgh, in the third week of January, and it should have been miserable outside. It wasn't. Our team wasn't afraid of harsh conditions; the Chargers, who played half of their games in Southern California, probably celebrated its absence. They must have known the cold was part of our home-field advantage.

As expected, we jumped out to an early lead, but it was still a close game. The Chargers just knew how to hang around. We held our lead for almost four quarters, but the Chargers scored with five minutes left to take a 17–13 lead. Nobody panicked. We responded by moving methodically down the field, and with two minutes left we had a first down on the Chargers' 9-yard line. With a minute left, we had a fourth and goal from their 3.

Three yards away from going to the Super Bowl, with one play to get into the end zone. I called a time-out. Neil O'Donnell came to the sideline and I told him what the play was. With the whole season three yards from the end zone, I wasn't going to put my fate as the head coach into the hands of Ron Erhardt, our offensive coordinator, or any other assistant coach. That wouldn't be fair to him or me. My team. My responsibility. My call.

This was the logic of the call: We put Barry Foster in motion, trying to get him one-on-one with linebacker Dennis Gibson. I didn't like Barry versus Gibson; I *loved* it—more than I could express. I didn't think the Chargers would have a good answer for what we had planned. The ball was snapped and Barry beat Gibson to the inside. But O'Donnell's pass was a split second too late, which allowed Gibson to get a hand on it and knock it down. The stadium was as silent as I'd ever heard it. The genuine shock was palpable; this was supposed to be our win and, perhaps, our year.

It felt worse than the loss to the Chiefs. A win over Kansas City would have been an upset by us, and in '94 we were the ones who'd been upset at home. It was a long walk across the field to congratulate the Chargers' head coach, Bobby Ross. I don't even know how I got there as I visualized my heart sinking and then breaking into minuscule pieces. Instead of going to Miami for the Super Bowl, my next stop would be Hawaii, where the losing head coach led the conference's Pro Bowlers. Surely, no one wanted that trip.

Mr. Rooney was waiting for me when I began to leave the stadium. "I'm sorry," I said. "We let one get away."

He patted me on the back. "That's all right. You did your best."

My wife and two of our three daughters were waiting for me. Meagan was nine, Lauren was seven, and our youngest, four-year-old Lindsay, was at home with a sitter. Kaye gave me a kiss on the cheek and said, "Hang in there. It'll be okay."

Meagan looked up at me with the innocent eyes of a child and sweetly said, "Dad?"

"Yeah?"

"Why didn't you give the ball to Barry Foster? He would've gotten three yards."

I began to explain to her that in hindsight everything . . . but Lauren interrupted and said, "Meagan, you shouldn't have said that to Dad. Mom told you not to say that."

Meagan shot back, "But you said the same thing up in the box!"

"Girls, girls. Please, let's not fight. In hindsight, maybe I could have made a better decision. But those are the things you learn in sports. And I will learn from this."

There was little conversation in the car as we drove home. No one wanted to verbalize the only thing that was on our minds. But when I pulled the car into the garage, I heard music coming from the house. I thought, *I've got one more child here to console.* She was young and was probably crying. But as I walked into the kitchen, there was Lindsay, dressed in a hula skirt, dancing around the table. If she had tears, they were tears of joy.

"Dad! Dad, we get to go to Hawaii!"

I got down on my knees and I explained to her, "Sweetheart, we wanted to go to the Super Bowl in Florida."

"No, Daddy. We've already been to Florida. But we've never been to Hawaii!"

I'd talked to my players and their wives and girlfriends about perspective, but here was my four-year-old daughter with the guiding light for this season, and others. Football consumed me and it was my passion. I'd loved playing it, and now coaching and teaching and thinking about it. It occupied my thoughts when everyone knew it, and sometimes even in secret. It was a huge part of my life. But it always operated against the backdrop of my life away from the sport.

I knew I wanted to be a champion. I thought about it all the time. But when I came home, after a while, all the girls in that house cared about was being around their dad. My girls never lost sight that I was Dad, who happened to coach football. I needed to figure out the perfect balance of work and home. I needed the calmness and normalcy of home to balance the intensity of work.

It's tough to get it just right. That was my mission going forward: trying to win it all, while also being a present dad and husband. I didn't exactly know how to do that. I was committed to figuring it out.

9

One Drive Away from a Title

One of the by-products of success is that people begin to pay attention to everything you do. Not only do they see the blueprint, they want to accomplish it themselves. Because of this, I should have known that in time I'd lose one of the core members of my original staff.

The NFL's 1995 expansion, from twenty-eight teams to thirty, meant new opportunities for everyone in the league, including my defensive coordinator for three years, Dom Capers. We gave up the second-fewest points in football in two of those seasons and ranked eighth in the other. The expansion Carolina Panthers could see Dom was ready to be the first head coach in their franchise's history. After he accepted the position, I promoted Dick LeBeau to defensive coordinator, which was one of the best decisions I ever made.

I knew I needed to be adaptable and to plan for change. When you hire talented and creative people, they'll eventually be in line to run their own programs, and I never wanted to hold anyone back; change is part of the league.

These types of big changes weren't just on our coaching staff. The final offensive play of our 1994 season, an incomplete pass from Neil O'Donnell to Barry Foster, was also the final play of Foster's Pittsburgh career. When he felt like it, he was one of the best playmakers we had. But when he didn't feel like it, well, I couldn't justify his roster spot as a Steeler.

We traded Foster to Dom's Panthers for a fifth-round pick. Then we refocused on the Super Bowl. We were so close in 1994, and that lingering disappointment drove us. Our mission had an urgency, based on what we and the league had become. We'd grown into perennial contenders, and the league now had unrestricted free agency and a salary cap. It meant that other teams were likely to look at free agent talent, especially from good teams, and offer significant pay raises. A couple of our better players, such as O'Donnell, tackle Leon Searcy, and pass-rushing linebacker Kevin Greene, were in their "contract" years in 1995. I loved them all, but I was realistic enough to know that we couldn't keep them all going forward. I knew we'd have to make the most of the '95 season.

Heading into that fourth season, I was comfortable with our team structure. I say that even though I used to tell the players every season, "Please be comfortable with knowing that I'm going to make you uncomfortable at some point." It didn't mean I was going to be unnecessarily harsh or unreasonable. I knew my job was to push myself, and everyone around me, to do things we either didn't think we could do or simply didn't want to do.

I wanted every coach and player to be open to all possibilities. Some people don't dream big enough dreams. I didn't want to begin any season by sending a message that our options were limited. The start of any project should have its ultimate success as the main goal. For us, that was the Super Bowl. Every meeting, film correction, coaching point, and practice was made with that in mind. Many of our team leaders had built their lives around the game, and I was no different.

In a typical home-game week during the season, I'd begin Monday mornings—usually around six—looking at game film. We'd have a team meeting at 1:00 p.m., and most players would leave after that. I'd start pulling out film on our next opponent so I could study them. I'd have dinner, do my televised coach's show around 8:00 p.m., then watch more film. If my daughters had a game or an event after school, I'd switch the taping time of the show so I could be there for my girls.

On Tuesdays, the players were off, but it was "game-plan day" for the coaching staff. I'd drop the girls off at the school bus stop, pick up muffins for the coaches, then prepare for one of the longest, multilayered days of the week. It included a meeting with the doctors for injury updates, a press conference with the media, and intensive game-planning with my coordinators.

I was self-aware enough to know my biggest strength. Defense. I was hands-on and vocal in those planning sessions. I'd stay in there from around 4:00 p.m. until about 9:00 p.m. Then I'd switch to offense. I observed and listened more and spoke less with Ron Erhardt and his staff. My main objective there was to hear their plan, get a sense of their call sheet, and remind them to leave space for me to insert some plays that I believed would work against the next opponent's weaknesses. I'd usually leave around 1:00 a.m.

Wednesdays began with a drive to the bus stop. It allowed me to have some quick conversations with my daughters and see what was on their minds. After leaving them, I'd go to the office and prepare for our team meeting. It was essential to get the team aligned on the tendencies of our opponent, what was at stake in the game, and the messaging we wanted to present to the public. That was important; we didn't want to say—or reveal—anything that could help another team. We'd practice and finish around 3:00 p.m. I'd have dinner and watch even more film.

I was never one for sleeping at the office. I thought it was important to be home and have some mental and physical distance from the job. If I pulled into the driveway and saw lights on in the girls' rooms, I'd stop in and get updated on their day. Then I'd talk with Kaye before going to sleep. Even though I was done for the day, the notebook on my bedside table was always open. I couldn't help it. Some play, some insight, some detail, wouldn't let me completely rest.

Thursdays were similar to Wednesdays. By the end of the week, on Friday, I'd kick the coaches out after our early practice. That was a day for them to get things done and spend time with their families. I still had a couple of obligations: another meeting with the doctors, a press conference with the media, and a racquetball game of some sort (in '95, that game was usually at a Y in downtown Pittsburgh). After all that, it was time for me to think and write.

I always tried to make each game personal. We played just sixteen, so each of them had significance. I wanted to find ways to make sure each individual's pride was at stake every game. I spent a lot of time crafting what I wanted to say and how I wanted to say it. If we were viewed as an underdog, I made sure everyone knew that the so-called experts thought that our opponent was better. *They think we can't do something? That's even more of a reason to show them we can.*

Respect may well be the strongest motivational tool for professional athletes. That's where the use of quotes or actions from the other team becomes valuable. Yes, we absolutely monitored what was said and written in the local and national media, and we collected the most useful material. Pro athletes are the best in the world at what they do and well compensated for it, but I guarantee almost all of them play with the same mindset they had in high school or college. I don't know a single one who won't talk at length about their biggest rival in high school. That includes me: That a coach on my staff, Marvin Lewis, was part of a Fort Cherry team that beat us my senior year at Carlynton—6–3 on a kickoff return—still bothered me twenty years later.

On Friday evening I'd finish writing and have dinner with Kaye and the girls at the Pittsburgh Field Club. This was our family's sacred time, just the five of us, and we relished it. A lot of families bond over Sunday dinners, but we couldn't do that. Friday nights filled that void for us; during the season, it was the only night of the week that we had a family dinner. We all looked forward to our time at the Field Club. There was nothing fancy about it: the girls would eat chicken and fries, and we'd all make several trips to the nearby popcorn machine. We'd give a detailed rundown of our week, and we'd share jokes and laughs. Anyone who knew us understood that those couple of hours on Friday were special and protected. At home, after dinner, I might have a glass of wine and be in bed by ten.

The next day, Saturday morning, was Steelers practice. I'd make sure one of our assistants compiled the juiciest opponent quotes from the week and stick them in the players' lockers. Our Saturday afternoons were free, and we'd reconnect as a team Saturday evening at a hotel.

On Sunday morning, I'd make the short drive home. Then, like many families in Pittsburgh, the Cowhers would drive downtown to Three Rivers Stadium for the Steelers game. The whole city would be blanketed in black and gold on game days. It was yet another reminder of why I loved this job. There were thirty NFL cities, but none with the quirks, traditions, and overwhelming passion of Greater Pittsburgh.

Mr. Rooney had a lot to do with that. He'd been part of the NFL when it was a struggling business, and he never forgot those roots. I don't think there's ever been an owner more concerned about fans than Dan Rooney. He was very much aware a large part of our fan base consisted of working people like my father. Accordingly, he tried to keep ticket prices as low as possible. He always insisted some tickets be available for single games so people who couldn't afford season tickets could get to at least one game.

When people stood in line in the cold for playoff tickets, he'd send pizzas down to them so they would have something to eat while they waited.

"We do things differently here," he told me, "so we don't forget that ultimately we're here to serve the average fan, not just the people who can afford luxury boxes."

‖‖‖‖‖‖‖‖

We were immediately challenged in our '95 season opener, at home against the Detroit Lions. We won the game, but Rod Woodson tore his ACL while trying to tackle Barry Sanders. It was so serious that we knew his regular season was over. I say it that way because of who Rod was. Not many corners in the league played like him, plus he was one of our valuable team leaders. The recovery time for his particular injury is generally one full year. But this was Rod. We didn't put him on injured reserve, which would have ended his entire season. We decided to carry him on the roster for the whole year, hopeful that he might be ready if we made it to the Super Bowl. It meant we'd be one player short for most of the season, but I felt it was a gamble worth taking.

Neil O'Donnell also got hurt during the game. He was scheduled to miss about a month. His backup was a veteran, Mike Tomczak, whom I had a lot of respect for. Tomczak would have to lead us for the next four games, or more, if Neil had any setbacks in his rehab.

My cord man for that game was my friend John DeMaine. He'd talked for years about being the person who walked behind me on the sideline, making sure the cords connected to my headset were untangled and in good condition. He did the job for the first time in the Lions game.

When the injuries were assessed, I took a long look at John. "Today, I lost my best cornerback and my starting quarterback. The only difference between today and any other day is you!"

I was only half joking. That was the last time John held my cord at home, and it had nothing to do with the injuries. He told me he didn't want to take that job from one of our ball boys. Instead, he paid his own way to each of our road games so he could hold my cord. Several years later, when NFL headsets went cordless, John kept his job. I referred to him as the only cord man in a cordless league.

Going into our fourth game of the '95 season, against the Minnesota Vikings, we were 2-1. Their quarterback was Warren Moon, who was a year older than me and still playing at a high level. Their defensive coordinator was my friend Tony Dungy, whom I'd worked with in Kansas City. Shortly after that game, I learned a humbling lesson. Fortunately, it had nothing to do with my preparation for Moon.

The Vikings led 10–6 just before halftime when they lined up to attempt a 48-yard field goal. They missed it. But the officials penalized us 5 yards for having twelve men on the field. This time Fuad Reveiz's kick was good, and it gave the Vikings a 13–6 lead. *Wait*, I thought. Twelve *men on the field?* I wanted to figure out what had happened so we didn't repeat the mistake. I started counting. That's when I realized it was a bad call.

I got ahold of a Polaroid taken from the press box, and sure enough, eleven Steelers were on the field. I approached an official.

"Listen, we only had eleven guys on the field." I held out the picture so he could see it. "I got the picture right here. Look."

He shook his head. "Coach, we can't look at that picture."

I was livid now. Their mistake had cost us 3 points in a close game. I went to the line judge to plead my case. He said, "You had twelve guys on the field. There's no doubt about it."

No doubt about it. He said it with such authority. I knew he was wrong. It was maddening.

"I'm telling you I didn't. I've got the friggin' picture right here!"

I lost all contact with my personal rule and refused to let it go. I was so mad that as we left the field at the end of the half, I took that picture and stuffed it into the shirt pocket of the official. That scene was quickly photographed and distributed. It got a ton of publicity.

I regained my composure by the time I reached the locker room, where I decided to use the incident to motivate the team. I was totally into it and definitely gave one of my best halftime speeches ever. We sprinted out of the locker room and got the ball at the beginning of the third quarter. Our second quarterback of the day, Jim Miller, threw two interceptions that went for touchdowns. We lost, 44–24. So much for my great speech.

After that incident, Pittsburgh fans were supportive of me. I heard, over and over, that what I did to that official was great. One of my daughters told me, "Daddy, I'm so glad you did that to that official because he was wrong."

I thought about it, then told her, "No, what *I* did was wrong. You don't treat people like that. You don't show somebody up on national TV like that."

I learned something that day. I realized I was in the entertainment business, too, and people are constantly watching me on the sidelines. To show up someone in a position of authority—even if I was right—was absolutely the wrong message. The league fined me $7,500. Both officials were fined for their mistake as well. Also, from that time on, the league took the pockets off the officials' shirts.

By midseason, we had bigger problems than an official's blown call. Our defense was unrecognizable; we were allowing, roughly, a touchdown more per game than we had my entire time in Pittsburgh. At 5-4, we were a solid team with obvious flaws in the secondary.

One of my defensive backs, Carnell Lake, was a consummate pro. He was as classy an individual as I've ever been around, truly a selfless leader. With Rod injured, I made a big request: I asked Carnell to move from strong safety, where he'd been a Pro Bowler the previous season, to corner, an unfamiliar position where he felt vulnerable. A young player, Willie Williams, was the other corner.

At times, both of them took their lumps. In a game at Cincinnati, they were repeatedly picked on by quarterback Jeff Blake. He threw alley-oop passes to his receivers, and Carnell and Willie struggled. I pulled Carnell and Willie aside, sat them down, and told them, "You guys are our starting corners. We're gonna go as far as you go. I got your back, and we'll live with whatever you do. Just play with confidence, be aggressive, take chances, and don't ever doubt yourselves. Because you guys are good."

I could see both of them grow into their positions. They were motivated by their own self-pride to be better. Carnell and Willie both needed positive motivation. Some players, such as those two, are self-motivators. What they needed was verbalized support and then the freedom to improve without me hovering or nitpicking.

This was one of the reasons I was so adamant about getting to know people and their backgrounds. I felt the more I knew about people personally, the more I could tap into the best way to motivate them. I didn't use a general approach to get the best out of players.

One example was linebacker Levon Kirkland, our second-round pick my first season. He was a preacher's son and was far tougher on himself than I or anyone on my staff could have been. Levon was confident, but he always thought he should be playing better. He pushed himself hard. The last thing I wanted to do with a player who was that self-critical was reinforce his doubts. As a manager, you have to be careful with people like that.

I remember that we once drafted a player and wanted to move

him to a different position. He struggled and became agitated with his inability to make the transition. We kept telling him, "Ask questions," but he finally admitted he wasn't comfortable asking questions because he felt his questions were dumb.

"What am I supposed to look at?" he finally asked. "Who's going to tell me if it's a run or a pass?"

He didn't want us to think badly about him. When we got over that hurdle, he quickly picked up his position and filled our need there. I was learning that many people just can't take criticism, and it's important to find out quickly who they are. Instead of responding to criticism and being motivated by it, they go into a shell. You can lose those people with a few words.

The trick, in 1995 and in all seasons, was to be mindful of specific personality types and learning styles, while also staying focused on our team culture and team goals. My standard for everyone was there would be expectations. Once those expectations were established, I'd demand accountability. The accountability flow chart started with me, then went on to my coaching staff, and finally to the players.

My job as the leader of our team was to identify where we had an issue, figure out why it happened, and find a way to correct it. In our meetings, I told coaches that when a player continues to make the same mistake, two things are happening: He either doesn't understand it or he doesn't care. If he doesn't understand it, then it's his coach's fault. If he doesn't care, then we have to do something about him.

Among the things I just hated to hear from a coach or a player after something went wrong was "I did my job" or "I told him that at the meeting" or "I threw it where he was supposed to be." Statements such as that would set me off. Maybe you did your job. Maybe you told him at the meeting. Maybe you threw it where he was supposed to be. But the job didn't get done. It means that maybe there's a better way of doing it as opposed to deflecting responsibility. I was never as concerned with assessing blame as I was with trying to correct problems.

I'd never won a championship, but I knew the journey there didn't seamlessly open itself up. Uncomfortable and blunt conversations are part of the process. On occasion, I'd sit in on unit meetings to observe my assistants. I remember one of them would use a certain profane word I didn't like, and each time he did it, I'd pull him aside and correct it. But then in the next meeting he'd use that same profanity again. Finally, I told him point-blank, "Listen, I don't like it when you use that word. That's why I keep correcting you."

"Oh," he replied. "I wondered why you were doing that."

Whoa. I was accountable for that. It was my fault, not his. I obviously wasn't clear about the way I wanted things done. I'd thought I'd made it clear that I viewed the meeting rooms like classrooms, and coaches as teachers. Good teachers don't use that language when teaching. That exchange taught me something, and I used it as a coaching point to the rest of my staff: They should never assume a player got their message. Our rule was simple: Be specific.

By the end of the regular season, we didn't resemble the team from the first month of the season. Our defense regained its identity after we made those changes in the secondary, and we won six of our final seven games. For the third time in four years, we won the AFC Central Division, with a record of 11-5. As the number two seed in the conference, we knew we'd be at Three Rivers for our divisional playoff game. But if the top two seeds won their games, we'd have to go on the road for the AFC title game. And that top-seeded team was in Kansas City, led by my old coach and boss, Marty.

We dominated Buffalo in our divisional game, winning, 40–21. The Chiefs, who owned the best record in the NFL, gave up just 10 points in their divisional game to the Indianapolis Colts—and still lost. The final was 10–7.

For us, it had been an unusual and unpredictable route to another conference championship game at home, but here we were. Like the previous season, the talk was that we were supposed to beat the Colts based on our regular season and theirs. I didn't buy it. They'd gone to Arrowhead Stadium and defeated an excellent, well-coached team. If they could beat them, they could beat us. I wanted to be sure everyone in our building gave the Colts the respect—and study—that they deserved. I was committed to learning from the heartbreak of the '94 AFC Championship against San Diego.

All week, I could feel the city pulsing with championship excitement. The energy reached its peak on game day, and everyone in the stadium clearly remembered last year's emptiness. Those who didn't remember were treated to signs such as 3 MORE YARDS, a reference to the failed fourth-and-3 play from that Chargers game.

As I expected, nothing was easy about the game. I knew we were the better team, but the Colts wouldn't go away. They made us work for everything. In a season of humbling lessons, I received another one on our first touchdown of the day. We'd drafted quarterback Kordell Stewart in '95. He'd been a second team all-American at Colorado and led his team to a Top 3 ranking. But as a rookie, he wasn't going to play over anyone in our quarterback group. Initially, we had him running our scout team, the group that mimics the plays our next opponent usually runs. We saw how fast he was and that he had great hands.

To take advantage of his tremendous athletic ability, we turned him into a receiver. When I discussed it with him, he understood the situation and told me, "I'll play receiver, but I want you to know I want to be a quarterback in this league."

"Okay," I agreed. "We'll call you quarterback-slash-receiver." And his nickname was born right there: Slash. He became a sensation with his speed, versatility, and showmanship. I knew how big he was locally just by listening to my daughters. He was one of their favorite players.

Slash caught a 5-yard pass from Neil O'Donnell just before the end of the first half to give us a 10–6 lead. But replays showed that in getting open, he'd run out of the end zone and then stepped back in for the score. That's illegal. The officials missed that call, but I don't remember an irritated head coach chasing them down with *that* Polaroid to show them that they'd missed it. You get my point. Officials will miss some calls that go against you and some that will benefit you. It's not wise to overreact to what they're doing and let it become a distraction.

The game ground on in the second half. With three minutes to play, we had the ball, trailing 16–13. The similarities to the Chargers game were eerie. We trailed in the final three minutes then, 17–13. As everyone referenced throughout the week, our season ended on that fourth-and-3 play against San Diego. Against the Colts, we faced a fourth-and-3 from their 47-yard line. We needed a conversion to save our season and we got it, with Neil making a great throw over the middle to Andre Hastings. Then, on the very next play, Ron Erhardt called for Neil to take a shot deep down the right sideline, where Ernie Mills was facing man coverage. Ernie was our big-play receiver, and he showed outstanding footwork to bring in the ball and set us up at the 1. Our bruiser of a running back Bam Morris scored two plays later, giving us a 20–16 lead. We *had* to be going to the Super Bowl, right?

Well, ninety seconds were left in the game. My players knew, and physically felt, my views on finishing every part of a job. Down to the final second. To make my point, I'd asked them all to do something that I hated to do myself: I asked them to be disciplined enough to run without headphones when they worked out on their own in the middle of the summer. We all do the opposite; I see it all the time. People run, bike, and train with their music on. It'll get them into their personal zone where they'll push harder. Some people can do that all day—with the music.

But when you're in the NFL and, say, ninety seconds are left in the AFC Championship Game . . . you realize how tired you are. There's no personalized playlist for the burst you need. You've got to find a way to push through fatigue because taking just one play off, one half-hearted play, can cost your team a win. I hated to run. Finishing was the best part. So I installed drills with the focus on finishing whatever we started. Those drills were conducted in front of a handful of people, but they were designed for moments such as this conference championship, played in front of thousands.

We used to do a running test in which a player had to run fourteen 40-yard dashes within a certain time based on his best previous time. He didn't have to beat that time or even match it, but we did want him to get close to it. Players would run, then take a forty- or fifty-second break, then run it again. And again. And again. But we did it in groups, so it became competitive, with pride becoming a factor. The biggest hurdle was just finishing fourteen 40s. A lot of our linemen struggled with it. I pushed them hard because I wanted them to get over the mental block about being able to finish. I wanted them to understand at those moments late in the game they had more to give than they thought they did. To do that, they had to finish.

The Colts made that test real at the end of the game. They moved from their own 17 to our 29. They had used their time well, and they had one more shot at the end zone to decide the game. Their quarterback, Jim Harbaugh, threw a great ball intended for receiver Aaron Bailey. We had five guys there, but the ball still wound up on Bailey's stomach before it slid off and grazed the turf. It was so close to being a catch, Harbaugh walked off in a daze. He stared around the field and kept saying, "I thought he caught the ball."

At first, I did, too. But then it began to sink in. We had finished the job. We were headed to Arizona for the Super Bowl and not to Hawaii for the Pro Bowl. My daughter would have to settle for the desert instead of the beach.

In the moment, I wished I had the ability to pause time. Or slow it down. I'd coached in a conference championship game at Three Rivers Stadium—my team's stadium in my hometown. We'd won it. My family and friends had watched it. At thirty-eight years old, I became the youngest coach in history to lead his team to the Super Bowl. And I got the chance to lift the Lamar Hunt Trophy—given to the AFC champion—in the sky before handing it over to the man who'd been like a father and teacher and mentor to me, Mr. Rooney.

The drive from downtown to Fox Chapel was much louder (and later) than it had been the previous year. There were big plays to recap and plans to make for the trip to Tempe. My wife and daughters knew how much time and thought went into the job, and the long stretches I wasn't at home because of it, so they were happy to exalt within our 24-Hour Rule. That's how long we all stayed on a win, or a loss, before moving on to the next thing.

|||||||||||

Our opponents in Super Bowl XXX were the Dallas Cowboys. When I was in high school and college, Steelers-Cowboys was the greatest rivalry in the league. Being from Pittsburgh, I was biased: We played the game the way it was supposed to be played, while Dallas finessed their way to success. Or so the story went then. I soon understood this was different. In my four seasons as head coach of the Steelers, the Cowboys had played either in the Super Bowl or NFC Championship Game each year. They'd won two Super Bowls already, and they were favored to beat us by just over a touchdown for their third.

The media had fun with the contrasts. The Cowboys had some of the league's biggest and most outspoken stars: Troy Aikman, Michael Irvin, Emmitt Smith, and Deion Sanders. Even their owner, Jerry Jones, had a celebrity swagger to him. There were reports that the Cowboys' top players would arrive for practice in limousines, while we would show up on yellow school buses. (I don't know if our buses were actually yellow, but the comparison was accurate. We were a blue-collar team and proud of it.)

I knew we needed our best game of the year to beat Dallas, and I was encouraged—and in awe—that Rod Woodson was declared active for the game. As soon as he stepped on the field, Rod would become the first player in league history to return to play in the same season in which he'd had reconstructive knee surgery. His mental and physical toughness, and his leadership, inspired our entire organization.

The two weeks leading up to Super Bowl XXX were a whirlwind of distractions. It was impossible to turn around without somebody snapping a photograph, asking a question, or warmly relaying well-wishes. There wasn't one moment of quiet or relaxation. About two hours before the game, I went to the field by myself. Supposedly I was there to check out the conditions, do my usual pregame walk-around. But that wasn't what I was really doing. I'd spent my whole life on football fields, from the beat-up Pee Wee football fields of Crafton to here, on a manicured field at the single greatest sporting event in the world. I was on the most important football field of my life, and I needed to take that in.

I walked around the perimeter and tuned out all the yelling around me. The sound system was playing music from the 1970s, and listening to those songs took me all the way back home. I never wanted to forget this moment. I reminisced about my life and what it had taken to get here. I thought of my beginnings, my parents, Kaye and the girls, and all the people in Pittsburgh who told me that they looked at me and saw and heard a reflection of themselves.

All we needed, for a perfect night in the desert, was a win.

Everything about playing in the Super Bowl is different. You have more delays before the game starts, a longer halftime, more media time-outs, and a lot of time standing around that you have to fill. Instead of the game's starting twelve minutes after you come out of the tunnel, it's twenty-three minutes later. You've got your team right on the edge, then you get deflated. You've spent the entire season following a routine that got you to the Super Bowl, then that routine changes. If you aren't ready for it, it definitely brings you down. Once the game starts, though, on the sidelines it really is like every other football game.

Unfortunately for us, we got off to a slow start in the game.

I'd talked with the staff all week about being ready to shake things up early against the Cowboys. They were too good and talented for us to go out and give them something predictable. I told Ron Erhardt, our offensive coordinator, "When we get our first, first down with our regular people in the game, let's go no huddle and spread out everybody. Go into an empty-backfield formation."

That was one of my first ten plays. I wanted to remind Cowboys head coach Barry Switzer that we had wrinkles like that, just so his quick defense couldn't line up and tee off on us. Neil O'Donnell and the offense understood that rather than being under center, Neil would be a few yards behind the center in a shotgun formation. We hadn't practiced it much the prior few weeks, but we had done it often enough during the season.

We were trailing 10–0 when we made our first, first down on the Cowboys' 36-yard line. Neil, as instructed, went into a shotgun formation with an empty backfield. We did everything right on that play—except our All-Pro center, Dermontti Dawson, thought that Neil was still under center. Dermontti was looking forward, locating his blocking assignment. Neil called signals and Dermontti snapped the ball—in a wide arc way over Neil's head. I watched the ball sail through the air, as if it were in slow motion, and thought, *Oh. My. Gosh.*

Neil turned and ran after the ball. He fell on it for a 13-yard loss. As a coach, you can't do much in those situations. These were two good football players who'd had a miscommunication. That it happened in front of 94 million people would make it easy to overreact to it, but at those moments everyone has to be reassured and stay focused.

We chased the Cowboys all day, and we needed another special play to stay in the game. You practice for these situations because you may face them, not because you want them to arise. At the beginning of the fourth quarter, the Cowboys were ahead 20–7. Our kicker, Norm Johnson, made a field goal with about eleven minutes left to make it 20–10.

Up to that point, my coaching reputation was that I was conservative on offense but tough on defense: I liked to play the percentages on offense, then rely on my defense to hold the lead. That was probably a fair scouting report; I usually needed to have a strong reason before I'd go against the percentages. I thought this was one of those times. Bobby April, the special teams coach, suggested the onside kick. I agreed with him.

An onside is one of the riskiest plays in football. It works less than one in every five attempts, and when it fails, it leaves your opponent in excellent field position to start their possession. But those percentages are misleading. A team almost always attempts an onside kick when it's trailing and time is running out. Everyone knows an onside is coming then, and the receiving team puts its most reliable ball handlers in position to catch the ball. When an onside kick is a complete surprise, it's close to a fifty-fifty play.

We'd practiced it during the week. It was just a matter of having the guts to call it. I decided to do it then for several reasons: The Cowboys didn't seem to suspect it was coming; they had a powerful offense that could melt the clock; my team had been disciplined and tough and focused all year; we deserved it.

Dallas was completely surprised. They didn't even have their hands team in the game. As Norm Johnson moved toward the ball, their front line was already moving backward to block for the return man. Norm kicked it perfectly. It bounced several times, and one of our corners, Deon Figures, recovered at our 47-yard line.

If you want to know the emotional level of a team, watch it as it recovers an onside kick. When your team gets it, it feels like a fresh start to the game. It didn't matter that we'd played almost fifty minutes and had just 10 points. When we got the ball, we felt that we were going to score. Eight plays later we got a short touchdown run from Bam Morris to make it 20–17.

When our defense forced the Cowboys to punt four plays later, we thought we were going to win the game. We had the ball on our own 32-yard line with 4:15 remaining. This is just what we'd hoped for. All we had to do was move the ball, at our own pace. Everyone on our sideline wanted a late touchdown to win the championship, but even a tying field goal would put us in position to play the first overtime game in Super Bowl history.

We'd been here before, with the ball in a big moment and in need of a winning drive. On a second-down play, we had four receivers in the game. I didn't mind that because we'd done it before during the season. But it also wasn't our ideal way of moving the ball. At the key moments in a game, you have to either win it or lose it with your best plays and people. The Cowboys came with a blitz, and Neil misread it and threw it early. It was a second-down play, so I didn't think that play would be the key to the game. But it was. Neil was intercepted by cornerback Larry Brown, and it wasn't even close. It looked like Brown was the intended receiver. I was sick and exhausted. The turnover gave the Cowboys the ball in the red zone, and they scored to make the final 27–17.

I could see some black-and-gold jerseys in the stands, and I'd heard Steelers fans—from Pittsburgh and all over the country—cheering during the game. But now our sideline was quiet, while Dallas celebrated its third championship in four years.

Before I walked through the tunnel and to our locker room, I saw Kaye and Meagan on the field. Kaye was dressed for a championship, wearing black and gold. Meagan had a hair elastic with the Steelers logo on it. I could see that they were hurting for me. I grabbed Meagan and told her what I always did about sports: "Sometimes you win, sometimes you lose." But what she said to me brought me back, once again, to my larger purpose.

"Dad, win or lose, you'll always be my hero."

It was devastating to lose the game. It was the worst defeat I'd ever experienced. But those words from Meagan lifted my spirits. There's a postgame party for both Super Bowl participants, win or lose, so the entertainment was already in place. Kool & the Gang was scheduled to perform, and I'd always been a big fan of their music.

"Play all of your stuff tonight, fellas," I told the group. "Except for 'Celebration.' It may not go over well tonight."

I was down, but I danced that night. I probably danced too long because Kaye whispered in my ear, "We should go. It's probably not the best thing for you to be dancing this much after what happened in the game."

She was right. I danced that much because it was one of my favorite things to do. As soon as the music stopped, we had to face some tough realities about the upcoming season.

10

How to Adapt and Still Win

NFL head coaches have been multitasking longer than the term has been in use. Major League Baseball got it right whenever it began to describe its team leaders as "managers." That's exactly the job of a head coach in pro football: manager of . . . everything.

In season, during a typical game, the head coach manages his staff, his players, the clock, and the rhythm of the game. He weighs a continuous stream of information—from numerous sources—that he instantly evaluates and turns into a decision. Every aspect of the game, no matter how minute, requires his attention and approval: offense, defense, kicking game, available players, injuries (and replacements).

The job is perfect if you like talking to yourself.

Do I use a time-out here?

Should I throw a challenge flag?

Can my kicker make it from here against the wind?

It's fourth and a foot; is this the time to go for it?

What are the terms if we accept this penalty?

Nothing prepares you for the quick-pace chaos and exhilaration of the sideline except doing it. And then doing it again and again.

Remember, I said that's for a typical game. Real life doesn't work that way, though. Once the games are over and players go their separate ways into the off-season, coaches are the sole decision makers. It adds even more unpredictability to the head coach's job because, most of the time, when you get a call about a player in the off-season, good news doesn't usually follow.

That's what happened at the beginning of my fifth season in the spring of 1996. I learned that our starting running back, Bam Morris, had been taken into custody in Texas. During a traffic stop, police said they found between five and fifty pounds of marijuana in the trunk of the car Bam owned and was driving. Another passenger was in the car as well.

I never sensed or had any issues with Bam, so I was surprised by the report. At twenty-four, he found himself in a position certain to affect his career. We couldn't jump to conclusions about guilt, but we also couldn't wait. Free agency had begun and the college draft was only three weeks away. This was the major period of roster management, and unexpectedly, running back shot to the top of our priorities list. And after coming so close in Super Bowl XXX, we had lots of priorities. Some bills were coming due, and the reality was that we couldn't pay all our important players.

After another solid season as our starting quarterback, Neil O'Donnell headed to free agency. I'd been comfortable with Neil as our quarterback, but we'd spent a second-round pick on Kordell Stewart and believed in his upside. We also had Mike Tomczak and Jim Miller to compete for the job. I was happy for Neil: He was twenty-nine and had a lot of teams willing to commit to him long-term with a significant salary. I didn't think it made sense to spend that much of our cap money on him. That said, we still offered him the largest contract in Steelers history, before the Jets offered more than we could compete with.

On the other side of the ball, we'd had three great seasons with Kevin Greene, who became a fan favorite in Pittsburgh. He was the perfect fit for our culture and scheme as soon as he arrived. He'd be thirty-four at the start of the '96 season, and I knew he could still play. But his backup, Jason Gildon, was ten years younger, and it was his time to become a starter. Greene signed with the Panthers, reuniting with Dom Capers. I also lost my first first-round pick, a young tackle named Leon Searcy. We'd drafted him, developed him, and looked forward to watching him reach his potential with us. But Jacksonville, in its second year of existence, signed him to a record contract for an offensive lineman.

It was a stinging problem we dealt with every season. Every organization wrestles with the same issue. The best way to deal with it is to be realistic: A good player may simply be worth more to another team than he is to you.

At times, signing a veteran free agent coming off the best season of his career can also be a gamble—although it certainly looks good in the media. When a player has a really good year, one of the first league-wide questions is, How many years does he have left on his contract? It's never surprising to learn a player who is having a career-best year is in the final year of his contract. The problem in many of those situations is that you don't know what kind of player you're getting. Is he the solid performer of the last year of his contract or the average player of the other years? Did he suddenly figure it out, or did he work harder than ever before simply with the money in mind?

Building a roster is a balancing act. As in any business, we worked within our personnel budget. Money was always a factor. But I don't know of any other industries except professional sports in which companies face the same type of budget constraints as we did. In the NFL, every team has to work with an identical salary cap; the variation comes with how much each team decides to allot to each position. What we *wanted* to do and what we could *afford* to do were often very different. As a result, we knew we'd lose a lot of good people to free agency.

As usual, a new season also meant coaching turnover. I had to react to continued league-wide interest in my staff. Marvin Lewis had done an excellent job with all of our linebackers since '92, and he had a chance to get a promotion and make more money with the Baltimore Ravens. He left to become their defensive coordinator. Chan Gailey, our receivers coach, was on a head coaching path. I wanted to keep him with us, and I needed to offer a job that would entice him to stay. I made him the offensive coordinator, the role Ron Erhardt had had since my first year in Pittsburgh. Erhardt went to the Jets and, once again, was Neil's offensive coordinator.

The Steelers were not going to be big spenders for players in the free agent market. Our internal philosophy was to draft or find talented young players, sign them, and develop them through teaching and experience within our system. Whenever possible, we liked to have our young players start on special teams and maybe get a few offensive or defensive plays as they earned them. Some teams have tried to rebuild quickly by bringing in several big-name and expensive free agents at the same time. Almost without exception it hasn't worked. I believe in team chemistry; it develops when you slowly create a mix of veterans and young players, then continue to bring in the young players to replace the veterans you have to let go. Bringing in a star player who has no knowledge of your system may create more problems than it solves.

The biggest challenge we faced when deciding which players to acquire—beyond talent—was projecting a player's effectiveness within our system. In business, that's like trying to judge a salesperson. You're thinking about hiring this person who relates well to other people. But the person wasn't especially successful with his or her old company. You have to look at that to figure out why. Maybe the person didn't have such great sales numbers because nobody wanted the product. Or if armed with the right product, the person could become special on the job.

Just before the draft, that's exactly how we viewed one of our options at running back. If we were going to hand the job to a rookie, I wanted us to find a way to get Eddie George from Ohio State. He was tall for the position—about six-three—and he had the ruggedness of a linebacker. I liked that. If not George, we were intrigued by another tough running back on the trade market.

<hr/>

Jerome Bettis had been a first-round draft choice of the Los Angeles Rams in 1993. He'd rushed for over 1,000 yards his first two seasons, but in 1995 the Rams moved to St. Louis and got themselves a new head coach, Rich Brooks. He came from the college game, at Oregon, and he installed a wide-open, pass-oriented offense. It was a bad fit for Bettis, a 250-plus-pound back who steamrolled people. The Rams were looking for a faster hybrid-type back who could catch and run on third down. Bettis had good hands, but he couldn't make a quick move to beat a linebacker in one-on-one coverage. His nickname, the Bus, told you what kind of player he was: He'd beat you by carrying you, running past you, or over you. The Bus, who was just twenty-four, was *made* for our offense.

We decided to make our move on draft day. Our player personnel director, Tom Donahoe, said the Rams wanted a lot more than the draft picks—a second and fourth—we offered for Bettis. We insisted on our terms and got the deal done. Admittedly, we weren't sure on everything about him. Some rumors were floating around that he was a bit of a malcontent, a "locker room lawyer," supposedly a disgruntled player who tries to influence others to see things as he does.

What we knew was we were desperate for a power back and Bettis was available. Any hesitation about his game or his personality went away the first time I saw him in our offense.

We had a minicamp on the campus of Duquesne University, a few minutes away from Three Rivers Stadium. Bettis showed up with the most contagious smile, and you could tell that his teammates wanted to be around him. He then ran a couple of basic running plays.

I looked at our running backs coach, Dick Hoak: "Oh my God. Did we get a special player here or what?"

Bettis was big, tough, and had remarkably quick feet. Everything about him—running style, personality, nickname—was going to make him a magnet for Steelers fans.

Heading into training camp, having dealt with the players' money matters, I was now in position to exhale. Our team would be built from the players in this camp. And Mr. Rooney had made it clear that he wanted me to lead the Steelers for a long time. I was honored. I didn't want to be anywhere else.

The big story of camp was, Who's going to be the quarterback? Neil had been my quarterback since '92, so it had been a while since our team began training camp with a true quarterback competition. I should either have picked a starter before camp or allowed two players to split reps and fight it out for the job. Instead, three men were trying to win one job: Mike Tomczak, who had started four games for us the year before when Neil was hurt; Jim Miller, who was a sixth-round choice from '94; and Kordell "Slash" Stewart. Each of them offered a different skill set. In training camp it was impossible to give all three of them enough opportunities to legitimately make a fair decision. Doing it with two people is hard enough.

It wasn't a good situation. While competition between players is healthy, at some positions continued competition isn't good for the team. A team, and any organization, needs clearly defined leadership.

Then you need everybody else to support the people you've put into leadership positions. When that line of authority isn't clear, you're practically asking for the creation of factions. They're the worst things that can happen, and they can split a team wide open.

If I knew then what I know now, I would have made a pick and stuck with it. It didn't happen in '96, but I've seen situations in which the backup quarterback roots for the starter to get hurt so he can get a chance to play. One reason certain backups survive for a long time is that they embrace their role and stay prepared but also go out of their way to show support for the starting quarterback.

Frankly, no one won the job in '96. I asked Kordell to be Slash for one more season because we needed his help at wide receiver. In deciding between Tomczak and Miller, I asked myself a question: If I pick the wrong guy, who would I rather have on the bench ready to replace him? I decided that if Miller failed, Tomczak would definitely give the team a spark. That was the primary reason I named Miller our starter, but I never had complete confidence in my decision.

We opened against Jacksonville and I decided to pull him at halftime. He didn't play badly. But as I watched him, I realized I just *trusted* Tomczak more. I couldn't point at anything specifically. I didn't like the look in Miller's eyes. Sometimes, even with reams of data, you just have to go with your gut feeling. That feeling was the result of every minute I'd ever spent playing or coaching football. Maybe I couldn't point out specifics, maybe there were things I couldn't identify, but it just didn't feel right.

It was the right decision. Tomczak was the starter the rest of the way, and Slash became the backup. With his dynamic athleticism, Slash provided a good change of pace from Tomczak, who was more of a pocket passer.

Some of our leadership came from our quarterbacks, but our

identity was in our running game. The Bus was the most talented and team-oriented back I'd ever coached. As expected, Pittsburgh embraced his straightforward and bruising running style. Add to it a genuine passion and enthusiasm for each game—sometimes it was each run—and we had ourselves a star. He had ten 100-yard games during the season, finishing with over 1,400 yards. He was an example of being in the right environment to achieve. So were we.

For the third year in a row, we won the AFC Central Division, with a 10-6 record, and we won our first playoff game. We played the Colts again at Three Rivers, but this time we put the game away early, winning 42–14. The next week we were in a fog, literally, in New England. At times it looked as if we were on the set of a film where the designers had lost control of the dry ice. We were all enveloped in that thick haze, which was also the best way to describe that game. We lost 28–3. The Patriots were coached by Bill Parcells, the former Giants coach, for whom I had a lot of respect. He'd always had an encouraging word in person, and he even taught me things when he didn't realize it.

I was overly defensive with the media in my first few seasons coaching. Watching the way Parcells used subtlety, deflection, and acknowledgment of the obvious inspired me. If a reporter asked me something like "Why were you guys so bad?," I'd start to get angry and reject the question: "Well, we weren't that bad; we did a lot of things well." When Parcells was asked that same question, he usually met it head-on: "You're right, we weren't very good."

I realized I wasn't being accountable. Because of that, I was setting a poor example for the team. How could I ask my players to be stand-up people if I wasn't doing it myself?

When Rod Woodson's contract expired at the end of the '96 season, we had to make a big decision. He'd earned a substantial contract, but when our doctors examined him, they decided he probably wouldn't be able to play more than one or two seasons. Based on that advice, his age (thirty-two), and the cost to sign him, we didn't offer him a contract. It was a painful decision. Rod was one of the best and toughest players, at any position, I'd ever seen. I knew from coaching him that he'd find a way to defy the odds; I'd seen him both study himself and will himself to greatness. He signed with the 49ers.

Chad Brown, whom we'd drafted and watched blossom into an All-Pro, signed a lucrative contract with the Seahawks.

Our cycle—our regeneration—was occurring again. With the loss of Woodson, we drafted a young cornerback, Chad Scott. With the loss of Brown, we drafted a young defensive end who could be a linebacker for us, Mike Vrabel. And once again, we had turnover on the coaching staff. Dick LeBeau left and joined the Bengals as their defensive coordinator. I hired Jim Haslett to replace him.

I didn't complain about our way of doing business. I think our philosophy forced me to be a better coach and talent evaluator. I recognized the temptation to stay with veteran players too long. It's better to trade or release a player a year too early than a year too late. By the time someone plays himself off the team, he's probably leaving some losses in his wake. But if you replace somebody a year too soon with a capable player, you might not lose too much production at his position.

Continual change is essential. A roster cannot remain static; if you stay with the same people too long, the sudden turnover at a lot of positions will make it impossible for you to compete. Loyalty to your people is wonderful, but you can't forget your ultimate responsibility is to the organization and to the fans. Sometimes that was hard for me. At times I'd look at a player and see vivid memories of how good he used to be. A play would take place that I knew he'd make because I'd seen him make it numerous times. But suddenly he was a half step slower. The first few times it happened, I ignored it. Then I'd look for an excuse. Finally, I had to be objective in rating a player's performance.

I learned my lesson from the previous training camp: I named Kordell Stewart the starter. Period. That was the end of Slash. Chan Gailey did a great job of installing all the things that Kordell could do effectively: we ran a lot of quarterback draws, short passes, as well as some of our playbook staples. We played to his strengths. He was nothing like Neil or Mike at quarterback, and it would have been our mistake if we'd tried to make him be them.

Even though I wasn't calling the plays, I had the ultimate responsibility for what we did on the field. I never forgot that. At times, if I didn't like something that Chan or Jim called, I'd say, "It's not your fault. It's my fault for letting you call that." I know that sounds demeaning, but it wasn't meant that way. I meant what I said: If I didn't like the call, it was my fault for not speaking up.

Once I saw us having success with a play, I wanted to keep calling it. One of my pet peeves with offensive coordinators is that they have 130 plays in the playlist and sometimes feel as if they have to run every one of them weekly. If the defense didn't show me it could stop Jerome Bettis, for example, I'd want to run the same play three or four times in a row.

"Call it again," I'd instruct. "Just flip it. Let's run it to the other side."

I didn't want to look at film on Monday morning and see a play that we ran twice for 42 yards and then wonder why it wasn't run three or four times. Professional football is complex enough without adding more complications. If our opponent couldn't figure out how to defend a play, why would I want to stop running it? That's Football 101: Keep doing what works.

During the game, I let my coordinators call the plays. But I'd speak to them. Push. Prod. Challenge. Remind. Point things out. Make suggestions. With few exceptions, I didn't interfere with their game plan. I did reserve the right to call a play when I sensed the coordinator was hesitating. I told my staff flat out, "If I call a defense or if I call an offensive play, I want you to call it."

We had a Monday night game in '97 when I looked up at the scoreboard and saw that we had a third and 3. When Chan Gailey hesitated, I told him, "Call the draw."

To his credit he stood up to me. "Bill, no."

I insisted, "Yes. Call the draw. H42 from the four wides. Flush right. H42."

Chan sounded skeptical. I could sense his reluctance. "Okay."

I watched with great satisfaction as the play went for 4 yards and a first down.

Then I heard Chan's voice in my headphones. "Are we punting or you want to go for it?"

Punting? "What are you talking about? We just got a first down."

After a brief pause Chan explained, "No, we didn't. Bill, that was third and eight."

That was when I realized I needed glasses to see at night. I had totally misread the scoreboard. The 8 had looked just like a 3.

When I did make a call, I thought it was important to let the coordinators know that I was willing to accept the responsibility for it: "When I make a call and it doesn't work, it's on me. But if it works, it's a great call by you."

There were a lot of great calls, all around, in '97. Our running game, with the Bus once again leading the way, was awesome. We finished with 572 rushing attempts, which was one of our highest numbers of the decade. Bettis had over 1,600 yards on the ground, and Kordell had nearly 500. We had good receivers in Yancey Thigpen and Charles Johnson; our tight end Mark Bruener was an excellent blocker. Our offensive line was rock-solid with Dermontti Dawson at center. Our defense was unbelievable. But it all came down to the quarterback. We finished 11-5 and had home-field advantage throughout the playoffs. Kordell was good within our system. But in the AFC Championship Game against the wild card Denver Broncos, he threw 3 interceptions, including 2 in the end zone.

That 1997 team might have been the best team we had in my fifteen seasons in Pittsburgh. I'm not blaming Kordell Stewart for those interceptions. The precise timing that takes place on the field every play is one of the things that makes the game so beautiful for those people who understand it. When you've practiced a timed route endlessly and then you see it work on the field just as it did in practice, the satisfaction is tremendous. But sometimes it doesn't work as well in the game as it did in practice. On a lot of pass plays a quarterback is throwing to a spot, and the receiver's responsibility is to be there; they have worked on it over and over in practice. The execution has to be precise. That ball is going to be thrown 17 yards down the field to the inside edge of the numbers off a five-step drop. The quarterback in that situation has to read the coverage; he has to determine where the free safety is going to be. If the safety has moved, then the quarterback has to trust his receiver to be there.

When the throw is made correctly, the ball is out of the quarterback's hands before the receiver has made his cut. The ball will be waiting for him when he makes it. But that means that if the receiver doesn't make the right cut at the precise instant, then the quarterback is going to be left hanging out there for the fans to boo. The ball looks as if it has been overthrown or thrown behind the receiver, but fans will immediately blame the quarterback—the player who did exactly what he was supposed to do. The relationship between a quarterback and his receivers is built in practice.

The night before every game, I projected good feelings about it because I wanted my team to feel good about themselves. The best night of sleep I got each week during the season was the night before a game. I always looked and sounded confident. Sometimes I was even cocky. But when I was alone with my staff in the locker room before the game, it was a little bit different. I'd sit there and kid with my assistants. Just before we took the field, I'd tell them, "Don't get scared now. It's too late."

It was after a game that I didn't sleep well. I'd lie there thinking about what I wished I had done differently and I'd focus on our next opponent. What didn't we do well in that game? Who played well and how am I going to get him the ball more? Who played poorly and what can we do to give him some support? What adjustments do we need to make?

The night after a game, in the regular season, is always long. Normally, the thoughts go to the next opponent. With no opponent scheduled, the thoughts returned to the process. How do we get to where we want to be, with more inevitable changes on the way?

11

Coaching through Conflict

On Thanksgiving Day in 1998, we found ourselves in Detroit for the Lions' annual holiday game. Four days earlier in Pittsburgh, we'd beaten the Jacksonville Jaguars, the team that now led our division by just one game. If we could pull off a win on Thanksgiving, we'd be 8-4 and in good shape for a season-ending run.

We had a 13–6 lead in the third quarter, but seemingly in an instant, the game was tied and headed to overtime. That's when I saw—and heard—something that I'd never thought of or imagined occurring in a pro football game. It was the first time I'd argued over the flip of a coin.

An official has to make a lot of quick analyses during a game, but I didn't think a decision on who won the coin toss was one of them. It's going to be either heads or tails. Not a tough call. But it was, and it did more than make some unintentionally funny NFL history. It also led our season on another trajectory.

Here's what happened: At the end of regulation, we were tied at 16 and on our way to overtime. Getting the ball first was a huge advantage since the first team to score (field goal or touchdown) won the game. When the referee, Phil Luckett, flipped the coin to determine who'd receive the ball, you could hear Jerome Bettis clearly say, "Tails!" Luckett looked at it when it landed, confirmed that it was tails, and then turned to the Lions captains and asked if they wanted to kick off or receive.

From our sideline, I saw Bettis having an animated conversation with Luckett at midfield. I was confused until one of our captains, Carnell Lake, came over and told me, "Jerome called tails." Carnell was adamant about it: "I'd put my reputation at stake."

That was good enough for me. Jerome and Carnell were people I'd trust my children with. When they looked me in the eye and told me Jerome called tails and the coin landed tails, I had no doubts. I protested, but Luckett told me, "He said 'Heads' first. That's what I heard."

"He's wrong, Coach," Carnell insisted. "He did not call 'Heads' first."

I felt like a parent standing between two children on a playground. *He did. . . . He did not. . . . Did! . . . Did not!* Of all the things that can possibly go wrong during a game, this wasn't something I'd prepared for. I argued, but the officials could do nothing about it. As linebacker Earl Holmes asked in frustration, "How do you blow the coin toss?" When the Lions went right down the field and kicked a 42-yard winning field goal, I was even angrier. I screamed at the officials as they left the field.

CBS's audio replay supported Bettis. But a few days later, an enhanced version of the audio was released. This time you could hear a voice saying, "Hea-tails!" Bettis had begun to call heads first, then changed his mind and called tails. By rule, the official had to accept the first thing Bettis said, which was "Hea . . ." Luckett had gotten it absolutely right. Practically the next day the league changed the rule and everything was clearer and better.

It was the opposite for our team. We lost to the Lions, then dropped our first three games of December to fall to 7-8. Going into the final game of the season against Jacksonville, I had to deal with our on-field problems as well as a few office conflicts. I'd managed to sail through the first six seasons of my head coaching career without an abundance of adversity, but in year seven it hit me from all directions.

We'd established a culture of success. We expected to win. Yet I hadn't learned how to lose. I hadn't developed the patience you need to get through an extended slide. When we couldn't get out of our rut, it was tough for me to accept. How had it gone so bad? Where was the button I could push to give the system a reset?

As usual, our off-season had been filled with transitions. We'd said goodbye to another iconic Steeler, linebacker Greg Lloyd, whose injuries and age had slowed him. He'd been one of the players who'd set and enforced our culture. No one wanted to get into it with Greg, who was fiercely competitive and intimidating. He spent the last season of his career with the Panthers. We also lost another coordinator. Chan Gailey had taken over for Ron Erhardt in 1996 and was masterful in his two seasons of play calling. He was so good the Dallas Cowboys offered him their head coaching job, and he had to take it. He'd learned the news in February at the league's scouting combine.

Awesome for Chan; horrendous for me.

By that time of year, experienced coaches were already locked into jobs. I didn't have a lot of options. I'd interviewed several people but hired Ray Sherman. He had a good background as an assistant, both as a quarterbacks coach and offensive coordinator. But toward the end of the '98 season, it was clear that this wasn't a good fit for us.

I made the decision to take play-calling away from Ray. I'd call the offensive plays for the season finale against Jacksonville. No matter what happened in the game, the Jaguars had already won our division, breaking our four-season streak as AFC Central champions. But taking immediate action with the play calling had to be done, and it was one of the hardest aspects of the job. Coaches have worked incredibly hard to reach this level, and I found it difficult to tell them that they weren't doing the job to my satisfaction and had to be replaced.

But my credibility was at stake: The day I fail to act decisively is the day I lose the respect of my team. Besides, the players all knew what was going on. I asked our tight ends coach, Mike Mularkey, to draw up the game plan. Initially, I'd decided Mike would call the plays. But if I did that, it would look as if Mike had gone behind Ray's back. Mike was a fine young coach who was obviously going to have many opportunities in the NFL, and I didn't want to risk getting him unfairly labeled. Mike had nothing to do with the situation.

While I'd never run an offense, I figured calling plays couldn't be that challenging. The night before the game, I told Mr. Rooney what I intended to do, and as always, he was supportive.

Well, he was supportive before he actually saw me start calling plays. I can't imagine what he thought as the game unfolded. It took just one series of downs for me to understand that being an offensive coordinator is like trying to juggle hot waffle irons for three hours. The job is complex, and I was a little surprised by its fast-and-getting-faster nature.

The offensive coordinator always has to be thinking *at least* one play in advance. He's got to know his options and, based on the result of a play, make an instant decision and get the right personnel package into the game. His key mission, for each play call, is to figure out which players to put on the field and at what time. Fans see a few players running on and off the field between each play, but some don't understand what it means and how potentially game-changing those jogs onto the field can be.

A specific group of players used in a certain situation is called a package. You start with a base package. It may consist of two tight ends, two receivers, and a back. On third down, you'll go to your third-down package. Packages are generally named for the number of backs that are in the game, followed by the number of tight ends. For example, if you call "10 personnel," you want one back and no tight ends, which means you've got four receivers. If you want "11 personnel," it means you want one back, one tight end, and three receivers. A "21 package" consists of two backs and one tight end, while "22" is two backs and two tight ends. Within each grouping there are specific plays. The offense is trying to create bad individual matchups, such as forcing a linebacker to cover a wide receiver. This strategic chess game goes on throughout the game between the offense and the defense, back and forth, play after play, with both teams eager to catch the other in a bad position.

I mention chess, and you might think of a game between two thoughtful participants in a public park or intimate family room. Now imagine chess with a play clock running down, seventy thousand fans screaming, and twenty-two passionate players on the field sprinting and colliding into one another.

As head coach, I was used to encouraging players between series, moving around, talking to guys. But as the play caller, if I took my attention from the field for even a few seconds, I was behind and had to hustle to catch up. At one point, Jerome trotted off the field after a nice run and I went to congratulate him. As I turned to him, I heard an urgent voice in my ear: "Bill! Bill! What personnel grouping? What do you want to do here?"

Oh, yeah, I remembered as I turned the other way and fumbled through the pages in my hand.

"Uh, give me 12 personnel," I stammered.

There was so much information to consider: the score, game flow, clock management, ball location, down, and distance. We lost, 21–3. I was never so happy for a game to be over. I was exhausted. It was a cool night in late December, but I was sweating through everything I had on. Mr. Rooney told me after the game, "You know, that's the best we've moved the ball this year."

To my credit, I didn't laugh. I was thinking, *But Mr. Rooney, we only scored 3 points.* I just accepted the compliment and told him flatly I was never going to do that again. Never. No chance.

|||||||||||||

The bigger issue was that we'd finished 7-9. We'd lost five games in a row, something I'd never experienced, whether as an assistant or a head coach. I knew some changes would organically happen: the expired contracts and player retirements. Also, I'd have to make some moves, in general, around football operations.

You learn a lot about your organization's collective will and determination when you win, and we'd done a lot of that in six years. But in a down year, with no signs of a quick turnaround, you find out about your character. Do the players still trust one another? Does the coaching staff have solidarity? Is the vision between the head coach, front office, and ownership still aligned?

I was grateful we had the ownership that we did. Some head coaches struggle with their team's ownership, for a variety of reasons, and never get on the same page. The real power in any franchise belongs to the owner, who may know finance better than football but exercises control over both areas. If an owner publicly exercises that obvious power, it can undermine the head coach with his players. They all know there's a higher authority, and at times they don't hesitate to go directly to the owner. Thankfully, that was never a problem. Mr. Rooney might have offered his opinion, but he never mandated anything. When things started to get tough, he was the same: He'd walk into my office, pat me on the back, and say a few words of support. It's amazing how much that little pat on the back meant to me. When other people were going through a tough time, I remembered that.

Mr. Rooney also had uncanny business and interpersonal instincts. He understood how to deal with people and get things done. He never made me feel that he was pressuring me to do something that went against my coaching principles.

I couldn't put my finger on what it was at the end of the '98 season, going into '99, but something was off in my relationship with our team's personnel director, Tom Donahoe. Like me, he'd grown up in Pittsburgh. His grandfather David Lawrence was a longtime Pittsburgh mayor before becoming governor of Pennsylvania. You couldn't walk through Pittsburgh—or even other parts of Pennsylvania—without seeing a building, monument, or plaque bearing David Lawrence's name. Tom Donahoe was connected and well liked by the business, political, and media communities in Pittsburgh.

I don't know if he believed I was trying to be more connected than he was in the office, but he was noticeably uncomfortable whenever I'd walk into Mr. Rooney's office. I'd go in for a routine check-in or to run a small item by him, but whenever I'd come out, Tom would want to know the sum of our conversations. It had never been that way before, but there was suddenly tension and eroding trust between us.

The high visibility of my job, and now losing, brought out some ugliness away from the office.

But even that wasn't the biggest issue. Criticism was never a surprise, and I accepted that it came with the territory. I didn't particularly like it; I don't think anybody likes being criticized whether it's legitimate or not. As long as the criticism focused on the game, I never objected too strenuously to it. When things became personal, and they did, I felt that was crossing the line.

What I didn't like was that the girls had to go to school and hear snarky comments about me. "Your dad is going to get fired" and

"Your dad is no good" were among the things they heard. I felt bad about it because I was insulated while I did my job. I was working while they were the ones regularly going to school, shopping, and interacting with people in town.

Kaye, as usual, had the right combination of loving perspective and clear-eyed analysis of the industry I was in. She'd take car drives with the girls and say matter-of-factly, "Coaches are hired to get fired. That's what happens in pro sports." She'd also let them know that we'd be all right because of the strength of our family, and as blessed as we were to have the lifestyle we did, we couldn't lose ourselves totally to the Pittsburgh Steelers.

That balanced outlook was always essential for me. Having parents who'd been scholarship and professional athletes, the girls knew sports were a big part of our lives. They also realized the high academic standard in our house. Kaye emphasized that point, and at times the girls would be ecstatic to see me when I came home because I was the good cop in the house. At all times, but especially when things at work weren't ideal, I needed to know I could walk in my house and be part of something that wasn't the Steelers. It felt good to close the door and simply be Dad.

With our '98 offense near the bottom of the league, I wanted to bring in an experienced offensive coordinator to work with Kordell Stewart. He'd been electric in his first full season as a starter under Chan Gailey but regressed under Ray Sherman, finishing with 11 touchdown passes and 18 interceptions. He looked like a completely different player. I leaned toward giving the job to Mike Mularkey, whom I viewed as a great coaching prospect. But I thought Kordell would benefit from working with a veteran, so I hired Kevin Gilbride, who'd had a decade of coordinating and head coaching experience. Gilbride, ironically, was one of the candidates I was competing against in 1992 for the Steelers job.

Change was inevitable in the NFL, and it had taken a while to keep my personal feelings out of it. For example, in my first couple of seasons, I'd talk with every player I cut. Then I realized the only person in the room who felt better about that approach was me. If I told a player that I regretted having to cut him, then why was I doing it?

It was tough to either cut or not offer a contract to the people I'd been with for several seasons. We'd been through the football wars together. I'd seen them play hurt, play in pain, make sacrifices for the good of the team. After a few seasons, these people had become much more than football players to me. They were people I'd come to respect and admire. I knew their wives and children. At times, I even knew how much they needed the income.

I had to remind myself nobody's playing career goes on forever, as much as we'd like it to. The time comes for everyone, and there was never anything personal about it. While generally it wasn't solely my decision to cut a player, making the decision was more complicated when I was aware of the human consequences. But that was my obligation as the head coach.

This was a leadership lesson that I couldn't forget: Each person in an organization has to take responsibility for his or her actions and be accountable for the result.

Building and maintaining a championship culture is a process. You have to create the structure and put your own imprint on it. You have to staff it with people who share your vision and have the ability to follow through on their own. You have to be able to communicate with precision throughout the entire organization, both to the entire group as well as to specific individuals, and you have to proceed as a team toward a common purpose.

Midway through the 1999 season, we were strong in several of those areas, despite some of the outside negativity and the fraying trust between Tom and me. I was committed to the organization and the city, and nothing was going to skew my perspective there. No matter what happened, I was fortunate to be in the position I was. I almost had to pinch myself.

||||||||||||||

On November 7, our eighth game of the season, we beat the 49ers in San Francisco for our third straight win. We were 5-3. I felt great about the game and our team. We didn't turn the ball over, we were tough to move the ball on, the Bus scored a couple of touchdowns, and one of our promising second-year players, Hines Ward, scored a touchdown and continued to show rapid improvement.

Then we suddenly caught hell.

We lost our next five games, all to opponents in our division. Then we went to Kansas City and lost another one. Six straight losses. We weren't just in a "bad stretch"; at 5-9 we were simply a bad team.

Most days I felt terrible. But I learned that it serves no purpose to spend a lot of time feeling bad about losing. You can feel worse about failing than anyone else has ever felt in history. You can wallow in it. But feeling bad isn't going to change a thing. The only way you can change the outcome is by eliminating bad or inefficient habits.

We tried to stay within our structure. That is, to be specific. We wanted to be specific about the things we weren't doing well—we're turning the ball over too often, we're not running the ball successfully—and then examine the alternatives.

We also tried to identify those things we were doing well. It's challenging to stay positive when you're searching for something to be positive about. Most of the time, even when you're on a six-game losing streak, you're doing at least a few things well. The problem was our lack of sustainability.

The idea was to figure out the things that worked and do them over and over. We isolated those things and tried to expand them. Sometimes it meant giving more playing time to someone who hadn't played regularly but was having success in a limited role. It meant tweaking an element of the passing game. It didn't matter what it was; I was willing to try anything. I never wanted to come to work on Monday morning thinking, *I wish we would have done this.*

If we had tried everything and our opponent was still better than us, I could accept it. But if something was wrong and we didn't adjust, that was on me. If one of our people got beat and we didn't give him help, that was our fault. If we couldn't get our offense going and we failed to make an adjustment, that was our fault. When we saw a problem of any type and failed to adjust, it just ate me up inside. People might see what appeared to be my stoicism, but I was absolutely sick and restless over what could have been.

I knew I couldn't show any of it publicly. It was important that no one on the staff gave off the slightest hint of defeat, exasperation, or panic. I never wanted the team to think that we weren't building something, even in the losses, or that I didn't believe in them.

With all the losing, it was important for me to speak with thoughtful people I respected and trusted. They had a range of backgrounds. First and foremost, I talked with Kaye because I knew how smart and insightful she was. She loved me, but she didn't seek to give me answers I wanted to hear. She was always a good and objective consultant. I'd be at the office and I'd call her at home. Just from the tone of my voice, she'd know that I needed to run something by her. I could hear her tell the girls, "I need to talk with your dad about work stuff."

Kaye heard a lot of my vents and rants. She'd listen and, without fail, she'd tell me if I had it right or if I needed to consider another perspective.

I sought the opinion of Dick Hoak and others who'd been in the league much longer than me.

What do you think is wrong with the team?

What are we doing differently that's keeping us from the results we want?

What do you see?

Often, I'd pick up the phone and talk to Marty.

I'd bring in the team leaders and ask for their observations.

Are we working too hard?

Is there something going on I don't know about?

Every coach and team have valleys. It had taken me eight seasons to hit my most concerning and puzzling one.

I tried to be realistic. I pushed, but not so much that players were afraid to make a mistake. I also stressed—just as I did when we were winning—that a *team* wins or loses, not individual players. Just as I didn't overly praise one player or one unit when we were winning, I didn't blame individuals or one unit when we were losing. No scape-goats and no heroes. In my press conferences after games, I was careful to spend the same amount of time talking about the offense and the defense. If someone was to be blamed, it was me. I almost never deflected responsibility. The worst thing a head coach can do is blame a member of his staff or a player. Do that and there's a good chance that your relationship with that person will never recover.

Unfortunately, I'd reached that point with Tom Donahoe. In my estimation, we were beyond mediation or a conversation to clear the air. I could not and did not want to work with Tom any-more. I explained to Mr. Rooney that this was about principle, not power, and I had no interest in being the football czar of the Steelers. I had so much respect for the Rooney family that I en-couraged them to accept my resignation if I was putting them in an awkward or uncomfortable spot. I assured them that I wouldn't ask for a dime of my contract, and they could have a clean break if they wanted to.

A few days after our 6-10 season, the decision was made. Tom resigned, and the search began for a new personnel director. In Pittsburgh, the story was positioned as a power struggle between Tom and me. It wasn't. I understood why the media would frame it that way because they didn't have all the information. Whenever Mr. Rooney brought in a candidate to replace Tom, I went out of my way to explain that I wouldn't be and didn't want to be that person's boss. I just wanted a collaborative and transparent approach to the job.

When Kevin Colbert got the job, I was happy. He was another Pittsburgher who'd spent his life in sports. He was unusual in that he'd worked in pro football since he was in his twenties, but he'd also been a head baseball coach at a couple of different colleges. Outside the office, I knew this move would put a new spotlight on me, but internally a weight had been lifted.

I'd talked with our team multiple times about the various elements that can make the difference in the result of a game. The same is true for an organization. All of these things have one thing in common: They require mental toughness and discipline. Sometimes the mind can be the strongest tool we have.

On occasion, I'd show the team clips of the great thoroughbred racehorse Seabiscuit. In all of those clips, Seabiscuit is wearing blinders, which prevented him from looking anywhere except straight ahead.

"He wore them," I explained, "because his trainer wanted him to focus on the finish line and not get caught up in all the peripheral things going on around him."

There will always be something to distract competitors from the finish line, but uncompromised focus will usually get you within range of your goals. We saw that at the beginning of the 2000 season, when an 0-3 start had some people wondering why the Rooneys displayed so much faith in me. There were more whispers. More cheap shots. More criticism.

But those were the peripheral issues for me, and the players had their own obstacles to overcome. We won our first game of the year on the road, then added another road win the following week. We won our third game in a row via shutout and added another shutout the following week.

Focus is a balm. It allows an individual to attain their goals, and it allows a team to sustain its level of play. Mental toughness, with focus, allows you to relentlessly pursue something—and sometimes you don't even realize you're doing it. It's just good habits.

As a coach, as a team, as an organization . . . we were able to get through the losing seasons of 1998 and 1999. We all have to be prepared for an ebb and flow. I learned that recognizing an event as simply part of a cycle is helpful.

We had those back-to-back losing seasons, then finished with a winning one, at 9-7, in 2000. Some years 9-7 is enough to qualify for the playoffs, but 2000 wasn't one of them. But I was proud of what we'd done, what we'd come through, and where we were headed.

12

Rebound and Reimagine

My first season as head coach of the Steelers, in September 1992, was also when Meagan, my oldest daughter, began first grade in the Fox Chapel school district. Kaye and I took comfort in our community's strong public schools but didn't realize just how long our girls would benefit from the school system. No NFL coach goes into a job believing that he'll be there for a decade.

It's a league and profession of constant relocation. You hope to come to an organization and help lift it up, making it better than when you found it. Sometimes that happens and it's still not enough to save your job. Since my first season in Pittsburgh, each franchise in our division had fired at least one head coach, and one—the Bengals—had fired two. So, in 2001, I felt blessed to begin my tenth season as head coach of the Steelers.

We still lived in the same neighborhood and same house we did when we first arrived from Kansas City in early '92. It was the same driveway hoop where Kaye and I played one-on-one, with the girls occasionally officiating. They'd give me a hard time about my game plan when I was losing to Kaye, who was clearly the more skilled player. I'd get myself back in the game by simply backing her down and using my size and strength to power in layups. It was the same driveway where we all played H-O-R-S-E, with the most daring attempt being something we named the Garage Shot. On Saturday afternoons during football-season home games, it's the house where I'd had the same routine for a decade: go to the back porch and take a nice nap before our evening team meetings.

By the fall of 2001, Meagan was a six-one sophomore and one of the best basketball players in western Pennsylvania. When I was a high school athlete, my father would watch my games and brag about them later. For Meagan, he'd go to each of her games with one pocket full of coins and the other one empty. Each time she scored, he'd put the appropriate coins in the empty pocket. He'd switch out pennies for nickels and nickels for dimes when necessary. At the end of the game, he'd pull the magic number out of his pocket. A quarter and three pennies? Well, that meant Meagan had finished with 28 points.

Lauren and Lindsay, eighth and fifth graders then, were also talented athletes. With parents such as Kaye and me, our girls were kind of expected to have opportunities to play in college one day. But how they were raised was important to us as well. We'd never go out of our way to give them anything or be overprotective. We were adamant that kids have to figure out some things on their own and problem solve among their peers, as part of growing up. I'd hear people say things like "I don't want my kids to go through what I went through," and I'd shake my head. Maybe what you went through, within reason, was why you became the person you became. It shaped you and taught you lessons.

Our one big nonnegotiable rule in the house was *Don't quit*. If you agreed to play a sport, you finished that season. Even if things weren't going well for the team or for you individually, you finished. Sometimes I'd finish saying a phrase and I'd have a flashback to Crafton;

my parents used to say the same things to me. Kaye and I loved the traits that being on a team emphasized: competitiveness, respect for teammates and opponents, commitment, winning with humility, and losing with graciousness. It was important for us to instill those values.

I was grateful we could raise our kids in a city where they were surrounded by so much love and family. The stability was refreshing, given all the professional changes happening around me. For example, I never imagined when I pulled out of our driveway and headed to work, I'd take the same route to Three Rivers Stadium . . . but Three Rivers Stadium would no longer be there. There's no way I thought I'd outlast *the stadium*.

As a kid, I'd gone to Three Rivers with my father to watch the Steelers take on AFC Central Division rivals such as the Browns and the Oilers. But the stadium, which opened in 1970, was toppled in 2001. Our brand-new home, Heinz Field, was just down the street. We still played in the AFC Central, but the Browns had left Cleveland and returned, the Oilers had become the Titans, and new teams such as the Ravens and Jaguars had joined the league and become part of our divisional schedule.

One thing I didn't want to change was our team identity, even if we needed different players to continue it.

Anyone who grew up in Pittsburgh knew about the lineage of great Steelers centers, going back to the 1960s. It was Ray Mansfield for a dozen years, Mike Webster for a dozen years, and then Dermontti Dawson. Dermontti made it easy for me: All I had to do was pat him on the back and send him out there. I don't think there's ever been a better athlete to play the position. But after playing 170 consecutive games, which is incredible, a serious hamstring injury caused him to miss 16 games over two seasons.

We released Dermontti at the end of the 2000 season. His salary took up too much cap space, and those injuries made him questionable. His departure left us with a massive hole in the middle of the offensive line, and we didn't see an available center—in the draft or free agency—who could fill it. In moments like that it's important to remind yourself what kind of team you want to be, the requirements of each of your positions, and the various paths you can take to fill the need.

We decided to sign free agent right guard Jeff Hartings, who had never played a single down at center. He'd never done it in college or during his five-year career with the Detroit Lions. But we believed he could do it for us. In our blocking scheme, the center had to be able to pull—or get out of his stance and run quickly to the left or right—and block on the run. Just like Dermontti, Hartings was quick, athletic, and smart.

Converting a player to a different position is always difficult and sometimes a questionable proposition. Some players just can't make the transition. Getting it done successfully requires a willing player with the right skill set, a coach to teach him how to do it, and patience to work through all the inevitable mistakes he'll make as he learns the position. Initially, Hartings had some difficulty with his snaps. But just as we expected, he put in the time and quickly improved.

I felt that our team had that collective spirit. I'd seen hints of it at the end of 2000, and there was some carryover in 2001. Several reasons for our mentality and style of play could be traced back to the culture we'd created. I disagree with anyone who suggests that any game in a season is meaningless. That couldn't be further from the truth. Even though we didn't make the 2000 playoffs, think about some of the examples our players, especially our young ones, saw:

There was Dermontti at the end of his career, injured yet still trying as hard as he could to get on the field. There was a free agent we signed that year, Kimo von Oelhoffen, who'd played six seasons for the Bengals. Everyone knew what we'd get from Kimo on Sunday; the problem was he wanted to give you that same intensity every single day in practice. We had to protect him from leaving it on the practice field, so we'd hold him out on Wednesdays and sometimes Thursdays. He'd fight with us to be on the field with the guys; he'd be furious when we'd shut him down. Not only could Kimo practice hard, but he could raise his game to another level when it counted. If he made a mistake in practice, he'd correct it before the game.

If you witness that toughness and professionalism during a season, whether it's a playoff season or not, it will have an effect on you. That's who we were as Steelers. If coaches and players weren't willing to bring that type of commitment and effort, they'd have a difficult time in our building. That was our standard and I didn't apologize for it.

||||||||||||

The embodiment of that commitment, effort, and toughness in 2001 was our twenty-five-year-old wide receiver, Hines Ward. At the University of Georgia, he'd played quarterback, running back, and wide receiver. He was still on the board in the third round of the 1998 draft, so we took him. His receiving stats in college had been good but not exceptional, because Georgia's offensive system properly utilized his talents. Because he was so versatile, we weren't sure what we intended to do with him. He wasn't spectacularly fast, but he had great hands, was an explosive hitter, and knew how to play the game. He was a winner. We wanted him on the team. After we'd drafted him, a reporter asked me, "Who's Hines Ward?"

"He's a football player," I said. "That's all I know, he's a football player."

Hines quickly became a model of versatility and leadership for us. Halfway through the 2001 season we were 6-2. Hines had an impact on every part of our offense, and if it's possible, he did it with both constant toughness and a constant smile. He was our leading receiver, willing to go over the middle and make tough catches in traffic. He was a big part of our running game because he *loved* to hit and often moved defenders back a couple of yards with his ferocious blocks; he took great pride in that aspect of his game. Most wide receivers, then and now, can't say that. You could look at Hines at any point during the game, big play or routine one, and feel the joy he had for football. He was an accountable and supportive teammate as well.

To play in the NFL you have to have talent, and as a coach it's nice to have players who can get by on theirs. But talent alone rarely wins championships. Every player will be tested through the course of a season. The ability to complement and enhance natural talent, technique, and experience with mental toughness is what helps extend careers.

We also drafted Deshea Townsend in '98, one round after Hines. Deshea didn't have great speed, but he was a smart, dependable, and resilient cornerback. Like Hines, he began as a special teamer. Eventually we asked him to contribute more and more on defense, and he responded each time. He'd made up his mind that nobody would beat him, and if someone did, he'd spring up as if to say, *You won't do that again.*

I loved these players and our team, including our quarterback, Kordell Stewart. I felt he needed to be in a specific offense that played to his strengths on the ground as well as in the air. Kevin Gilbride's approach, which relied heavily on downfield passing, wasn't the right fit. Mike Mularkey was already on our staff, and he was ready to be promoted to offensive coordinator. I had a lot of confidence in Mike. I knew he'd structure a system suited to Kordell's strengths and the rest of our offensive personnel.

By early December, we'd already passed last season's win total. Kordell, the Bus, and Hines all thrived and made the Pro Bowl in Mike's scheme. Yet another of our '98 draftees, guard Alan Faneca, became the leader of our offensive line and a first-team All Pro. We secured our twelfth win of the season, and the division title, two days before Christmas with a big win against Detroit. In that game, we displayed all of our potential and possibilities: defensive touchdown, production in the running and passing game, and even a late score from our backup quarterback, Tommy Maddox.

One week later, against the Bengals and the man who was now their head coach, Dick LeBeau, I can tell you about a "coaching first" for me. It was so rare and odd that I still remember even the smallest details of it. The game was in Cincinnati, and the first thing that stands out is how cold it was. I looked at the temperature pregame—supposedly twenty degrees—and I said to myself, *There's no way it's that warm out here.* I was told that the windchill made it feel like nine degrees, and that still seemed too high.

We were better than they were, and you could see it early. We went up 14–0, and in the second quarter, our kicker went out to attempt a 47-yard field goal that would have given us a three-score lead. Instead, the snap sailed right through the hands of our holder. One of the Bengals scooped it, lateraled it to linebacker Brian Simmons, and 56 yards later it was a Bengals touchdown. Even with that, we'd been up 23–10 late and blown that lead, too. We lost that game. I remember it so well because it was the only loss a team of mine had after leading by 11 points or more.

I hated the loss, but I was (and am) proud of the stat. It's what my coaching philosophy is all about. Whenever we were in position to close out a game, the math teacher in me came out and we played the percentages. Keep that clock running. Use every possible second before running a play.

When we were at least 10 points ahead midway through the third quarter, we'd slow everything down and begin using the clock. We'd stay in the huddle until about ten seconds were left on the play clock. We'd snap the ball with no more than three seconds left. We tried to keep the ball on the ground, and when it became necessary, we threw quick, short passes. We did that to slow down the tempo of our offense, because once we had the lead, taking minutes off the clock was as important as scoring. Some of my players hated the tactic. Especially some wide receivers over the years who walked the sideline complaining, "This is crap. We can throw on these guys! Why aren't we throwing the ball?"

The answer was obvious: We had the lead and I wanted to win the game. I wasn't trying to pile up stats. I'd tell them, "This is still about winning, right? And we are winning. I just want to run down the clock." I believed that in football, as in anything else, short-term gains weren't as important as being on top at the end.

I know some coaches never want to ease up. They've got the lead, the offense is moving the ball, they're completing passes, why change the tempo? I just disagree. When you're ahead, the clock becomes your ally.

We entered the 2001 postseason as the top seed in the AFC. When we beat our new number one rivals, the Baltimore Ravens, we set ourselves up to host the AFC Championship Game. It was my fourth home championship game as head coach. Our opponent was the New England Patriots, who'd had different head coaches every time we'd seen them in the playoffs. In '96 it was Bill Parcells. In '97 it was Pete Carroll. In '01 it was Bill Belichick.

Not only had Bill and I exchanged information over the years, we had similar approaches to roster construction. He was one coach in the league who I was certain valued special teams as much as I did. I thought the game might come down to that because I didn't believe they had many offensive weapons who could beat us. They were led by a first-year starter at quarterback, Tom Brady. When we looked at him on film, his poise and pocket presence stood out to us. He'd replaced Pro Bowler Drew Bledsoe during the season, and my staff could see why; he presented a completely different challenge for our defense.

Unfortunately for us, an officiating mistake factored into the first score of the game. It wasn't even a bad call. Worse, it was a bad spot.

Early in the first quarter we punted from our 13-yard line. To prevent a runback, we were directional punting into the sideline from the left hash mark on the field. Our coverage was set up for that punt. Josh Miller hit a beautiful 64-yard punt that bounced over receiver Troy Brown's head and out of bounds, giving them the ball close to their own 40. It was just a great punt.

But an official threw a flag, as he should have. The flyer, as I referred to him—our special teams player running down the sideline—had run out of bounds to avoid being blocked and then come back in. You're not allowed to do that. If you get blocked out of bounds, you can come right back in, but if you go out of bounds to avoid being blocked and come back in, it's an illegal procedure.

Bill Belichick accepted the penalty and forced us to punt again. The problem was that when the official respotted the ball, he mistakenly put it on the right hash mark. The distance between the two hash marks is nearly 15 yards. If you look at a grass playing field near the end of the season, the middle is always worn down because that's where most of the plays take place. It's also where the worst footing is late in a game. We'd wanted Josh to put his first punt outside the left hash mark, which would cut down the width of the field.

Josh wasn't sure what we wanted him to do now. He'd punted to the left sideline from the left hash, and now he wondered if we wanted him to punt this ball to the right sideline. He looked at us on the sideline for an answer. In the confusion nobody made the call. The official placed the ball and started the clock. I think everyone assumed we wanted to punt to the left sideline again. I don't know what Josh thought, but he punted into the middle of the field. Bill liked to play his starters on special teams, so his best receiver, Troy Brown, was also his punt returner. Brown received Josh's punt right in the middle of the field. Our coverage wasn't set up for it, and the players who were close to Brown slipped and fell in the middle between the hashes as they pursued him. He ran straight ahead for 55 yards and a touchdown.

We'd gone from being in good shape to trailing 7–0. Even that early in the game, one play made a dramatic difference. We had another special teams breakdown in the third quarter when our field goal attempt was blocked, and that turned into a Patriots touchdown that put them ahead, 21–3.

It wasn't our day. They had four times as many penalties as we did, yet we turned it over four times. Kordell had played great all season, but he finished the game with three interceptions. A big pregame story line was that a trip to the Super Bowl for Kordell would mean a return home because the game was in New Orleans, his hometown. I knew the Patriots were motivated by the perception that we had overlooked them and made our plans for the Super Bowl. The truth is that each of the final four teams, including them, had to make contingency plans, having just one week to essentially pack up operations and travel from the conference championship site to New Orleans. Yes, we prepared well for the Patriots. We just didn't play well, and it hurt us. We lost 24–17.

During the season I talked often with our team about perspective. A loss, or a losing streak, was never as bad as the public thought. And a win, or flurry of six or seven in a row, was never as impeccable as our fans and media thought. *Perspective.* But feeling that in the minutes, hours, and even days after the conference championship loss was hard. I knew that a season in which we won 14 games was in no way bad. It just had a deep sting.

At times the themes I emphasized to Meagan, Lindsay, and Lauren were similar to what I told the team:

—Make good choices. As Marty used to say all the time, "You control your choice, but once you make your choice your choice controls you.

—Surround yourself with positive, purpose-driven people. The people you spend a lot of time with say a lot about what you'll do. Spend a lot of time with negative people, and you're almost guaranteed to take the most negative views of everything. Spending time with strong, positive people has the opposite effect.

—Nothing good happens after midnight. I'm not sure who I said that more to, my daughters or my players.

Whether I was talking to my three daughters or fifty-three sons, I wanted them to know that they can't stay down long. They can't walk around feeling sorry for themselves. Take the defeats when they come, rebound from them, apply the lessons, and bounce back ready to fight.

That's where the Steelers were in the spring of 2002, ready to restart and refine our team building. On occasion, Mr. Rooney would tell me stories about the formative days of the league. He remembered a time after the NFL draft when he and his general manager would fill a suitcase with cash and go out on the road signing free agents. They'd drive from college to college signing undrafted players on the spot, opening the suitcase, and paying them in cash. I loved hearing the stories about where the league was and what it had grown into.

I still had the first check I'd ever received, from the Cleveland Browns, framed and hanging on the wall in my office. It amounted to

$713.70 after taxes. At times a player would complain that he wasn't being paid enough, that the front office was only offering him a large enough signing bonus.

"Come over here," I'd tell the player. I'd point to my framed check. It was always worth a smile. At least one player looked at it in amazement and then asked, "You were really worth *that* much as a player?"

I didn't run away from our organization's conversations about money. In the salary cap era, you had to accept some franchises were going to swoop in and take guys whom you'd drafted and developed. Instead of whining about it, the assignment was to draft, develop, sign, trade for—whatever you had to do—more good players. The franchises who did that the best were the ones that would consistently win and compete, and that's how we saw ourselves. As a leader, you have no credibility if you can't be honest. So when a player we wanted to keep became a free agent, I'd meet with him and tell him, "I hope we can keep you, but tell me what you've been offered and we'll see what we can do."

At least a couple of times a player gave me the number and I told him flat out, "I'd take that offer if I were you. We can't match that."

As expected, one of our inside linebackers, Earl Holmes, was a big name on the open market in '02. He'd led our team in tackles for three straight years, and we offered him a contract to stay; the Cleveland Browns offered him more years and more money, so he signed with them. Suddenly we needed an inside linebacker.

Five years earlier, James Farrior had been the Jets' first-round draft pick, but he never established himself in New York. They had moved him around, didn't play him regularly, and in his five seasons he'd played for three different head coaches. As a first-rounder, he had a lot of pressure on him in New York. As a free agent signing in Pittsburgh, it would feel like the opposite.

For us, signing a player such as Farrior was worth the chance.

He obviously hadn't tapped into his talent level. He desperately needed an opportunity, and we needed a linebacker. He got his chance, and we got a hungry ballplayer. We signed him to a reasonable and incentive-laden three-year contract. We moved him to inside linebacker and assured him that was where he was going to be. That certainty, even before the season began, seemed to put him at ease. We knew then that Farrior could be a force on the field and in our locker room.

As we got ready for the draft, I felt good about our franchise alignment. It would be my third draft with Kevin Colbert, and we'd developed that collaborative approach that I'd wanted all along. We were in constant communication and never had any surprises about where one of us stood. During the season, he was one of my racquetball partners (I teasingly called him the Washington Generals because I beat him so much). After I'd watch game film, I always wanted to hear Kevin's game analysis because he might have seen something that I didn't. It was helpful to work with someone who was in it solely for what was best for the team.

On the first day of the 2002 draft, Indiana University quarterback Antwaan Randle El was available when we picked in the second round. He was the first player in Division I history to pass for 40 touchdowns and rush for 40 touchdowns. He also played basketball for Bobby Knight as well as baseball. With Kordell and Tommy Maddox, we didn't need a quarterback, but we all agreed that Randle El was just too good an athlete to pass up. We drafted him because he was unbelievably quick and had good hands. He'd played wide receiver for the first time at the Senior Bowl, but that didn't discourage us from our plan: We'd convert him to wide receiver and use him as our kickoff and punt returner.

One of the hidden parts of the draft is the scramble when it's over. We felt good about the players we'd selected, from Chris Hope and Larry Foote to our seventh-rounder, Brett Keisel. But just as Mr. Rooney mentioned about the early days of the league, there was still a frenzy around free agent players who could sign with anyone. Most of the time, those players wouldn't make a roster, but it had a bargain-shopping element; you just might come up with a gem.

We were interested in looking at an undrafted cornerback, but his agent insisted that if we wanted him, we'd also have to consider an undrafted linebacker from Kent State named James Harrison. He was six feet and 245 pounds, too small to play linebacker in the NFL, and we also didn't think he was quick enough. We signed him anyway, unsure of what we'd get.

Some rookies were so eager to play that they'd show up hours before they were required to be there. Harrison? He showed up late to his first minicamp. I almost sent him home right then. On the field, if he couldn't figure out a play, he would literally stop in the middle of it, throw his hands up in the air, and tell us to get him off the field. He definitely was a challenge.

But the more we saw him play, the more we could see how much talent he had. The question was if his attitude would prevent him from reaching his potential. When do you give up on someone and decide the headaches aren't worth the potential gain? Some people get it right away, some people never figure it out. Harrison was a fringe roster guy whom we kept our eye on. He was raw, but he had something about him that we couldn't ignore.

I always tell players to keep working during the season because you never know when your opportunity will come. I'd say it often on the practice field as I had snippets of conversations with players, trying to make sure they knew that I saw their efforts. I think a lot of coaches say that, or something similar, to many players on their roster. I'm sure no coach ever says that to their backup quarterback. And neither did I.

1

Young Billy Bowtie, circa 1964.

2

3

From my NC State days, circa 1977.

My high school playing days, from my 1975 yearbook.

4

Kaye Young during an NC State game, circa 1977.

6

5

My father and mother, Laird and Dorothy Cowher, on their wedding day in 1947.

With the family in 1994. Clockwise, from top left: Bill Cowher, Kaye Cowher, Lauren Cowher, Lindsay Cowher, Meagan Cowher.

7

The family in Bald Head Island in 2018. Left to right: Ryan Kelly, Tess Kelly, Lindsay Kelly, Nile Kelly, Bill Cowher, Veronica Stigeler-Cowher, Mac Westgarth, Meagan Westgarth, Kevin Westgarth, Finn Westgarth, Jason Hill, Lauren Cowher (Hill).

Mom and my brothers, circa 2016. Clockwise, from top left: Dale Cowher, Bill Cowher, Doug Cowher, Janet Cowher, Mary Lou Faett, Dorothy Cowher, V. Stigeler-Cowher, Joady Cowher.

With my family at training camp in 1994.

From my days as a Cleveland
Brown in 1982.

Running down the field as a Philadelphia Eagle in 1983.

(Above) At training camp with the guys in 2006.

(Left) With Art Rooney II during practice.

With my friend and mentor, Marty Schottenheimer.

Having a talk with my defense.

Shaking hands with Dan Rooney after taking the job on January 21, 1992.

With Patricia and Dan Rooney after we won a preseason game in Dublin, Ireland, 1997

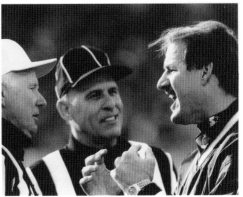

A friendly discussion with the refs.

Raising the Lombardi Trophy on
February 5, 2006.

Among my CBS friends, my family, and David Baker, who
surprised me on air with the announcement.

You don't go into a season expecting the backup to surpass the starter. Communicating something like that would sink a team. I fully expected Kordell to be our starter again for the entirety of the 2002 season. But then we lost our first two games, and in game three we trailed the Browns by a touchdown with nine minutes to play. Kordell made some good passes as he was driving us down the field, and we were set up nicely at the Cleveland 22. When Kordell's next pass was intercepted in the end zone—his fifth interception in our first three games—I decided to make a change.

Tommy Maddox went in, threw a late touchdown pass to tie it, and put us in position to win it in overtime. I knew what was coming next: Everyone would ask about a starter for our next game. I already had an answer: Maddox.

These decisions are hard to make, especially at that position. A lot of guys can look good in shells or when no one's wearing pads because they're fast or athletic, but putting on the pads takes away all posing and pretense. The position where it's most revealing is quarterback, because a quarterback knows that he's not going to get hit in practice. In practice he can stand back there and hit his target every time. But when he gets in the game and gets hit or pressured a couple of times, how does he respond? Does he get antsy? Is he the same player? Does he maintain that practice composure?

Maddox was confident in the pocket. He could throw with accuracy and wanted us to put it in the air. With receivers like Hines Ward and six-foot-five Plaxico Burress, we had the personnel to play that way. That's what we did. After a loss in his first start, Maddox quarterbacked us to four wins in a row. His sixth start, against Michael Vick and the Atlanta Falcons, was the perfect illustration of the offense we'd transformed into.

With ten minutes remaining against the Falcons at Heinz Field, we were ahead by 17 points. You already know my thoughts about that: I liked our chances. We went into a prevent defense, and we couldn't prevent a thing. Vick picked us apart. He threw for 114 yards and ran for 30 in the fourth quarter alone. At the end of regulation, we were tied at 34 apiece. In the sudden-death overtime period we kept moving downfield into Falcons territory . . . and we kept stalling in Falcons territory. On the final play of the game, Maddox threw a Hail Mary to Plaxico—who got stopped a yard short of the winning touchdown as time expired.

The previous year we'd blown a rare big lead and gotten a loss. This time we'd done it and earned a tie. Our record was 5-3-1, and our starting quarterback had passed for 473 yards and 4 touchdowns. Plax caught 9 passes for 253 yards.

Halfway through the season, I could tell Mike Mularkey to dial back the offense and play in the ball-control style that we wanted. Or I could adjust to who we were. The ball-control coach now had himself a passing team.

Maddox and Kordell were nearly the same age, thirty-one and thirty, so I didn't know if either was the long-term answer at quarterback. But Tommy had the job, and Kordell's contract was up at the end of the season. I knew another team would likely sign Kordell and that he didn't want to be in Pittsburgh as a backup.

I thought we could be successful going forward with Maddox. We won our division again, beat Cleveland in a wild card game, and lost in the divisional round to the Titans in a high-scoring game. Our high scoring wasn't a fluke. It's who we'd become. Or so I thought.

Every team, every season, is completely different. Even if there hasn't been a substantial turnover of personnel, the team is going to be different from the previous year. While we spend all winter working on the roster and preparing for the season, training camp is the time to realistically identify your strengths and, more important, your weaknesses. That old saying is true: You're only as strong as your weakest link, so the best way to start the season is to identify those things you don't do well and figure out how to fix them. Every team has problems, but the winning teams find a way to compensate for their weaknesses.

In training camp a team establishes its identity. A coach has to look at the team he's got and design a strategy to utilize what's there, not what he *wishes* he had. A quarterback might be a great thrower, for example, but if the offensive line can't protect him, then you're limited with what you can do. If your receivers can't get down the field, then you have to find an alternative way of moving the ball. The broad decisions you make will impact the entire season. The beginning can predict the end. So as hard as it is, you have to be realistic.

We had a great training camp in 2003, for example, and we went into the season believing we could throw the ball. That was going to be our identity. But when the season started, we found out that in reality we couldn't throw it efficiently, for a lot of reasons. Problems with the offensive line and inconsistent play were the major ones. But clearly we'd turned ourselves into a passing team that didn't pass well.

Midway through the 2003 season, we tried to become a running team. But we were never able to successfully establish a consistent ground game. Then we decided we were going to be a tough, physical team that could run the ball and throw it when we had the opportunity. That didn't work, either. We never figured it out, and for the final eight weeks of the season we won every other week.

After most losses, I was churning with emotions. I was angry and frustrated, but I tried to never show that publicly. The first few minutes after a loss can be devastating. I always needed five or ten minutes to just calm down before I said a word. At times during 2003 I didn't wait long enough. After we lost to Cincinnati, now coached by Marvin Lewis, I was upset that the replay official chose not to review a fumble at the end of the first half. When I was told the replay official was a retired referee from Pittsburgh, I said, "That's who the replay guy was? Is he from Pittsburgh? I guess that's why he retired."

Ooh. Totally unnecessary. That was pure frustration speaking. The next day I apologized, publicly and privately. I was out of line. The league thought so, too, and fined me $10,000.

A few times (especially my first few years as head coach) I was upset by a reporter's question and maybe got a little short with my answer. It's hard to claim when you're looking someone right in the eyes, jutting out your jaw and answering their question, that your answer isn't personal. But that's true; it's rarely personal.

People are always watching the leader to see how he reacts to adversity. The leader has to remain above the storm. The leader has to project an aura of control. If the captain runs for the lifeboats, you can be sure the passengers won't be far behind in a panic. Confidence breeds confidence.

Our problems in 2003 had nothing to do with the officials or the media. We finished 6-10, and what hurt more than the lost games was the loss of our identity. I viewed the next off-season as one of the biggest of my career. It had been over a decade, since my first season in 1992, since the Steelers had needed to establish an identity. That was the top priority. We'd all have to search and find ourselves again.

13

Another Chance to Get There

The first time I met Ben Roethlisberger was during our interview at the draft combine in Indianapolis, a couple of months before the 2004 NFL draft. The chip on his shoulder was impossible to miss. He had an edge to him, and tremendous confidence that bordered on cockiness. Our general manager, Kevin Colbert, noticed it, too.

We weren't sure what it was about the twenty-two-year-old quarterback, but we both decided we wanted to speak with him again in a few weeks. This time we flew him to Pittsburgh. I talked with him first, then pointed him toward Kevin's office down the hall. After Ben left our building, Kevin and I compared notes.

"Well, what did you think?" Kevin asked.

"Um, he was . . . better this time than he was in Indy?" I answered with a laugh.

Ben was rough around the edges—but he was also fiercely competitive. One of the things that bothered him about the predraft analysis was how he was rated. Of the three great quarterbacks in the 2004 draft, most experts rated Ole Miss's Eli Manning and North Carolina State's Philip Rivers higher than Ben, primarily because those two had played in stronger college programs in higher-profile conferences. Ben had starred at Miami of Ohio, known more for its historically strong football coaches than its star quarterbacks. Legends such as Paul Brown and Woody Hayes and Sid Gillman had coached or played there, but it wasn't known for the same level of competition that Manning and Rivers had played against in the SEC and ACC. But when we looked at Ben's physical capabilities, we thought he was equal to (and even better) than the other two quarterbacks.

He was six-five and could make any throw needed. The raw talent was there, but often that isn't enough. We had the eleventh pick in the first round. Kevin and I decided we wouldn't trade up to get him, but if he was available at eleven, he wouldn't get past us.

We didn't desperately need a quarterback. Tommy Maddox hadn't had a great 2003 season, and that wasn't totally his fault. Our offensive line wasn't good, so he never had a chance. We probably needed an offensive lineman more than a quarterback. But when a potential franchise quarterback—a player who might elevate the whole team—comes your way, you take him. You don't wait. You don't weigh other possibilities. You just call his name. Manning was the first overall pick, Rivers was taken fourth, and when Ben was still available for us at eleven, we happily picked him.

Soon after that, I heard from an unhappy Tommy Maddox. We met face-to-face in the office because, as I always told the players, they were welcome to ask me any questions about their role. My promise was I'd always give an answer, even if it was one the player didn't agree with or want to hear.

Tommy felt I had promised him in exit interviews he was going to be our quarterback of the future. I listened at first, then both of our voices got louder. I told him I wouldn't be doing my job if I didn't do everything possible to help our team, and when this player became available, we took him because it was in the team's best long-term interest. I told Tommy that as a player, his job was to compete, regardless of our personnel decisions. After this emotional conversation, in which Tommy got his feelings off his chest, we moved on. It wasn't the answer he wanted, but he asked and he was entitled to an honest response.

I liked the mentality we had in the spring of 2004. Ideally, I wanted us to be a team that craved competition and thrived in competitive situations. When we didn't do that naturally, I'd find a way to challenge the players (and coaches) so they'd get there. We'd lost our way in 2003 during the 6-10 season. I didn't want us to go through that again.

When we got to our minicamp just after the draft, I was hit with a couple of pleasant surprises. One was Ben's athleticism; he was much better than I had originally thought. Kordell was my quarterback for five years, and he was an athlete who was a quarterback. Ben was a quarterback who was really athletic. For a big man, he moved around the pocket extremely well. He could run and throw to both his left and right. He had a strong, accurate arm. He could even punt with his left foot. We could see he'd be a special player one day, but we didn't expect him to play much during the season.

Tommy remained our starter; Charlie Batch was his backup, with Ben there to watch and learn. He'd have a year in our system without any pressure or responsibility. He'd begin to understand just how long the season is and the preparation required to be successful in the NFL. We wanted to be careful about giving a kid too much responsibility before he was ready for it.

We told Ben the plan and he said he understood and accepted it.

The second surprise? The performance of a rookie running back whom we didn't even draft.

From our experience with James Harrison, now one of our star special teamers and occasional starter, we knew how successful an undrafted free agent could be in our system. A kid named Willie Parker had been a third-string running back at the University of North Carolina because the coaching staff felt he wasn't big enough to be the featured back in their ground-and-pound offense. He never got the chance to play.

Dan Rooney Jr. had just started scouting for us, covering the South. He's the one who found Parker. "He's fast," Dan reported. "There's nobody who can catch him when he gets out to the corner."

I was surprised that Parker wasn't on anybody's radar. It's hard for good football players to stay hidden. I asked Dick Hoak, "What's the hole in this kid? How come he didn't play at North Carolina?"

Dick shook his head and said he didn't know.

"Is he smart?" I asked.

"Yeah, he gets it. He doesn't make any mental mistakes."

"Can he catch the ball?"

"He doesn't catch real good. But he's fast."

Fast Willie.

We signed him and hoped for some success, just as we did with James Harrison. Like Harrison, Fast Willie had a real chance to stick around in some role.

In the summer space between minicamp and training camp, I was in a relaxed and celebratory mood. Every year since my friend John DeMaine had let us stay at his Bald Head Island home in the early 1990s, our family had vacationed in North Carolina. After our first trip there, we decided to become island homeowners. We'd had some of our best times as a family on that island. The summer of 2004 was particularly fun because Kaye and I officially had a high school graduate. Meagan finished her Fox Chapel High career as a perennial first-team All-Section basketball player. In the fall, she'd be on her way to the Ivy League to play at Princeton University. Kaye and I were beaming with pride.

All of our girls were great student athletes, so we knew there'd be more college recruiting over the next several years. Lauren was about to begin her third straight year as Fox Chapel's starting point guard. At five-seven, she wasn't as tall as her sisters, but I used to tell her she had the type of athleticism that would make her a cornerback if she played in the NFL. Lindsay was in the eighth grade, but her height and skills were certain to draw the attention of several college coaches.

I was optimistic about what the fall would bring for the Steelers. The plan was to get back to our core, from our coaching staff to our style of play. We needed a new offensive coordinator because Mike Mularkey became the head coach of the Buffalo Bills. I replaced Mike with Ken Whisenhunt, who was already on our staff and knew our schemes and terminology. It was the same thing with our "new" defensive coordinator, Dick LeBeau. He'd been fired as head coach of the Bengals after the '02 season, spent '03 in Buffalo as assistant head coach, and now was back with us after being gone for eight years. It was great to have Dick back at home.

While Jerome Bettis was thirty-two years old and slowing down a little, I still wanted us to get back to being a reliable team on the ground. He needed support back there, so we added Duce Staley, a power back with quickness, as a complement. Both of them needed our line to be better, and I was confident that it would happen through the draft, free agency, and better coaching.

In training camp and through the preseason, we saw the same things we had seen in minicamp: a lot of good things from Ben and Fast Willie.

Ben could make something positive out of a broken play, which nobody can teach. He also had that big ego on the field that great quarterbacks have. He just didn't know enough to be hesitant. And that competitiveness, which Kevin Colbert and I'd noticed early, shone. When a play broke down, he improvised, he took chances, he did unconventional things to make something good out of something bad. With some quarterbacks, a broken-down play is their opportunity to extend it, not lose yardage. But Ben was all about turning it into a plus-yardage play. Right away I could see our challenge would be to make him work within our system while not taking the special ability out of his game. With a player such as him, a real danger is that you can overcoach him into mediocrity.

Fast Willie, meanwhile, had exceptional natural ability, which needed to be honed for him to significantly contribute. As the scouting reports had warned, Willie initially had trouble holding on to the football. He fumbled three times in preseason games. But he was a great kid, full of energy with a willingness to learn, and we decided to keep him. Dick Hoak worked with him and refined his abilities. Every time he got the ball, his instinct was to head for the outside, turn the corner, and take off downfield. But he began to learn that sometimes you just have to hit a hole. The best models of that were the guys he was sitting behind, Jerome and Duce.

When Charlie Batch had to have knee surgery, Ben suddenly became our number two quarterback. We gave him a small package of plays just in case we ever had to play him. "Just in case" didn't last two full games.

Tommy started our season-opening win against the Oakland Raiders. But in the third quarter of our second game, against the Ravens, we didn't pick up a blitz. Tommy took a blindside hit, fumbled, and left the game injured. We now had no choice: The kid whom we'd wanted to watch and learn became our starting quarterback. So much for not giving him too much too soon.

When Ben stepped on the field for the first time, his team trailed 20–0 on the road against their biggest division rival. He threw an interception on his first series, but then settled down. I think he surprised the Ravens with his savvy and his arm strength; one of his completions was a 58-yarder to Hines Ward. Two plays later, he threw a short touchdown pass to Antwaan Randle El. He did a good job getting us back to a reasonable level of competitiveness. In the fourth quarter, we went no huddle, and Ben barked out, "Nine ninety! Nine ninety!" That's a go route—which is a downfield play—and he thought he was calling a hitch, which calls for a receiver to run 5 yards, stop, and turn. He threw the hitch without looking to see if one of our guys was there. The pass was intercepted and returned for a touchdown. That was the game.

We couldn't blame him. He showed more than we would have expected in that situation. After that touchdown return made it 30–13, I told our offense, "Let's just run the ball and get outta here. Ben's the only quarterback we've got, and we can't get him hurt."

The next week in Miami against the Dolphins, Ben started his first game. We didn't have any other option. To make it work we planned to limit the process, and Ben had to embrace it. It was an exercise in week-by-week coaching. The question that we had to answer each week was *How much more can he handle?* We could easily have asked him to do too much, and we didn't.

The biggest advantage we had was the players surrounding Ben. They included Jerome, Hines, Plaxico Burress, and Alan Faneca. We had a diverse offense that was built to utilize their skills rather than depend on the quarterback. We decided to let Ben be part of us winning, but not part of us losing. That meant we would take as much responsibility away from him as possible. We'd run the ball and use a lot of play action, the things he did naturally. As the season progressed, we'd add to the mix based on what Ben showed us he could manage.

Leading up to that game in Miami, I addressed the entire team. I wanted to remind them we were all responsible for the rest of this season, and no one player could carry us or undermine us. "This is an opportunity to show a sign of strength. If you play hard each down, if you play with a passion and a purpose, if you can overlook adversity and obstacles, we will win this game." It was a Sunday night game, played in a torrential downpour. We won by holding the Dolphins to 3 points and forcing 4 turnovers.

Whenever I gave a speech to our team, I wanted to be sure of two things: that I didn't go too long, and that I held their attention. Chet Fuhrman, our strength and conditioning coach, knew me better than most people. He was a part of my first coaching staff in '92 and, along with Dick Hoak, was the only coach who held the same position a dozen years later.

Chet would time my speeches to make sure I'd given equal talking time to the offense and defense. He'd also sit in the back of the room and scan the audience while I talked. He'd let me know how my words landed with the players.

In 2004, no matter what I said and what the players did, things seemed to fall in place.

The next two games were divisional games at home, against Cincinnati and Cleveland. We won them both to move to 4-1.

We tried to correct Ben and advise him, without overcoaching him. We kept it as simple as possible. Some things he did naturally that under normal circumstances we'd try to deter, such as making certain throws into coverage and getting out of the pocket before he should have. But in this situation we didn't press. He loved to run, scramble, and throw the ball downfield as opposed to sitting in the pocket to go through his reads. And that was the other thing: We never gave him more than two reads. *Look here first; if you don't like that one, look over there.*

Most of the time we kept those options to the same side of the field. "You know you're going to this side of the field," we told him.

"Don't even bother looking at the other side. There's nothing over there for you." In addition to the options, we limited the information we gave him because we didn't want to slow him down. Young quarterbacks don't usually process information as quickly as veterans, who have seen all the possibilities.

While Ben began to get a lot of attention, the whole team had raised its level of production. Everybody was contributing, so in some ways Ben had become the lead supporting player in the offense, not the focus.

In mid-October, we traveled to Dallas for a game against the Cowboys. As I walked the field before kickoff, I had a brief chat with Cowboys head coach Bill Parcells. I'd always had great respect for him, going back to the days when he offered me a job with the New York Giants. Coach Parcells had retired a couple of times in his career, only to return. I asked him why.

"When you first get into the league, it's a part of your life," he explained. "After a while longer, it *becomes* your life."

This quick comment was powerful. I loved what I was doing, and no one could convince me that I didn't have the best job in the world. But I didn't want that to be me. I was forty-seven years old, which meant I'd been in the NFL as a player and coach for exactly half of my life. I didn't want to spend the rest of my life in a locker room. I was proud that I'd been able to achieve some stability in a profession that wasn't known for it. Still, wasn't that somewhat of a compromise? Meagan was already off at college, and Lauren and Lindsay would be there before I knew it. Time goes quickly.

Coach Parcells's comment stayed with me for a while.

We beat Dallas to move to 5-1. Then we prepared for the toughest part of our schedule. When we gave 6-0 New England its first loss of the season, then did the same thing the next week to 7-0 Philadelphia, all of us clearly saw that something special was happening. A big part of our job during that run was to prevent the team from getting caught up in the media hype. With each succeeding victory the one thing we continued to emphasize was that we could not lose sight of how we got to that point. "Results are one thing," I said. "But the thing you have to remember is that it's the process that got you here. If you don't understand that we're achieving these results because of your commitment to the process, then you're simply playing week to week."

Some of our veterans knew exactly what that meant. Ben didn't yet know it. How could he? He'd started six games in his NFL career and was 6-0. Our problem was he was having success doing things that weren't going to be successful in the future. But what were we going to say: "Don't throw that touchdown pass?" We didn't want to stop him, but we also didn't want him to develop habits that would hold him back. The coaching staff walked the edge; Ben and the team kept winning games.

And the *way* that we were winning inspired me. Against those two great teams, the Patriots and Eagles, we possessed the ball for more than two-thirds of the game. They can't beat you if you don't let them touch the ball. The combination of the Bus and Duce was devastating. Our offensive line played like the best line in football.

We got two more wins over the Browns and the Bengals to push our record to 9-1.

It occurred to us that Ben didn't realize what he was doing was so extraordinary. I cautioned people from talking about it too much, telling them, "This is not normal, but don't tell him. It shouldn't be this easy for him." We'd write plays for him on a wristband. He'd go into the huddle, read the play on his wrist, and break out of the huddle. He probably had no idea who was in the huddle with him; he was just trying to read the right play.

We also wanted him to be accountable, which was a way of putting restraints on him. He wanted to do things his way, and we told him flatly, "No, we're going to do things our way right now."

Winning one week is the result of a game plan, but sustaining it week after week is what happens when you embrace the process. What we had become as a team was the by-product of the work we had done to create a structure our players could rely on. Building confidence in the system began the first day of our minicamp and continued through every day of practice throughout the season.

When talking with aspiring coaches, I was often asked what I'd learned as an experienced coach that I didn't know at the beginning of my career. The best answer is pacing. How to manage a team through a long season so that we're as healthy as possible and ready to play at the end of the season. How to keep a good perspective and keep things on an even keel.

It's a cliché in the NFL that football players would play for free on Sunday. The reality is that they're getting paid to practice. Practice *is* the job. It's hard work. We tried to make it fun and lively, and going to work when on a winning streak certainly helps. But the job is tough.

One thing the players wanted from my staff was a disciplined, scheduled practice. They didn't want to get to the field and stand around. They didn't want their time wasted. I always thought practice was a good opportunity for me and my staff to send a message: We know what we're doing. A process is in place here. We're following it and you can rely on it, too.

We gave the players a plan for every practice and every meeting. Coaches and players knew exactly what to expect and when to expect it. During the season, practice time was broken into six or seven different periods. It might be special teams, defensive blitz, offense third down, defensive team red zone . . . and we moved rapidly through each one.

But despite the great record or what had happened in the previous game, if any one of those segments was sloppy, we'd just start it over. If it continued to be sloppy, we'd start the whole period over. At the beginning of the season we'd have pads on for practice. But by late November and December, we had to make sure our people were fresh for Sunday. We might put pads on for a period and take them off for the rest of the practice. Or, if I didn't feel we were practicing well, we'd put them back on. Admittedly, players sometimes had an agreement with their counterpart on the opposing unit, and neither would hit as hard as possible. I used to call that being a brother-in-law. If I didn't hear the pads cracking after eight plays, I'd tell the team, "Okay, now you guys are warmed up, let's start at the top again," and we'd repeat the whole series from the top.

Teams tape their practice sessions and review them. I'd pull players into my office to watch practice sessions with them. It wasn't that different than being brought into the principal's office. When players were confronted with tape of their effort, they couldn't deny it. "I'm watching you run and I'm watching him run and there's a whole difference in urgency. See what I'm talking about?" Seeing definitely was believing.

What we'd been able to do to good teams in 2004 was impressive. We hosted the Jets, who were 9-3, in December. We didn't allow them to do much all day and won the game, 17–6. It was our eleventh win in a row and boosted our record to 12-1. In that Jets game, our versatile safety, Troy Polamalu, had an interception. We'd drafted Troy in the first round of the 2003 draft. He was such an unusual prospect that an evaluation of his special teams play alone would have made him a draftable player. But he was so much more than that.

There was no better student of the game than Troy. What excited me was he had the confidence to take risks when he felt it was the right time. He was "conservatively aggressive," if that makes sense.

He knew our defensive system, understood its principles, and respected it. Yet he never felt restrained by our system. He was always thinking, detecting the rhythm of the game, ready to make a play. One time he did just that and I thought he'd lost his mind.

We were in a Cover 2 defense, in which Troy was responsible for covering half the field. Prior to the snap, sometimes Troy lined up in different places to disguise his coverage. In this instance, Troy lined up right next to the inside linebacker. I couldn't believe it. From that position on the field, it made it nearly impossible for him to fulfill his assignment. When I saw it, I thought, *My God, he doesn't know what coverage we're in! He'd better get outta there.*

I started yelling to and pointing at him: "Two! Two! Troy! Two!" He looked at me and waved me off, as if he wanted me to be quiet. I could see him telling me, "I'm okay! I'm okay!"

I didn't think he was okay. The ball was snapped, and instead of moving into coverage, he stayed right in the flat. Completely out of position. I watched in total disbelief; I never expected that from an A student such as Troy. I couldn't believe he blew the coverage. Fortunately, the play went nowhere.

When he ran to the sideline a few plays later, I was right there to meet him. "What were you doing there? We were in Cover 2. You were up on the line of scrimmage."

"I know, Coach. But we've been calling it so much I wanted to give the quarterback a different look. I told the corner, you take half the field, I'll take the flat. Me and him just switched responsibilities."

Now that was smart. That's the mind of a great player and thinker at work.

I exhaled. "You know what, Troy? That's a great thought. But do me a favor: The next time you do something like that, would you please tell us so I don't have a heart attack?"

I loved coaching, competing, and teaching. The one thing I always wanted to avoid was interfering with a player's instincts. The last thing you want is a player who's afraid to trust his instincts because he's afraid he'll lose his job. You want your people to be confident enough to take risks. The question every leader has to answer is, How much is too much? How much information and teaching are too much? When does it become counterproductive? How do you develop a young person with great potential without burning him out early?

Some of the questions can be answered when you know the personalities of the people who are playing for you. I knew some of my risk-takers were also hard workers who had a method to what they were doing. In Troy's case, he had the thought and immediately told a teammate to cover where he was supposed to be. That's intelligent, quick thinking. It's hard for a coach to argue with that.

On the day after Christmas, we beat the Ravens 20–7. The win put our record at 14-1 and allowed us to clinch the top playoff seed in the AFC. The following week, we played against the Bills, coached by my former assistant Mike Mularkey. I was proud of him. He had that team in playoff contention in his first season as head coach. I let most of our regulars play the first quarter, then put in our reserves. It was a tough game. Buffalo was fighting for a playoff spot, and no yard was easily gained. In three quarters of work, Willie Parker rushed for 102 yards, including a 58-yard run. We won that game, and Willie continued to open our eyes.

Fifteen and one. I'd never been on a team that had won so many games in a row, in a variety of ways. We'd run the ball well all year, yet we were also an explosive, big-play team. We had young stars and veterans. We'd finished first in the league in defense. It was tough to categorize us.

I wish I could tell you that I'd seen a sign that our postseason would play out the way that it did. At no moment was I worried that we didn't have enough, weren't focused enough, or had some hidden weakness that was suddenly exposed. I didn't have that thought then, and I don't have it now.

The New York Jets took us to overtime in the divisional round, and we won it 20–17. The next week, at Heinz, was the conference championship. This was my fifth conference championship as head coach of the Steelers, and all of them had been at home. It had become a talking point in the local and national media: We were 1-3 in these games.

I wasn't concerned about the record or any talk about my legacy. As a highly competitive person, I wanted to win. I always did. I tried to do all I could to make sure my team was ready. When we lost the 2001 conference championship to the Patriots, they went on to upset the Rams in the Super Bowl. They'd won it again in 2003, and in 2004, they'd lost just two games in the regular season. One of them was to us, which gave them their first defeat of the season and snapped a 21-game winning streak they'd had over two years.

They were tough. The young quarterback who took over for Drew Bledsoe in 2001, Tom Brady, now had two Super Bowl MVPs and was one of the best quarterbacks in the game. His play-action passing got us on the second series of the game. He faked a hand-off and then threw deep—which he wasn't known for—to Deion Branch for a 60-yard touchdown.

The bigger play, a game changer, happened just before the half. We trailed 17–3 and desperately needed points. A touchdown would have us in good shape; a field goal wouldn't be great, but it was better than nothing. Ben was driving us down the field, and we had plenty of time to get a play we liked. Unfortunately, Ben didn't anticipate veteran safety Rodney Harrison's jumping the out route, which he did. Harrison intercepted the pass and returned it 87 yards for a touchdown.

We lost 41–27. It was another year without a chance to play in the Super Bowl. When your team wins 14 games in a row and still doesn't get to the Super Bowl, it starts to mess with your mind. That was a great football team. It was hard to walk into that locker room and say thank you and goodbye to those proud men. It was painful. Some of my leaders were in tears. Players, who loved Jerome Bettis, thought this was their best chance to get him to a Super Bowl before he retired. Hines Ward cried more for Jerome than for himself.

"There's not really a whole lot I can say that will ease the disappointment we all feel," I said. The room was quiet. Deflated. "Each of you is going to deal with this in his own way, as you should, but I promise you this: The pain is temporary; the pride is forever. The one thing I want you to do is not let this game define this season. Look at the whole season, sixteen and two. I'm just asking you to do two things: Don't let people on the outside, who don't ever sacrifice or compete, influence your emotions. And don't dwell on the worst of all emotions, self-pity."

Growing up in Pittsburgh when I did, the expected finish to a Steelers season was a hoisting of the Lombardi Trophy. We'd fallen short again, and I wondered how many more chances we'd get. If any. For all I knew, this might have been my last opportunity with a team as loaded as this.

Then 2005 happened.

14

Champions, at Last

I had a surprise for our players as we began our team meeting on the first Monday in December 2005. Although we'd started the season strong with a 7-2 record, three consecutive losses left us at 7-5 and in a rut. The most recent one, at home to the Cincinnati Bengals, put us in trouble. If we dropped one more game, we'd miss the playoffs.

We were all feeling down, and my job was to find a way to restore our confidence and focus. Usually, the players came to work and saw a goal board. They could see the entire schedule with what they'd done previously and what was to be done ahead. It was normally all there before them.

But not this time. When they walked in, all they saw was one game there. Our next opponent was the Chicago Bears, and I wanted to illustrate the message so everyone got it. What we had done didn't matter. What we might do in three weeks didn't matter. The playoffs, if we wanted them, needed to begin immediately. We needed to home in on our next "playoff" game, against the Bears.

I looked around the room and, before checking in with Chet Fuhrman (my audience engagement expert), I knew that I had the players' full attention. I believed in this group, and I wanted them to see how close they were to controlling and winning games. I decided to challenge them in a new way. I had some homework for each of them. It's something I'd never asked a team of mine to do. I wanted the players to grade themselves on every play based on the completion of their on-field assignment, if they knew what they were doing, technique, as well as passion and effort. I did that because I wanted people to take a good look at their own performance. My coaching staff graded them on the same factors.

It was shocking when we got a look at the players' grades of themselves versus the coaches' grades of them. Even though we told them they hadn't played well, they still believed they had done a good job. When we sat down with them and showed them the two grades, with only a few exceptions the players insisted that the coaching staff was wrong. Until we showed them on film the specific problem, most players refused to accept that we were indeed talking about them.

A typical exchange would be something like this:

Coach: "You weren't taking a good angle to the ball."

Player: "You were talking about me? When? I definitely had a good angle."

Coach: "Yeah, I was talking about you. C'mon, I'll show you. Look right there."

Player: "Ohhhh. That. Now I get it. Yeah, that's what you want?"

What I learned from the exercise was that the players weren't getting the message because we hadn't delivered it with enough specificity. It was an eye-opening lesson for me as a coach, and as a leader. I had to remind myself that when I spoke to a large group and had a specific message for a few individuals, I couldn't assume those persons in the crowd would get it. If I or my coaches wanted to target players, it was always best to pull them in and repeat it directly to them. That's how they knew precisely what the expectations were.

There's no better way of communicating with someone than face-to-face, eye-to-eye. When he walked out of that room, I knew for *certain* that we were on the same page.

We were 7-5 and on a three-game losing streak, but it felt as if we'd made progress simply by looking at ourselves through different lenses.

With that said, there was nothing easy about our upcoming game. The Bears, winners of eight games in a row, were one of the hottest teams in the league. They had the number one defense in the NFL. I respected what they were doing, but I believed in our team more. For this game, and the rest of the season, I wanted us to reestablish ourselves as a tough, physical team. I wanted to make sure that thought sunk in at our Saturday night meeting before the game.

"Tomorrow we have to reestablish our identity," I told them. "Everything has a life cycle. Each life cycle has an end but also a start. Isn't that where we are right now? We're a good football team, and I don't believe we're that far away from playing like it. What happens going forward is about *us*. It's about *our* team. Tomorrow is not the end of our life cycle; it's the start of a new one. For the Chicago Bears, it's their end. For us, it's our beginning."

On Sunday, I had a great feeling. And it wasn't because of my usual sugar rush. Before every game, I ate two Hershey's chocolate bars with almonds. Then for the game itself, I'd have a pack of gum to chew for stress relief. I knew we had a good plan against the Bears, and it was evident from our first offensive and defensive series. We forced them to punt on their opening drive, and we performed like champions on ours. Willie Parker was good as a runner and receiver as he picked up 45 yards on a catch. Three plays later, Ben found Hines for a 14-yard touchdown.

It was a cold and windy Pittsburgh day, and we played the game on our terms all afternoon. We got strong running from Willie and Jerome, and that allowed us to hold the ball for 37 minutes. We won, 21–9.

When we went to Minnesota the next week, we had a chance to end another team's winning streak—the Vikings had won six in a row—and we did it. We won, 18–3. That was 12 points allowed in two weeks. Could we be better on Christmas Eve against the Browns in Cleveland? I thought we could, and so did the players. We crushed the Browns in a shutout, 41–0, for our tenth win. We finished the regular season by beating the Lions, 35–21.

The win over Detroit was special because of what Jerome had been able to do in the game. His status as a beloved member of our locker room and city hadn't changed, even though his role had. He and Duce Staley had both been injured earlier in the season. Willie then started against the Titans and rushed for 161 yards. When he rushed for more than 100 the next week, he became our starter. Willie finished the season with 1,202 yards to become the second undrafted running back in NFL history to rush for more than 1,200 yards in a season. While Jerome had become an excellent mentor, he still managed to be a productive player as well. He scored 3 touchdowns against the Lions, his hometown team.

Detroit was also the site of the 2005 Super Bowl. As the sixth—and last—seed in the playoffs at 11-5, we'd have to play our entire postseason on the road to earn a trip to Detroit. Our team had so much love for Jerome that winning it for him, in his city, became one of our missions, too. I knew we believed, collectively, that we could beat any team in the NFL. Still, no sixth seed had ever advanced to the Super Bowl and won it. The players would hear that stat over and over before playing one minute in a postseason game. So in our first meeting as a group before the start of the playoffs, I wanted to encourage the players about accomplishing things that critics view as impossible. I started with an unexpected history lesson.

"I'm going to tell you about Christopher Columbus."

I looked around the room and could see the puzzled looks: *Christopher Columbus? Where's he going with this?*

"Christopher Columbus put together his own team and got three ships. And as those ships were about to leave port, people were standing there on the docks screaming at the crews not to go. 'Don't do it,' they shouted. 'It's a death trap. The world is flat. You're going to leave here and never come back. There's nothing out there.' People had no respect for him. Nobody thought he had any chance of succeeding.

"But Columbus had surrounded himself with people who believed in him. While other people were telling him he had no chance, he didn't care. He believed in himself and he believed in his crew. It didn't matter to him what anybody else thought. So he set off, and he went on and eventually he discovered America.

"My point to you simply is this: If you guys believe in yourselves, if you have confidence in yourselves, anything is possible. Don't let history dictate your future. Let your future make history."

I thought it was a great speech. I'd even motivated myself. But then from the back of the room, I saw Troy Polamalu's hand go up, and I knew this was the start of the avalanche.

"Troy, what's up?"

"Coach, Christopher Columbus didn't discover America. He discovered the West Indies."

The room was initially quiet as everyone waited to see how I'd turn it around. Then I heard a couple more one-liners about my version of world history. They were all paying attention.

"I know that," I finally answered Troy. "But there's an important lesson to be learned here."

The mood was light, and the message had stuck. Everyone in the room could sense the urgency and novelty of what was ahead of us. No one had done what we were attempting to do, so why not be the first team to accomplish it? We had championship talent, but for us to win a title, we'd have to do it in an unusual way. I had a one-liner of my own for Troy: "Never let the facts get in the way of a good story!"

A couple of days later, Mr. Rooney popped into my office, as he often did.

He smiled and handed me some rosary beads. "These will bring you good luck."

I thanked him and put them in my pocket. I knew that prayer wouldn't hurt us, but we also needed to perform on the road.

We didn't think anybody wanted to play us. All we had to do was go out and prove it.

|||||||||||

There wasn't a playoff team we knew better than our first-round opponent, the Bengals. We played them twice every year, and we'd had memorable games against them even when the result didn't affect the playoffs. I remember one season when we had a mini losing streak prior to a game with the Bengals. At the team meeting the night before the game, I told the players our problems had nothing to do with technique. What we needed was more passion and investment in the job. I then showed the great scene from *Network* in which Peter Finch's anger builds and builds until he finally is telling people to shout out their window, "I'm mad as hell and I'm not gonna take it anymore!"

Unlike some coaches, I wasn't big on bringing in outside speakers to talk to the team before a game. I've found people listen more carefully to people they know and respect, people they have shared experiences with and a common goal. I wanted our players to leave our pregame meetings feeling inspired, confident, prepared, and excited to play the game.

I knew that being in the playoffs against the Bengals was motivation enough. But I couldn't resist something else. The Bengals were the last team we'd lost to before starting our winning streak. They'd beaten us in Pittsburgh, 38–31. After that game, Bengals wide receiver T. J. Houshmandzadeh took our team and city symbol, the bright yellow Terrible Towel, and wiped his shoes with it. As soon as I saw that clip, I thought, *I'll remember that one.*

I doubt the Bengals expected to play us in the wild card game a month later. At our meeting the night before the game, I told the players, "I can show you clips of our last two games this year against the Bengals, but I think you know them and I think they know us. But what I'm not so sure you're aware of is what happened the last time we played them. I want to show you what one of their players did, something that I think may be as disrespectful as any act I've ever seen."

Then I showed the clip. There wasn't a sound in that room.

"When we win, we win with humility. And if we lose, we lose with grace. That wasn't humility. So tomorrow, when you go out there, just think about him wiping his shoes with something that signifies us as a team. And if you have a chance tomorrow, let him know you didn't appreciate it. That's it. Good night."

That clip did the trick. Throughout that whole game, at every opportunity someone hit Houshmandzadeh. I suspect he walked around wondering what he did. We won, 31–17. I thought we already matched up well with them, but the lack of respect raised our pissed-off factor and put each of our players in the right mental state.

Our next game was in Indianapolis against Peyton Manning and the top-seeded Colts. I worked closely with Colts head coach Tony Dungy when we were both assistant coaches in Kansas City. I could only imagine what he—or someone on his staff—was doing with *our* explosive quote now. As if we hadn't just experienced how one statement or action from a player can motivate an entire team, one of my favorite players went out and did just that.

I liked Joey Porter, one of our outside linebackers. Joey was always ready to play, and to play with passion. He was a leader whom guys followed. I liked to find ways to make games personal for our whole team, and Joey seemed to do that naturally on his own. Leading up to the game, Joey called out the Colts and said they were a finesse team.

"They don't want to play smashmouth football, they want to trick you," he said. "They want to make you think. They want it to be a thinking game instead of a football game."

Maybe the last thing you wanted to tell Peyton Manning was that his team was soft. The Colts had a Top 3 offense and defense. At 14-2, they had the best record in the NFL. To most experts, it didn't matter what Joey said about them: The Colts were clear Super Bowl favorites.

I couldn't have been happier about the flow of the game through three quarters. We were in the temperature-controlled RCA Dome in January, which was nothing like being out in the wintry elements of Pittsburgh, but this still felt like a classic Steelers game. At the end of the third quarter we led, 21–3. The Colts scored early in the fourth when Manning completed a 50-yard touchdown pass to Dallas Clark. Even with that, I felt that we were in control with a 21–10 lead.

The Colts needed at least two scores and a 2-point conversion just to tie, and our defense had played well. We'd blitzed all day, and Manning never got comfortable. With just over five minutes to play in the game, Manning had the Colts on the move and toward a score when Troy Polamalu made one of his instinctive plays. He jumped a route, dived, and intercepted a pass on our 48-yard line. He rolled over, got up, and took a step. Then he fumbled—and recovered his own fumble on a bounce.

When Tony threw a challenge flag, I had no idea what he was doing. My first thought was that he threw the flag out of desperation. At the very least, Troy's interception would allow us to burn some clock, if not flat out win the game. I wasn't worried about that flag.

But when the delay seemed longer than it should have, for something that seemed obvious to me, I started to get anxious.

The officials told me Tony was challenging the call on the field that it was an interception. He claimed that Troy never had control of the ball. I was confused: There were a lot of things that play might have been, but an incomplete pass wasn't one of them. Troy clearly had possession of the ball. He'd rolled over holding on to it and then gotten up and taken at least one step. How was that an incompletion?

They kept looking at the tape, and now I was the one feeling like Peter Finch. This was infuriating. Here we were five minutes from the AFC Championship Game, and the officials were trying to take the ball away from us at midfield. I knew they were misinterpreting the rule, and I could do nothing about it.

Finally, the referee called it an incomplete pass.

We couldn't believe it; it was a terrible call. Even though I was furious, I had to keep everyone focused. I couldn't get caught up in the emotion of the moment.

"Just keep playing," I said to as many players as I could. "Keep playing. Don't get yourself caught up in it."

I knew the league would eventually have to walk this one back, but that didn't help us now. We had to deal with Manning at midfield, directing an offense with momentum. It sounded as if the entire state of Indiana was in the building, cheering wildly for the Colts. Given life now and a second opportunity, Manning had his offense in the end zone less than a minute later. Then he completed a pass to Reggie Wayne for the 2-point conversion.

In less than a minute, we'd gone from a certain win to clinging to a 21–18 lead. It got even more tense when they kicked off and held, forcing us to punt. They took over at their own 18-yard line with two and a half minutes to play. That left them plenty of time to drive for a tying field goal or to beat us outright.

I'll give Joey Porter credit. He usually talked and played a good game. He'd made three Pro Bowls and finished 2005 with 10.5 sacks. He sacked Manning for a big loss on second down, and on a desperation fourth-down play, Joey and James Farrior combined for another sack that gave us the ball at the Colts' 2. They had all three of their time-outs left, so we couldn't just run out the clock.

If we scored a touchdown, the game was out of reach. In that situation the only risk you take is a fumble. I wasn't concerned about that. Jerome hadn't fumbled once the entire season. We knew he was going to retire at the end of the year, and it was poetic that he'd be the one with the ball in his hands as we moved on to the conference title game. Ben handed the ball to Jerome, and the nightmare began. A Colts linebacker hit the ball with his helmet, and the ball popped loose and into the hands of Nick Harper of the Colts.

The overturned Troy interception was bad. But this was sickening. And it was like that for us and all of our fans. Jerome was adored in Pittsburgh. The entire city wanted to give him a championship send-off to end his career. Now he was about to be on the wrong end of one of the most memorable plays in NFL history. Who could dream up a 98-yard fumble return for a game-winning touchdown?

We had all our big guys on the field because we were running the ball. None of those big, slow guys were going to catch Harper. To make the situation even more dramatic, the night before the game Harper had been in some domestic dispute with his wife, and his knee had been cut. That may have cost him some mobility. Ben was the only one with a shot of catching him. Harper made a move at midfield and spun Ben around, but as Ben was falling, he reached out and swiped at Harper's legs. It was enough to trip him and bring him to the turf. It was a season-saving tackle . . . by our quarterback.

I felt awful for Jerome. We still had a 3-point lead, and we had to focus on stopping the Colts from winning the game. Even though we'd had at least two moments when we thought we'd won it, a tie game headed to overtime didn't seem to be the worst option. With fourteen seconds left, the Colts were on our 28-yard line. The Colts brought out Mike Vanderjagt, the NFL's most accurate kicker, for a 46-yard field goal attempt.

I called a time-out to ice him.

Who knows if it made a difference? Opinions differ about the value of using a time-out to freeze a placekicker, but I always believed in it. If I had a time-out left, and I did against the Colts, there was no reason to save it.

Kickers are very much a product of routine. They're like golfers; they have a routine and get into a rhythm. The whole purpose of icing a kicker is to disrupt that routine. It's one thing to run onto the field, kick a field goal, and run off, just as you do every day in practice. But when you run onto the field and the other team calls a time-out, then you have to stand there with nothing to do but think about it longer than usual. A kick is very different when the whole season is on your shoulders. The pressure is tremendous, and it builds. Athletes are never supposed to think negative thoughts, but in that situation it's hard not to think, *What happens if I miss this one?*

Vanderjagt missed so badly to the right that we knew, as soon as his foot hit the ball, that we'd escaped with a win. The last five minutes of that game were probably the most exciting five minutes of football in my career. Those minutes seemed to hover and last longer than the entirety of the game.

After the win, as they had the previous week, the players shouted, "This one's for Chris." As in Columbus. We were having fun, and the only way for the running joke to remain funny was to keep winning. I didn't just make references to Columbus during the week. After what we'd experienced in Indy, I talked to the team about Winston Churchill. During the worst moments of the Battle of Britain, Churchill was able to keep his country calm. I spun that into a point about the importance of remaining calm, even when facing adversity.

I couldn't help smiling about the oddity of this run, our games, and my career. Before 2005, I'd been involved in five championship games as head coach of the Steelers. All of those games had been at home, and all of them had had surprise and drama. In four of those five games, I'd left the stadium shaking my head, trying to piece together what had gone wrong.

So it was totally unpredictable that my sixth conference championship—and first on the road, in Denver—would be relatively drama-free. I guess anything would be that compared to the Colts game. The only controversy was early in the Broncos game, and most people watching at home had no idea that it was happening.

As you might imagine, I had good reason to check in with the supervisor of officials after our win over the Colts. We might have avoided all the excitement in the final five minutes if the proper ruling had been made on Troy's interception. The league released a statement acknowledging that it had been an incorrect call. Another issue in Indianapolis was that the fans were so loud that our tackles couldn't hear Ben call the signals. We'd had several false-start penalties because of it.

To prevent them from happening again, we went to a silent count. The linemen would look in at our center, Jeff Hartings, and he'd bob

CHAMPIONS, AT LAST **211**

his head once, twice. The ball would be snapped on the first bob or the second bob. It worked well; we eliminated a lot of false starts. Our plan was to do the same thing in Denver with its rabid fans—seventy-six thousand strong—in Mile High Stadium. Earlier in the week I'd sent film to the supervisor of officials, Mike Pereira, and explained, "This is what we're going to do and why we're doing it. I want to make sure it's okay. This is not head bobbing by our center. We're not trying to draw anybody offside."

Mike told me we could do it.

After our first series of downs in Denver, the umpire came over to me and said, "Listen up, if your center keeps doing that, I gotta call a penalty. That's an illegal movement."

"No," I told him. "You can't do that. I know Mike Pereira is here. You'd better get him on the phone." I don't know if he did or didn't, but there was never a problem after that.

We controlled the game from start to finish and had a 24–3 half-time lead. We won, 34–17. We'd gone steadily west, from Cincinnati to Indianapolis to Denver, just to get back to Detroit and the Super Bowl. I was so excited for our players. They'd faced a critical point twelve games into their season and had to accept that what they'd thought was high effort wasn't high enough. And they'd done it.

The feeling you're playing an important and dependable role on a winning team is an incredible motivator. When you think you can't go any further, you keep going because you're not willing to let your teammates down. You're not going to let them see you quit. The more people you have who share the same feeling and the same energy, the more each individual will be able to draw from that. There's real power in numbers.

Inevitably, a little doubt will seep in. You start to wonder if you're going to be successful, but if you look around and everybody else is focused, you'll suck it up and get ready to go, too. You'll draw energy from your teammates. When a team displays that mental confidence, people say they're "in a zone." That's exactly where we were, riding a seven-game winning streak into Super Bowl XL against the Seattle Seahawks.

It crossed my mind that this might be my last Super Bowl. Earlier in the season, during the bye week, Kaye and I had quietly bought a home in Raleigh. It wasn't a move-in-right-now home, but the plan was to be there soon. I couldn't deny the coaching lifestyle was putting a strain on my marriage. Kaye wasn't happy. She never told me she wanted me to leave coaching, but I knew she wasn't in a good place.

I'd seen how people would literally push her aside to get to me for an autograph or a picture. I knew how hard she'd worked to make sure our daughters were being raised as the young women we wanted them to be. My job required long hours, and at times she'd done some things alone.

Plus, we had some decisions to make. We'd agreed that once any of our girls reached their sophomore year of high school, we were going to stay put until high school graduation. Lindsay, our youngest, was in her freshman year at Fox Chapel. If she returned there next year, we'd be in Pittsburgh. Maybe that was in Pittsburgh as head coach of the Steelers or not, but we didn't want to see our daughter change schools halfway through high school.

Several times over the fourteen seasons of my coaching career, I'd instructed my teams to be in the moment. That's what I focused on as we prepared for the game. I knew all of my girls would be there, and I was excited to share this moment with them.

Meagan was in the middle of her season, on her way to being a first-team all–Ivy League forward at Princeton. She planned to play in back-to-back games, on Friday and Saturday, then fly to Detroit for Super Bowl Sunday. The Steelers were nice enough to send a private plane for her and, if she wanted, her new boyfriend. Meagan was unsure if she wanted to invite a newcomer to what she considered an intimate family moment. But Kaye had met Kevin Westgarth, a Princeton hockey player, and made her recommendation: "Invite him; I really like him." Even better, Kevin was from Amherstburg, Ontario. The town is about fifteen miles away from Detroit, so not only did Kaye push for Kevin to come, I made sure his parents had tickets to the game.

The plan for Lauren and Lindsay, Fox Chapel teammates, was to come out for the Super Bowl but not miss school. If they missed school, they wouldn't be able to play in their game. They wanted to play, and I wanted to be there to watch them do it. I hadn't missed one of their games in fourteen years of being a head coach, and even the Super Bowl wouldn't stop me.

As for the Super Bowl against the Seahawks, I felt good about our plan—until the day before the game. As we did a morning walk-through in the hotel ballroom, I noticed one of our defenses, when matched against a popular Seahawks offensive formation, left their slot receiver uncovered. That afternoon I sat down with Dick LeBeau and drew up a new defense—we called it Tight Sam 2 Backer—against this formation. The only time we got to practice it was in the ballroom on Saturday night. We talked it through and decided that we'd use a four-man rush with some zone behind it. The twist was that we'd utilize Troy Polamalu in a "robber" position, which freed him up to be a playmaker. We'd use the just-created defense eighteen times during the game with no issues. That's what happens when you have disciplined players who are smart. They trust that the coaches are giving them something that will be successful, and they know we'll trust them.

When I think about the journey to Detroit, which I believe started with our team meeting at the beginning of December, I can see how it utilized every aspect of our organization. Everything we'd taught, everything we'd practiced, came together during our run and in the Super Bowl itself.

We scored 3 touchdowns in the 21–10 win, and the story behind those touchdowns gives a glimpse of what it means to be a Steeler. Ben, our first-round draft pick quarterback, scored first; in the beginning of the third quarter, our undrafted running back, Willie Parker, broke off a 75-yard run, the longest rushing play in Super Bowl history; in the fourth quarter, the versatile Antwaan Randle El became the first wide receiver to throw a touchdown pass in the Super Bowl . . . and he threw it to another all-around player, Hines Ward.

As the clock ran down, I felt a rush of cold Gatorade over my head and shoulders. I was drenched and ecstatic. Then I saw my girls: Kaye, Meagan, Lauren, and Lindsay. Our family was really, really close. Me and those girls. This was our small moment to share, surrounded by thousands and watched by millions. This was our bubble. I told them this was their Super Bowl, too, and they were the most important people in my life. *We won it, girls.* That's what I told them. *We endured. We persevered. We kept coming back.*

We hugged, kissed, and had a family high five.

When I saw Mr. Rooney, I hugged him and whispered, "I still have those rosary beads with me right now." Seeing him smile, knowing that he was leaving Detroit with the Lombardi Trophy, was beyond satisfying. For a moment, standing on the championship stage, I wasn't Coach Cowher. I was Billy from Crafton again. I'd rooted from afar for Steelers teams that I didn't personally know but felt as if I did due to the way they played. Now, this was a team that I knew. This was my team, as it was when I was growing up, and this was my team—my guys—that I coached. I did know these players; I loved these players. I thought of Marty, too. A good western Pennsylvanian who talked to his team about the gleam in the Lombardi Trophy. He'd never gotten a chance to see his own reflection in it. Since I was his student, his mentee, I held the Lombardi for Marty as well.

Even though we were in Michigan, all I could see was black and gold. And all I could hear was the singsong "Here we go, Steelers. Here we go . . ."

Someone threw me a Terrible Towel and I waved it, freely and excitedly, above my head as I celebrated with the crowd. In those few seconds, the only one who could have handled the Towel better was Myron Cope himself.

What a night.

Soon, the Super Bowl party would begin, and I'd be able to enjoy it with those I loved the most.

Back at the hotel and on the elevator, I let it be known that there wouldn't be any restrictions on our fun. The Commodores were performing at the official team party, and my announcement produced immediate silence.

"I'm a huge fan of the Commodores," I told everyone. "I can't wait to meet Lionel Richie."

There were stares for a few seconds before someone broke the news.

"Lionel Richie isn't with the Commodores anymore. He's been solo for years now. He's not here tonight."

Everyone laughed, knowing how special the night was—and was going to continue to be. Laughter. For the first time in my football career, the last game of the season ended with laughter, a party, and a championship.

15

The Final Season

In the fall of 2006, I'd reached a point that was hard to deny: I was lonely in our Fox Chapel home, either talking to myself or in dialogue there with the family cat, Stew. Sometimes both.

Our house, the one we'd bought in 1992, had never been so quiet. As a family of five with three athletic girls, we were always on our way somewhere. We double-checked schedules constantly, either Fox Chapel's, an AAU team's, or the Steelers'. We were an expressive family of talkers, the worst people in the world with whom to share your secrets. We laughed a lot together. We competed at everything together.

Over the summer, Kaye and Lindsay had moved into the Raleigh house that we'd bought in 2005. Lindsay was a high school sophomore, a star basketball player for Ravenscroft School. Meagan was a Princeton University junior, and one of her new teammates on the basketball team there was Lauren, who was beginning her freshman year. The new routine, though, was strange. Kaye and I had talked about it and planned it, but now that I was doing it, I wasn't myself.

I was in my fifteenth season as Steelers head coach. With my contract set to expire after the 2007 season, this was the closest I'd ever come to my contract year without some type of easily agreed-to extension with Mr. Rooney. There was lots of chatter on sports talk radio and in the newspaper about the "real reason" I was doing this. The theory was, I was unhappy with my contract and wanted to be one of the highest-paid coaches in the league. And if I couldn't do that, I'd leave the Steelers, sit out until my contract expired, then return to the NFL with a market-setting deal.

None of it was true. I'd never haggled over money with the Steelers. They understood I wasn't motivated by that. The Steelers, more than any other franchise, were a well-run *family* business. Family was emphasized and valued there. I think that's one reason I was never pressured to give answers about my future because I was in the midst of a family decision.

The Super Bowl win had changed all of the Cowhers. The spotlight became brighter, the demands more frequent, and day-to-day living more intruded upon. I remember my daughters planned a shopping trip one afternoon. When I told them I'd come with them, they said, "Dad, you stay here. It's a lot easier for us when you're not with us."

I'd become a prisoner of success. When I was away from the facility, I found myself walking around with my head down and a baseball cap pulled as low as it could be without covering my eyes. I didn't want to live like that. It brought me back to that conversation I'd had with Bill Parcells a couple of years earlier. And that aside, something was stirring in me: Did I want to have a life consumed by football, whether it was a "celebrity football life" or not?

That was the question that usually triggered those conversations with myself and Stew (the girls named him after their favorite player, Kordell Stewart). Despite our 2-6 record midway through the year, I was more focused on coaching than ever before. I had no family obligations waiting for me at the house. There were no bus stop drop-offs, rides to practice, or hustling to a game. There was no event

Kaye wanted me to attend. Kaye and Lindsay would fly into town for Steelers games, then go back to Raleigh afterward. Otherwise, it was me, the empty house, and Stew.

Is this what you want? Is it?

I'd ask myself that when I walked in the door. As crazy as it sounds, sometimes I'd turn to Stew and answer, "No, this isn't what I want. My family is the reason I can do the job. They provide the balance that I need."

The contrast stood out most on Friday evenings. When we were all together, we'd had a routine: We'd get dinner together at the Pittsburgh Field Club. Then we'd head back home either for family time with all of us, or as the girls got older, they'd make their plans and I'd have a relaxing night in with Kaye.

That's how it used to be. But now many things had changed.

My parents, now in their early eighties, sold the house I grew up in on Hawthorne Avenue and were genuinely touched when I told them what I wanted them to do: keep the profit from the house and allow me to purchase a condo for them in Mount Lebanon, a Pittsburgh suburb. My father reacted as if he'd won the lottery. My new Friday routine was to drive to Mount Lebanon and stop in a restaurant called Il Pizzaiolo. It was right down the street from my parents' condo. I'd head to the back, have a glass of wine at the bar, and watch a few minutes of the classic Italian movies they'd show on their screens. Then I'd take a pizza to my parents, spend some time with them, and go home.

As I prepared in my office or stood on the practice field, Mr. Rooney would come up to me and simply ask, "How are you doing with this?" He was concerned about my being away from what he knew to be my backbone. Mr. Rooney, who was in his mid-seventies, would sometimes say, "Beware of retirement, Coach. It's not all it's cracked up to be."

While retirement had crept into my mind, it wasn't my top priority in 2006. I liked our players, their talent and their togetherness. I'll never forget walking into a team meeting one day and preparing to begin a speech. As soon as I started talking, at least half of the room began coughing.

My first thought, honestly, was that my zipper was down or something. Was something in my hair? On my face?

"What am I missing?" I asked. "Are you guys all right?"

No one said anything unusual, so we moved on. After the meeting, I approached Chet Fuhrman.

"What was the deal with all the coughing?"

And that's when I learned that the players had made a pact. They knew how much I hated any kind of cell phone noise in meetings, and there'd be some consequence if I heard any ringing or buzzing there. They'd agreed to cover each other if someone slipped up and forgot to silence his phone. That's what happened when I began to speak. They heard a phone ring and they started coughing to drown it out.

I told Chet, "I love these guys. I love teammates who protect each other." Not only did I love the team, my job was to keep coaching them as hard as I could as defending Super Bowl champs. That started with Ben. For the first time in my Steelers career, we had a quarterback who was consistent and who was only going to get better. Kordell and Neil before him had been good, but Ben was something special.

He also wasn't quite himself during the year because of a motorcycle accident he had had over the summer. I heard about it when we were in Bald Head. I returned to Pittsburgh to see him in the hospital. Ben hadn't been wearing a helmet when he crashed, and he was fortunate that his injuries weren't worse. His off-season had been abnormal, and he wasn't as sharp as he could have been because of it.

With Jerome now retired, Willie Parker entered his second season as the featured back. Dick Hoak did a great job with him, and the results showed. Willie's 213-yard rushing day helped us snap a three-game losing streak to beat the Saints at Heinz Field. The next week, in Cleveland, he showed his hands and caught a late touchdown pass to beat the Browns. With those wins, our record was 4-6. I always wanted to make the playoffs, but I didn't coach just because of them. As always, I insisted that our players and coaches stick to our process.

The foundation of that process was a positive mindset and positive approach, even when players were being pushed to do something that they might not want to do. I believed our achievements started with the way we thought. Confidence is the result of positive thinking. From day one, we tried to instill mental toughness in our players. *We can do it. We will do it. We can go one more play. We will get up and pursue.* Success may require great athleticism, but it begins in the mind. If you believe you can do something, you may well be able to do it, but if don't think you can do it, then I guarantee you won't be able to do it.

I'd tell our players (and my daughters) often, "You are a product of who you surround yourself with. If the people around you are negative, it's almost impossible to maintain your own level of enthusiasm. But if enough people buy into what you're doing and believe in your approach, then you actually start to feel invincible."

In my career, I'd coached many players who became better when they changed the way they thought. For example, some performed better when they were angry and not self-satisfied. Those are the kind of players whom you're afraid to compliment, because they'll take any praise and immediately coast.

For players like this, I'd give specific instructions to their position coaches: "Do *not* tell them that they played great. Because if you give them just a little bit of a cushion, they're going to lay back a little."

Our chance to make the 2006 playoffs ended on the Sunday after

Thanksgiving. We were shut out by the Ravens, 27–0, for our seventh loss of the year. We'd have to go on a five-game winning streak and then still look for help from someone else to get into the postseason. Those losses, especially the shutouts, were tough to take.

I remember a conversation I'd had with Mike Sherman a few years earlier, when he was head coach of the Green Bay Packers. Win or lose, I didn't sleep on Sunday nights. But if we'd won, after Kaye and the girls had gone to sleep, I'd stay up with the cat (the other cats over the years were Blitz and Steel; my daughters named them after things I valued to insure that I'd love the cats). I'd watch *SportsCenter*, have an extra beer, watch all the news shows, and look at the tape of our game.

After being in the middle of all the game emotion, all that noise, I would enjoy just being there with the cat. I was content. Mike laughed and told me he could relate to everything but my pet; he had dogs.

"I'll check next year," I told him. "When you win a game and I win a game, and I'm sitting there having a beer with my cat, I'll know you're having a beer with your dogs."

But that was about as much of a celebration as I allowed myself to have. It had been like that for years. The savoring was rare. I'd always keep moving on to what was next, just moving on, trying not to be overwhelmed by the job. It's what I'd always done. Each week, there was a new set of challenges I'd feel unprepared for on Tuesday, and then, day by day, the vision of how a game would be won began to come into focus. I told Mike, "Here's the best piece of advice I can give you: Enjoy those Sunday nights. Because the longer you stay in this business, you're going to realize how hard it is to get those wins. Enjoy them."

At the beginning of December, we put together our longest win streak of the season: three games. This was nothing like 2005, when we rode an eight-game streak all the way to a Super Bowl title. The focus then was on seeing how we could advance in the playoffs. But this season, as much as I'd tried to prevent it, had been about what I would do next.

It started as far back as training camp. Even in retirement, Jerome created some talking points when he told the Pittsburgh media that he thought I was going to retire. He explained that he'd had a conversation with me and that I'd been more reflective than usual. He talked about the house in North Carolina and the love I had for my girls. All of Jerome's points were good—and true—but his comments were read as if I'd made my decision, and I hadn't. I thought that I *might* step down, but I wasn't sure. I wouldn't know until the season was over.

Our last game of 2006 was on the last day of the year, New Year's Eve. We were in Cincinnati taking on the Bengals. This was the stadium where our playoff run began in 2005, and the Bengals were trying to do something similar this season. If they beat us, they'd make the playoffs. We were 7-8 and already eliminated from the postseason. We were playing for pride, and that was fine with me. That's exactly what Bengals coach Marvin Lewis and I used to do as kids.

Back in high school, his team beat us on a late kickoff return. In the final seconds at Paul Brown Stadium, his team had a chance to win it with a 39-yard field goal in the final seconds. When the kick went to the right, the game went to overtime. We won the toss, and three plays in, Ben hit our rookie receiver, Santonio Holmes, for a 67-yard touchdown pass. As I walked across the field to shake Marvin's hand, I'm sure his mind was on missing the playoffs. But I was inspired to tell him something that was in my heart, just in case I didn't have a chance to do it in a head coach-to-head coach setting:

"Thanks for everything. You're a good football coach. I'm only a phone call away if you need me."

Even with those words, I didn't know if that win was my last game as head coach of the Steelers.

With a new year in front of me and the season behind me, I took a couple of days to clear my head. My thoughts were indicative of my next move. I found myself reflecting on what we'd accomplished as an organization. In fifteen seasons in Pittsburgh, we made the playoffs ten times. We won eight division titles, played in six AFC Championship Games and two Super Bowls. We won a Super Bowl, the fifth in Steelers history. We got "one for the thumb." It was a great run. Truly, there were dozens of players and coaches who contributed to the success and standards of the franchise. There were people behind the scenes, too, people who never got publicity yet were integral to our success. I would have been lost without people such as Mia Daudet, my administrative assistant. There were stadium workers, office workers, doctors, nutritionists, fans. I never lacked support.

||||||||||||||

I'd been able to achieve many of the dreams I had growing up in Crafton. I played college and pro football. I coached in the NFL. I won a Super Bowl for my beloved childhood team. My parents and brothers had been able to witness it. It doesn't even sound true, but all of it is. It's true that I had a crush on a girl in my psychology class when I was nineteen, and thirty years later we were married with three incredible daughters.

Those were all dreams that had blessedly come true. At forty-nine, I was much too young to be out of dreams. We all need goals to pursue. Having dreams and objectives provides direction. I've told anyone who will listen to never be afraid to chase a dream. I'm proof that sometimes they come true. If you have one, why not just go for it? Don't try to figure out if it's realistic; just . . . go for it. If it doesn't come to life, move on and find another one. You can't let yourself get caught without a dream.

I knew the Steelers were a team ready to win for a long time when I told the Rooney family I was leaving. I think they knew what I was going to say before I said it. I couldn't thank them enough for what they'd done for me and my family. No matter who the coach is, no one is bigger than the Pittsburgh Steelers. It's an honor to say you've coached a team like that, and all you ever want to do, humbly, is leave it in a better place than when you started.

No single event triggered my decision. Everything in my life had been structured around football. And I was afraid. My fear was, the longer I stayed as Coach Cowher, with a life completely tailored to football, the more difficult it would be to ever experience a different type of life. Mr. Rooney knew exactly what I meant when I said that to him, and that was important to me. I was at peace knowing that a lot of people might not understand what I was doing. Or that they might ascribe motives to me that had nothing to do with my actual reasoning.

As everyone does as they grow and learn, I'd changed. But my life hadn't changed; I was still doing the same things I'd done a decade earlier. I just had this feeling that it was time to take what I knew and try something different. I knew how lucky I was. Not many people get the opportunity to leave a job they love just because they're ready to move on to the next stage of their life.

I'd hear from and see Steelers fans, both from Pittsburgh and around the country. A lot of them would tell me they appreciated my passion; they could tell I cared about the team as much as they did. Well, what they saw was my heart, for a city and team and game. I followed my heart for fifteen seasons. I left because in my heart it was time to leave.

I had led a scripted life until then. I'd always gone from one thing right to the next and knew within a certain range what I'd be doing the next year. I knew where I'd be. I'd gone from high school to college to professional football to coaching. My adult life had always been attuned to the contours of a football season. I'd had small blocks of time, here and there, for vacation or some way of renewing myself. Following that life script had provided comfort.

The idea of having some *unscripted* time to be spontaneous was undeniably appealing. I still couldn't help writing things down, so I had a postcoaching-life list. It had just a few items on it, things I wanted to do—spend more time with my family; travel more; improve my golf game; learn to play the piano—and I was excited to add to it.

The difficulty in walking away from a situation such as I had is almost impossible to describe. It would have been much easier to continue doing it. I heard a stat once that the two most frequent days people die is at birth, due to the high rate of infant mortality, and after retirement. But as I stood at the dais at my retirement announcement on January 5, 2007, looking out at a roomful of reporters and photographers, I felt no fear or sadness. Just gratitude. It was time to do something else. For the first time in a long time, I was all right with not knowing what that would be.

16

At-Home Dad, TV Coach

Two and a half weeks after I left Pittsburgh, the franchise where I'd worked for fifteen seasons no longer had a head coaching vacancy. It was official now. The opening with the Steelers was filled by Mike Tomlin, who was the same age I was—thirty-four—when I took over the team.

I talked to Mike shortly after, and it was even clearer why Chuck Noll had advised me the way he did all those years earlier. Chuck didn't have any to-do or watch-out-for-this lists for me in 1992. If he had, no matter how well-meaning, it would probably have slowed me down. Chuck had been a young guy, too, when he began in Pittsburgh at age thirty-seven. Over time, he'd developed his routine, made some mistakes, and discovered his best path to success. I'd done the same. Now it was Mike's turn. When I talked with Mike, I told him one important piece of information.

"Hey, I left an Iron City beer for you in the office fridge."

"I know," he said. "It's still there."

I don't think anyone can tell you specifically how to be a head coach. Every dynamic is a little different. You begin the job and feel as if you're in the middle of a two-minute drill. Everything is coming your way and you have to catch it, quickly decide how to handle it, and keep moving. A glance at each of my fifteen seasonal notebooks tells that story.

In the first couple of notebooks, I was all over the place. They didn't have the same order, rhythm, and continuity as the later ones. With experience, I found myself writing more in each of them, and writing with authority. After a few years, I'd also begun going back and using them as reference guides. So, when we went through our losing streak in 2003, I'd go back four or five years to see how I handled similar situations in 1998 and 1999. I'd make notes to myself about discipline, leadership, and inspirational points for the players and coaches. What had I said in team meetings? What types of illustrations had I used? How was my communication with the coaches, and had I evolved in the way I coached them?

The more I learned about the league, the organization, the players, and myself, the more a clear and effective system came into view. I could sense it as I became a more seasoned coach, and I could see it right there on those pages.

In some ways, I'd have to do that now in Raleigh. For twenty-seven years as either player or coach, I knew what I had to do based on the calendar. Some periods were busier and faster than others, but there was always movement.

What do you do when things are hectic and there is no gradual slowdown to prepare you for the change? What do you do when all football activities abruptly stop?

Our youngest daughter, Lindsay, could see I was searching for answers when I first got back to Raleigh. Some days she'd find me in the house strumming a guitar. Sometimes I'd play the piano. At times I'd take off for a walk with our new yellow Lab, Huey, and the walk would be four or five miles. My days were suddenly wide-open for golf, shopping, or just hanging out.

"Dad needs a new hobby," Lindsay would joke.

Lindsay had the right idea about how to start her life anew. She never wanted to be solely known as Bill Cowher's daughter, so when she arrived at Ravenscroft, at times she tried to hide her last name when meeting people. That was a challenge for her to do there for a few reasons. Now at six-two, Lindsay was one of the best high school basketball players in North Carolina. She immediately gained the respect of her teammates and was named team captain.

Lots of people knew who she was, including the head of the school, Doreen Kelly. Doreen had been an athlete in her college days, playing volleyball at Penn. She eventually married a Yale basketball player who went on to play professionally in France. One of the Kellys' sons, Ryan, had a lot in common with Lindsay. Ryan also attended Ravenscroft and was the basketball team's star center. He and Lindsay became friends and began dating.

By overstating my racquetball skills, Lindsay also introduced me to someone who quickly became one of my best friends. Lindsay and her friend Jessica had been talking about their fathers and mentioned how racquetball obsessed their dads were. It didn't stop there. They determined that the fathers should meet—and not just meet but also play racquetball. Neither father was there to temper the hyperbole that was surely taking place between the girls.

That's how I met George Richards. Having been in commercial real estate for years, he was plugged into the Greater Raleigh community. I enjoyed talking with him. Lindsay and Jessica were right: We *did* have to play racquetball, and I had no idea what to expect. Had Lindsay set me up to fail against the best player in the state? Or would my new friend be ready to intensely compete?

The first time we played, we went back and forth for a while. As the sweat poured down my face, I paused to shout my analysis to George: "Hey! I feel like I'm playing against myself in the freakin' mirror!"

He was tough.

George and his wife, Judy, were the couple Kaye and I spent the most time with. The four of us got along great, and with my flexible schedule, planning things wasn't difficult. Kaye was in her element in North Carolina. She'd grown up about thirty-five minutes from where we lived. This move was her return home, and she was excited about it. She'd always supported me at Steelers games, but she had no interest in the spotlight as a celebrity wife. She didn't look at it that way: I understood that I couldn't have done my job without her, and it was fine with her that I knew it even if others didn't realize or consider the extent of it. She didn't want or need any credit. She was an independent Southern girl who loved and was protective of her family.

Kaye and I had spoken for years about traveling to different cities, places we'd go to without having any business reason to be there. Traveling, within the States and internationally, was part of the plan. But those conversations suddenly became less prominent after the spring of 2007.

iiiiiiiiiii

I'd never paid attention to a small mole on Kaye's shoulder until my sister-in-law Cathy mentioned it. Cathy is a nurse and noticed the mole had begun to darken. She advised Kaye to get it removed, and she followed up on Cathy's advice.

The mole tested positive for melanoma. Kaye was a poster child for the disease: She was blue-eyed and blonde and had grown up spending hours in the North Carolina sun, working the tobacco fields. Her doctors had some good news, though: Kaye's lymph nodes checked out fine.

I learned later that melanoma can lie dormant in the body for ten to fifteen years. Stress can be one of its activators. As soon as she was aware of the mole, Kaye changed. She became anxious. It was difficult for her to approach anything in a carefree way because her mind raced with worry. She wondered what was inside her; she thought of all the things that could happen to her one day.

I tried to assure her it would be okay. The reports were clean, so I tried to put the focus on them. She agreed, but the idea of traveling all over was tabled. She was self-conscious about spending time outside, particularly in the sun. The subject made her nervous, so we didn't talk about it.

Kaye was smart and hands-on, so one thing she became passionate about was planning and designing a new house for us in north Raleigh near North Ridge Country Club. It would take nearly two years to get the house the way she wanted it, which meant we might not be ready to move there until 2009. As usual, Kaye was thoughtful about each detail. One of my favorite plans: We'd walk off our back porch and be steps away from the first tee at North Ridge. For the most part, we enjoyed our new lifestyle. We could shape the weeks any way we wanted.

Even though I was now a retired football coach, I still was excited about the game itself. I remember when my agent, Phil de Picciotto, came to my final press conference in Pittsburgh. I'd talked with him before and after that press conference. I never wanted to be without options, so I had a simple message for Phil before that day: "I can't go cold turkey here. See if you can find me something."

I was open to media work, especially if the travel demands were minimal. Phil called several networks to present myriad opportunities. Many of them put a caveat with their offer: This sounds good, but what do we do if he accepts another coaching job? Does he still want to coach?

One of the best conversations Phil arranged was with Sean McManus of CBS. I wanted people I worked for to understand how I viewed this period in my life. This wasn't about money for me, or about taking a break before jumping back into the coaching cycle. If I wanted a short break from the game, I would have found a way to say that. My view was that I was finished with coaching. I'd keep the "maybe" alive not because of opportunity but reality: We're all capable of shifts for a number of unpredictable reasons.

I was grateful to receive an offer from McManus and CBS. Beginning with the 2007 NFL season, I'd join former players Dan Marino, Shannon Sharpe, and Boomer Esiason, along with host James Brown, on *The NFL Today*. It seemed like the perfect job. It would allow me to stay connected to the game while not having the daily pressure and grind of coaching. I understood from watching changes in the media that it also was an industry of programs and personalities with a brief shelf life. But it still wasn't as temporal as coaching. While with the Steelers, I can't say that I sat around worrying about getting fired, but part of coaching is learning you'd better appreciate every single day. And, as I'd told Mike Sherman, appreciate every single win. At times in every coach's career he wonders about the future, and I knew I wasn't going to miss that part of it.

That said, late July and August had made me a bit nostalgic. I couldn't remember the last time I hadn't been around football in late summer. As a kid, it was football camps. Then there was training camp, from college to playing days to the three cities where I'd been a coach. I tried to be careful to manage what I felt and what I missed because not a day went by without someone asking, "Coach, do you miss it?"

The answer was more involved than the questioner had time for. Simply put, I missed big *parts* of it. How could you do something that you love for so long and not miss it when it's over? I missed coaching. I missed the camaraderie with the players. The joking in the locker room. I missed the incredible feeling of leading a determined team with an attitude and a purpose. Nothing equals the act and the feeling of leading a team out of a tunnel and into a crazed wall of sound.

I also missed the strategic element of the game. I think most coaches crave the challenge of coming up with something new and finding an effective way to compete by constructing thorough game plans. There's the plan, and then things happen in real time that you have to make spontaneous decisions on. I understood TV was a fast-moving medium, but I knew nothing in media—maybe not anywhere—where seventy thousand people were one move away from a raucous cheer or boo. On top of that, you constantly worked with energetic and creative young people and had the opportunity to watch them grow as players, husbands, and fathers. Nothing out there could substitute for any of that.

At the beginning of my first season on TV, I didn't go in with the thought that it was going to totally fill the football void I had. But it did help. My first experience in a studio had taken place in 1998. After we were eliminated from the playoffs, Jim Nantz invited me to work a wild card game. Jim made me feel comfortable, telling me to keep my comments short, make one or two points, and not try to be someone or something different.

"Just be you" was how Jim put it.

I'd talked with ESPN's Chris Berman, who advised, "Just look at the camera as if you're talking to a friend in the living room. Someone who doesn't really know football that well who you're trying to explain the game of football to. Just try to keep it simple for them."

One of the CBS cameramen, Fred Shimizu, was even more succinct. He noticed that I was trying to say everything I knew. He shook his head. "You know a lot," he said. "But keep it short and sweet."

So that's what I did. Or what I tried to do.

My entire first season I was nervous. I used to get butterflies before an NFL game started, but they'd go away at kickoff. On

TV, I got butterflies and never got as comfortable as I wanted. But the opportunity to watch the games with Shannon, Dan, and Boomer—former players who *understood* football—was good for me. In meetings and on the air, they referred to me as Coach. It was good to have a blend of our perspectives. Sometimes they, as players, would rip coaches for their in-game decisions, and I'd respond just like a coach: "Wait a second, fellas. What about execution? Let's hold the players accountable."

We had a lot of laughs on set and off the air. James Brown—or JB—was great at listening to all of us, getting a feel for where everyone was strong or passionate, then setting us up perfectly on the air. He'd been an all–Ivy League forward at Harvard, but on TV he was our pass-first point guard. He was also deeply religious. Beyond the show, JB was a Christian with whom I could always have a meaningful conversation about spiritual life.

My job at CBS was perfect for our family, too. Kaye and I would spend the week together, then I'd fly to New York early Saturday. I'd have a meeting on Saturday, do the show on Sunday afternoon, and be back in Raleigh on Sunday night. Since Meagan and Lauren were both at Princeton, I was close enough to see them if Princeton had a Saturday night game.

As I got more comfortable on the air, sometimes I'd hear comments coming out of my mouth I hadn't thought about; I'd surprise myself. They'd often be strong opinions that had been stirring in my mind for a while that I hadn't verbalized. I also found that, similar to coaching, I needed to prepare to get the results I wanted. Initially, I didn't know how to prepare because I had to learn another skill first: *Take what you know about football, make it digestible for casual fans, and do it in fifteen- to thirty-second bites.* It was a different version of time management, and it took some time for me to adapt it.

When my primary audience had been players and coaches, I'd spent hours speaking in jargon and using insider terms only people in our locker room would understand. This was the opposite. My primary audience wasn't other players and coaches, it was casual fans, and I didn't need to hit them over the head with thick playbooks. I set my objectives, I did my preparation, and I moved ahead.

This is how different my life was in 2007 and 2008. In those years, the calls from NFL owners and general managers started coming again. It's incredibly complimentary to be considered for these jobs, and I always appreciated it. For me, saying yes meant going all in. There'd be no going back, no less of an effort. In almost every situation the job would require changing the culture—and making everyone there embrace the process. That's more than a full-time job. It would require a total commitment, and I didn't miss the NFL enough to dive into that commitment.

Plus, I had other coaching to do. In all my years with the Steelers, I'd spent countless hours at the office while Kaye was spending hours in cars, classrooms, gyms, and practice fields with our daughters. She was firm and had high expectations for our girls. She was serious about sports, too. At times she'd coached them, whether they wanted it or not. For example, Lauren used to say that she'd decide on whom she wanted to ride home with based on how she'd played. A bad game? She'd ride with me because I was the parent who would encourage and then pump up for the next game. Kaye, meanwhile, was the coach, pointing out poor technique and position.

Lindsay was with an AAU travel team, and the group needed a chaperone. Kaye volunteered me for the position, and off I went to such places as Atlanta and Washington, DC. Lindsay's teammates were great. Whenever I relaxed in gyms and prepared to watch them play, inevitably a fan would recognize me. The girls would be my fence and say, "That's just Lindsay's dad. He's here to watch her play."

As many as six of them would pile into my SUV. I made the mistake of taking them to McDonald's a few times and they cleaned me out. I was their coach, their chaperone, their chauffeur, and their caterer. They started referring to me as Uncle Bill.

These were the simple things I'd missed over the years. This was my life now. And I loved it.

17

Heartbreak and Resilience

For nearly two years, Kaye planned every detail of our dream house in Raleigh. Every entrance, every view, and every small finish had a purpose. From 2007 until the spring of 2009, Kaye was singularly focused on creating the most beautiful home she could imagine for our family.

I'd gotten used to coming home to see Kaye huddled with an interior designer, the two of them envisioning perfect layouts for each room. A specific brand for the kitchen ovens. A particular vanity for the master bedroom. I was excited to see her like this. She deserved it. Kaye was instinctively selfless; our entire family knew how much she'd put our needs in front of her own. We all went to her with our problems because she usually had something—her intelligence, her good advice, her inherent goodness—that would bring clarity to a situation.

In some ways, having a daily canvas on which to plan was exactly what Kaye needed. When she oversaw the construction of the house, she was the decisive, confident, and assertive woman we all recognized. But when the house was fully done in April 2009, there was no distraction. We'd changed.

For one, we were a couple on our way to an empty nest. Meagan had graduated from Princeton and lived in New York. Lauren was about to complete her junior year at Princeton. Lindsay was about to graduate from Ravenscroft and begin her freshman year at Wofford College in South Carolina.

We still called them "our girls," but they were the independent young women Kaye raised them to be. She'd invested so much of herself in them (and us), as a stay-at-home mom, and now that was changing. Our daughters could sense that their mother was searching for her next chapter. They encouraged her to try her hand at real estate. Or to do things for herself that made her happy. But the changes in her life dominated her thoughts. And those changes led to a return of her anxiety and stress.

I'll never forget the day in July 2009 when a nurse came to our house to give us routine physical exams for life insurance. After I'd completed mine, I went to my home office to look over some paperwork. A few minutes later, the nurse knocked on my door.

"Mr. Cowher, can I talk to you for a second?"

"Of course."

She looked concerned. "I'm in the other room with your wife, and she can't remember her birthday."

I told the nurse Kaye's birthday: April 17, 1956.

"Well, she can't remember that and she can't remember her Social Security number. I just want to make you aware of that."

I wasn't sure what to think, but it made me more attentive to Kaye. Over the next few weeks, I could see, clearly, that she wasn't herself. She'd carry something in the house—a cup, a plate, car keys—then suddenly lose her grip and drop them. Normally, she had the reflexes of an elite athlete; this wasn't like her at all. We were concerned enough to see our doctor, and in September, Kaye was diagnosed with early Alzheimer's disease. A lot of emotional,

life-changing things were converging at once: the Alzheimer's diagnosis, menopause, empty nesting, and a renewed focus on the
cancerous mole that had been removed in 2007.

We'd looked forward to a life in which we'd schedule what we
wanted, and when. But that was suddenly out of our control. There
was no more downtime. Most of our weeks had a similar pattern:
Monday through Friday, we'd meet with doctors and physical thera-
pists; Saturday morning, I'd fly to New York for my CBS work; Sunday night, I'd fly back to Raleigh.

That schedule was the entirety of our fall 2009. During that
time, Kaye learned that her twin sister, Faye, had cancer. Now
Kaye began to openly wonder, "Wow, do I have cancer, too? We're
twins. I might have cancer, too."

CBS had the broadcast rights to the Super Bowl in Miami that
season. I traveled there in late January 2010 in advance of the game,
which was on the first Sunday in February. As soon as I returned to
Raleigh, Kaye told me she was convinced she had cancer. Her sister
had a benign tumor on her chest she'd had removed. Kaye wanted
to be tested as well.

In early February, via needle biopsy, our doctors found something on Kaye's chest. They said it was hardened and benign and that
this wasn't likely to become something worrisome.

My wife was insistent: "I want it out of there. I know my body.
Something is not right."

Later that month, we prepared for what was supposed to be a
routine surgical procedure. I vividly remember that day. Kaye's sister
Cathy was there as well. Cathy, the registered nurse, was the one
who'd identified the mole in 2007. I remember where I was sitting,
and then standing, as I heard the string of stunning words from the
doctor:

She was right. . . . She's got melanoma . . . and it's spread all over. . . . I

240 HEART AND STEEL

have to ask you for your permission on this. . . . Can I put a balloon in her? Because I need to empty out a lot of liquid that's in her chest.

Everything had happened so fast. And was happening fast. I didn't even have time to process my sudden heartbreak.

Melanoma?

All over?

And she's still in surgery, with a tube in her chest?

"Yes," I said. "Do it. Yes."

I don't think I ever exhaled. I tried to separate all my emotions from the key question: What do we do now? Ultimately, that's what I wanted to know. What steps do we take with this? After a consultation with doctors, I began to get some answers. None could be characterized as optimistic. Three treatment options were presented. Of the three, her best chance of survival was 8 percent.

Kaye and I were soul mates for many reasons; one was a willingness to fight. I knew she'd fight to boost those odds, and I'd be right there with her. There was no time for reflection. I didn't have the luxury of sitting back and taking a big-picture view of what we'd learned and what we were about to go through.

In early March 2010, all of my days were spent working the phones and gathering research. *Whom do I know that may know someone else? What can we do? Think! There must be . . . something.* I talked with a range of people, sometimes hoping to hear something that would spark an idea. I reached out to Sean McManus at CBS; Sanjay Gupta, America's doctor; and the best employer I've ever had, the Pittsburgh Steelers. I'd spend my days in my office, the one my wife had thoughtfully designed and decorated a year earlier. Now I was in there hoping for a lead on something that could save her life.

I'd be in the office at night, and Kaye would stop in before going to bed.

"I know you're going to find a way to cure this. You always do. You always find a way to make things better."

I'd look back at her and say, "I'm going to take care of you, honey."

The first week in March, I thought we got our break. We had travel limitations due to the tube in Kaye's chest. We got her into a trial in Pittsburgh. Four years after leaving that city, we were on our way back.

Most people didn't know we were there, and those who did were extremely gracious in respecting our privacy. We rented a house in Shadyside, about fifteen minutes from where we used to live in Fox Chapel. It was a monthlong trial. Every morning I'd take Kaye to get her injections. I knew how tough she was, and I'd tell her that every day. This trial, though, was hard on her. She'd come back to the house in the afternoon, and sometimes she'd have a fever of 103, 104. She didn't want to eat anything. I'd beg her to do that, just to take a few bites of something. She'd either sleep or, when she was awake, stare. Just staring off, long moments of not being lucid. The treatment exacerbated things. It was too much.

After three weeks, we knew it was best to stop the treatment. We planned to regroup, pack up our things, and head back to Raleigh. That was entirely my focus. My mind wasn't on anything except finding the next place for treatment. But before we left Pittsburgh, I was reminded life doesn't work that way. There's no convenient pick-and-choose option to it. When life unfolds—or, in 2010, steamrolls—toward you, you have to stand and confront it. That confrontation might happen with tears in your eyes, or pain in your heart, but you have to do it.

That's what I told myself when I got a phone call from my mother, a couple of days before Kaye and I were to leave Pittsburgh and return to Raleigh.

As soon as I heard my mother's voice, her *tone*, I knew she was calling about my dad. She said he'd been hospitalized with pneumonia. He had water in his lungs. He was on a respirator to help with his low oxygen levels and breathing. I couldn't help thinking about the timing of it all. Kaye and I could have been anywhere on the East Coast: Raleigh, Washington, New York. Anywhere. But we were in Pittsburgh, so it allowed me to see my father before we left town.

Whenever I saw my dad, I knew what to expect. He'd preached the three principles I'd never forgotten: Never quit, because that speaks to perseverance; work harder than the next guy, which meant working when no one was watching; and never be intimidated by anyone or anything. No matter what, don't back down.

He was eighty-seven years old. I was almost fifty-three. His emphatic messages were still firmly in my mind. He was tough, but that was his way of encouraging me. That's how he did it. When I walked into his hospital room and saw him, hooked to oxygen as he lay in bed, I knew it was my turn to encourage my father. I'd done the same thing with Kaye during the trial.

With Kaye, I'd told her, "You can do this. You're so strong. I'm so proud of you. I love you. You're going to push your way through this."

When I saw my father, I was prepared to do the same thing.

"Dad, how ya doing?"

"Billy, I'm not doing very well."

"Dad, you can fight through this."

It was something he'd say. I sounded like him. But he looked at me, and I knew.

"No, Billy. You know what? I'm tired of fighting."

It reminded me of that old Kenny Loggins song "This Is It." Every time I hear that song, I think of my father. It was that look in his eyes when he said it. *I'm tired of fighting.* But as his son, I'm trying to hold it together as I think, *But this is it, Dad. Stand up and fight.* I couldn't say that, though. Dad was ready. Dad had fought for years and modeled that fighting spirit for my brothers and me. It was up to us to keep living and teaching what he'd lived and taught.

I grabbed his hand. "I get it, Dad. I love you."

Short of a miracle, I knew that would be the last time I saw him. I left his side, got back into the car where Kaye had been waiting, and we went straight to the airport.

We had a different plan when we got back to Raleigh. We wanted a treatment that wouldn't be as aggressive as the Pittsburgh trial. We also needed another plan for our house: aides. At first it was for three to four hours a day. Then six. Then, when Kaye slept all day, got up at night, and attempted to leave the house, we needed help around the clock.

Sometimes Cathy and Kaye's twin, Faye, would stay in the house and help out. I slept on an air mattress in our gym. My morning routine was to take over for the nurses who were watching her overnight, take her to the kitchen, and feed her. I'd then take her to her favorite chair so she could sit there for most of the day. Many of her days were just like that. There were fewer and fewer moments of lucidity.

For four or five hours a day, I'd have someone relieve me so I could run errands, make phone calls, or just clear my head. One Saturday afternoon in April, George Richards and I went to the golf course behind my house. George had become my best friend, and he knew when I just needed to play. As usual, I brought my cell with me because any call was likely from Kaye or about my dad.

As we approached the tee box at the fourteenth, my phone rang.

"This is about my dad," I guessed as I looked at the phone. "I think my dad just died."

That's exactly what the phone call was about. I'd consistently struggled on fourteen, hitting the ball to the right into the woods. At times I'd hit it in there so deep that we'd never find the ball. Fourteen was one of Dad's don't-back-down situations.

"Dad, this drive's for you," I said as I hit it. It was as if he were there looking over me saying, "Billy, you can do this. You'd better believe in yourself."

It was the best drive I'd hit all day. George called it "a rocket," and it was: It was as straight as could be, right down the middle of the fairway.

My dad was gone, yet all I felt was gratitude, blessed to have been raised, molded, and loved by a father like that. He had solid and simple values, and he stayed true to them. Work hard. Live within your means. Treat people well. Persevere.

I'm glad he'd seen his granddaughters, in his city, for fifteen years. And just as important, I'm glad they'd seen and learned from him.

In May, I contacted the girls and told them to come home. They were all in different parts of the country, at various stages of life, career, and school. I told them their mother was not well and they needed to see her, spend some time with her.

Once they saw her, there was a mix of denial and fear. She was deteriorating in front of us. It was extremely hard for all of us to reconcile. She was Mom, and Mom was the center of our family's conscience and strength. How could this be happening to her? How was this fair? In one-on-one moments with each of my daughters, I saw their tears and tried to appropriately answer their biggest questions:

Is Mom going to get better?

Is Mom going to die?

I didn't want to take away their hope. I didn't think it was my place to dash that. We all should hold on to hope. Finally I said, "If I'm giving your mother hope and she's still in there fighting, I want you to have the same hope that she has."

Some moments, from each of us, brought out her warm smile. Those connective moments let us know, despite how unfamiliar she looked and sounded at times, she was still there.

She was happy Lindsay, having transferred from Wofford to Elon, was closer now. Lindsay was still dating Ryan Kelly, who was down the road playing basketball at Duke. When Lauren graduated from Princeton, Kaye traveled to New Jersey to see it. And when Meagan and Kevin announced their engagement, Kaye was there with a joyful smile again. She'd always liked Kevin and had encouraged Meagan to invite him to the Detroit Super Bowl.

For me, I'd get her smile when I came down the stairs in the morning to walk her to the kitchen. I'd take over for the night nurse. Kaye would look to the nurse and say, "See? I told you he was coming."

By June, my full-time job was caring for Kaye. Each morning I needed updates on her medicines, dosages, and how to regulate her pain with drugs. I had a lot of information to consider and a lot of opinions were coming my way. I can't say everyone agreed with all of my decisions. But I knew Kaye, and I understood what kind of life she'd like to live. She was so vibrant and full of life, she wouldn't want to be just holding on.

In an odd way, I was pulling my inner head coach back out of me. Not in the sense real life is analogous to a game. It was more the analogy of handling emotions. And not letting the emotions get in the way of making correct decisions. Coaching helped me do that. It's the first time I had to stay focused with a truly broken heart, stay focused and ask, *What's in the best interest of Kaye? What's her best quality of life?*

At what point does anyone say, "No more"?

It was the toughest decision I've ever had to make. On anything. Ever. As a father, I wanted to make sure my daughters didn't have any regrets from what were inevitably their mother's last days. I didn't want Kaye's sisters to have regrets. I didn't want to have any, either.

After a while, Kaye didn't talk much, if at all. We'd sit with her, or talk with her, and she'd make eye contact. But those blue eyes would well with tears. It was as if she had so much to say but was frustrated by her inability to express herself.

We could all see how dire things were, but we were told by the nurses that we should go about our activities as we normally would. Based on their projections, Kaye might live like this for several more months. As awkward and strange as it was, we tried to resume some aspects of our lives.

Meagan and some of her friends had a trip planned to Thailand, but she decided not to go. Instead, she visited with Kevin and his family in Ontario.

In July, Kaye's health surprisingly and rapidly deteriorated. I wanted us all to be together. I remember calling Meagan in Canada and telling her that she needed to get back to Raleigh immediately. She rushed to get a flight out of Detroit for Raleigh. Kevin wasn't too far behind: While Meagan got a flight, Kevin got in his car and drove the eleven hours from Amherstburg to Raleigh.

Pam, an incredible hospice nurse, was at the house with us. She and her staff monitored Kaye's breathing, and they let us know that it wouldn't be long. I knew when Meagan was coming in from the airport, so I was there to pick her up. I can't remember ever driving faster than I did that day.

As soon as Meagan and I arrived at the house, we went to Kaye's room. Our whole family was there as we said goodbye and Kaye took her last breath. It was Friday, July 23.

The year was already hazy for all of us. There was so much to process. We all had our raw emotions and questions, too many to be dealt with in a short time. What could any of us have done differently? Should we have brought in hospice sooner? Should we have made more inclusive family decisions? How had a "minor procedure" in February gotten to a final goodbye in July?

It was different for each of us because Kaye had held deep and uniquely different relationships with each of us. We'd all been in the same house for years, experiencing similar events in different ways. Now we'd have to do that again, spread all over the country to live and grieve.

Kevin was going to play for the Los Angeles Kings, and Meagan was going there with him. Lauren had a job in New York to work for Edelman. Lindsay, at Elon now, was about to start school in a couple of weeks. I'd be between Raleigh and New York.

I didn't know how any of us would handle Kaye's passing. I didn't. I'd been through a year where I'd tried to will my father and wife through sickness. It didn't happen. I can't tell you that I didn't have questions. Was it too soon for Kaye? Yes. It was too soon. But that's what life throws at you.

I'd never imagined that the same Bunn, North Carolina, church where we'd gotten married in 1983 would be the same place I'd part with Kaye at a memorial service in 2010. We'd never gotten the chance to enjoy our to-do lists. We'd never gotten the chance to casually and freely figure out our early fifties together.

I'd always thought the good Lord is never going to hand you something you can't handle. I've always believed that there's a reason why—but sitting in our empty house in Raleigh, I didn't know the reason. I'd often look up and say, "You're testing me right now. I know you are. What else do you want to throw at me?"

18

A Family in Transition

At the end of August 2010, I sat alone in our Raleigh home and stared. *Our* home. It had been ours, with every part of it touched by Kaye. Now with her gone and the girls based in different parts of the country, I thought, *Why am I coming back here?*

I was set to begin my fourth season as a CBS analyst, which would begin the routine I'd known with Kaye: Monday through Friday in Raleigh, weekend in New York. But why do that now? I'd return to a beautiful, completely empty home. It was too much house for one person.

I remember being out with my best friend, George, one night in Raleigh, and he brought up dating, something that hadn't crossed my mind in thirty-plus years. The last time I'd thought about dating was in the late 1970s, when I'd first noticed Kaye at NC State. And that had developed so naturally I wouldn't be able to repeat it if I tried.

"Well, are you available to date?" George asked. "A friend of Judy's asked on behalf of another friend."

"George, uh, I don't know how this goes. How's the whole process supposed to work?"

I didn't think about being with anyone after twenty-seven years of marriage with Kaye. I wasn't necessarily for or against it. It just wasn't on my mind. From the time of the diagnosis to my father's death and then Kaye's, I didn't have many days where I thought of anything besides what I could do to help them. I had full-time workers assisting me with Kaye, and that allowed me to take care of daily business. Before that, it was hard for me to leave the house for any reason. One of those rare days was in April 2010. Knowing that I had professionals with Kaye, I went to a one-night event in West Hollywood in support of the Iraq and Afghanistan Veterans of America. It was at the legendary rock club the Viper Room. I talked with a few people there, including one of the musicians who performed. Her name was Veronica Stigeler, and she went by "V."

We had a good conversation, and V told me about her life and career. She mentioned some tough things going on in her life, and I offered my advice on how to manage your life through tumultuous times. Suddenly, I'd been able to speak on the subject with conviction. It was good for me to talk with someone else about something else.

As I prepared for the 2010 NFL season, I decided to alter my Raleigh–New York travel schedule. I rented an apartment in a New York high-rise on the Upper East Side. If I needed to arrive in the city earlier than usual or stay an extra night, I'd do that. I'd never thought of spending more time in New York, but the more I was able to walk around the city and see different parts of it, I liked it.

In September, on our first *NFL Today* show, I briefly spoke about losing Kaye. The support I got from the network, coaches, players, and fans was incredible. I was so appreciative of all the people who reached out with acts of kindness. One of the most powerful gestures after Kaye died was that of my colleague JB and Tony Dungy calling together and praying for me.

I knew it was going to be a challenging year for my girls and me, but I also knew what their mother would say to us: *Don't dwell in self-pity. Come on. A lot of people have things worse than you do.* The difficult part is knowing that's true but still processing the emotions and questions and new realities of life that block you from that truth. There's not one universal way to do it, to go through the emotional terrain so you can move on. Everyone goes through different paths on the way there and arrives at different points. I realized all three of my daughters needed to work through the stages that led to their mother's death. And now they had other questions, too.

When I was in New York, I'd usually talk to V. She'd grown up in Montclair, New Jersey, and lived in New York. I considered her a friend. The more I talked with her, the more ease I had with discussions about anything, including extremely difficult conversations. As we talked, she revealed more and more about who she was, beyond her musical branding.

That's one of the things that got the girls' attention. Veronica was Queen V for the stage. If you googled her, and they did, there were risqué pictures of a hard rocker with spiked hair. She'd shared stages and collaborations with artists such as Twisted Sister, Bon Jovi, Tom Morello, and Vernon Reid. She was also fifteen years younger than I was. The girls weren't happy. What had happened to their father?

They hadn't met V, and they didn't want to. Not then. They just weren't ready.

When I talked with her, yes, I saw she was the rock-and-roll girl. But she had these other sides to her. She could be with so-called distinguished company and hold her own gracefully. We could go into a SoHo restaurant and she'd connect with strangers there, too. She could relate to people. It was a gift. She was a good person.

I could see V was strong when she needed to be strong, but inside she was a nurturer. Smart. Talented. Well traveled. Her father was Swiss German and her mother was from Algiers. Her family sometimes traveled to Switzerland during the summer. V spoke

French and a little Hebrew, too. She could easily have thrived in corporate America, but she'd gotten the music bug when she was five years old and it never let her go.

This was not the Queen V that the world knew. She'd been in a tough marriage, and we talked at length about her experiences. Neither of us held back any of the issues or insecurities that had been—or still were—part of the journey.

As I'd said to George in Raleigh, I didn't plan to date anyone. I didn't know what that was. But I guess *this* is what it was. V and I saw each other all the time, and as 2010 became 2011, I had more reason to spend a bulk of my time in New York City. We found ourselves becoming inseparable friends.

Meagan, as the oldest, has always had the gift of intuitiveness. She has a knack for displaying intelligence and calm, even when others appear to be frazzled. I used to say that if you went to one of her games and didn't look at the score, you'd have no idea what kind of game she or her team was having. Down by 20 or up, Meagan would take care of business. She'd finished her Princeton career as the second-leading scorer in program history. On the court and off, she knew how to get things done.

She came up with an idea for her sisters and me. In March, she wanted us to go together on an African safari. We hadn't spent time together and talked since Kaye died. The trip would be an opportunity for us to vacation together, bond, and honestly share our grieving experiences.

We flew into Kilimanjaro Airport in Tanzania. Our first two nights were spent on the Serengeti in a custom tent. The next two were at a campsite. And the final two were at a five-star hotel at the top of the Ngorongoro Crater. We'd go down into the crater during the day and then come back at night.

The aesthetics of the trip were everything you might imagine and more. The African landscape was breathtaking. It was educational to observe the Maasai culture and to learn about the scenery all around us. I remember the first night, when our tour guide gave us a dose of reality as we sat around a bonfire. It was a magical scene, with people cooking and talking around the fire.

"You can't see them right now, but there are hyenas surrounding the perimeter. They're watching," he said. "Once the fire goes out, they're going to come up. They'll be looking for food. They won't come into your tent. But you also don't want to leave the tent."

Got it. No problem.

On that trip, during those six nights, I spent two nights with each of my daughters. They each had a different relationship with their mom, so sometimes what they needed to hear and understand was different from what concerned their sisters. One thing they all had in common was concern about my relationship with V.

"Dad, who is this that you're seeing? We're worried about you."

I explained they had to get to know her before understanding why I was seeing her. The pictures that they'd seen online didn't begin to capture the good person that she was. They had to meet her, I knew that was going to take some time, and that was all right.

"Did you meet her before Mom died?"

That had bothered all of them. I made it clear that my interactions with V in 2010 were wholly appropriate and friendly. "Your mother and I went through a lifetime together, and nothing will ever take that away. And I was there with her, fighting to help her, to the very end."

"But you just . . . moved on."

I completely understood, from their perspective, why they'd say that. Kaye's death had hit all of them hard. They're all such wonderful, positive daughters. They held on to hope. And they never thought things could turn so quickly. Kaye had been diagnosed in

February, and she was gone just five months later. How could I just bounce back from that?

"Let me tell you something, girls," I said. "I started grieving the day I got the three options we had to cure her. I started grieving right then. I knew it was a very, very slim chance she would survive. But I was going to fight as she was going to fight."

We spoke about grieving itself and what we'd learned from it. We were a family of talkers, and some people with that background can talk about grief and get through it. Some people have a problem talking about it at all. It takes a while for them. For the communicators, at times verbalizing things is part of the healing.

With Kaye, I'd felt that I'd let her down. And others down. I did everything I could and tried to deal with all options as someone whose primary objective was getting to the place that was best for Kaye. My daughters felt we could have sought hospice assistance earlier and that they could have been more involved in the decision-making. I thought it was a good point, and I could have handled it differently.

We were all sorting through feelings of sorrow and abandonment. Meagan was getting married in the summer. Lauren was at the beginning of her career. Lindsay was at a new school. These were all areas where Kaye had uncanny insight and could have been an invaluable resource for all of us.

We learned on our trip that some strong fiber is in our family. We knew that time would make us all better. My daughters also seemed to be flexible on meeting V. Of course, the two younger sisters volunteered Meagan to go first.

Before Meagan could meet her, I had to bring V with me to my brief return to coaching. I'd portray the head coach of the fictional Gotham Rogues in *The Dark Knight Rises*. The filming took place in Pittsburgh, at Heinz Field, and it gave me an opportunity to see many of the players I'd coached. They were also in the film. I saw Hines Ward, Troy Polamalu, Aaron Smith, and Ben Roethlisberger. They'd all added one more Super Bowl title after the 2008 season, bringing the franchise total to six.

It was hard for me to believe that it was 2011. I hadn't coached in the league in five years. I'd get phone calls from owners, and I'd listen. Then I'd honestly ask myself, "Can I give all I have to this situation? Because that's what it will require." I could never get myself to yes.

While I was in Pittsburgh, I told V I had someone she absolutely needed to meet: my mother. I wasn't testing V at all, because I already realized how much I enjoyed spending time with her. But I also knew my mom would see things few others could. She was the most intuitive person I knew. She had a great feel for people. My drive came from my father; my instincts came from my mother, who was open to people and also a great judge of character.

She met V and was quickly at ease. She gave me a look and a nod. If Mom didn't trust someone, she'd tell you. She liked V.

In August 2011, five months after the safari, Meagan met V in Hermosa Beach, California. V didn't know exactly where the conversation would go, but she believed it was important for her to say at least four things to Meagan:

—Thank you for taking the time to meet with me.
—I'm sorry for what has happened to your family the last year.
—I already love you because I love your dad.
—There's no pressure for this relationship; I'm here any way you'll have me.

They talked for a while after that, and it was a positive conversation. A couple months later, in New York, V and Lauren talked for the first time. And when Lindsay was on Christmas break, she and V had their talk as well.

I had no illusions about what would happen with these relationships. Maybe all four of them agreed to meet because of their love for me, and that would be the extent of it.

In 2012, on the verge of beginning my sixth season as a CBS broadcaster based in New York, I decided to buy in New York. Actually, *we* decided to buy in New York. V and I moved in together, on the Upper East Side, to find out what we really had. I always thought it was a good idea to move in with someone before marrying the person. I'd advised my girls to do that, and I know it's not something most fathers would say. But my view is that you need to know someone, 24-7, to see how the person lives—and see if you can live with that.

I had a good idea of how it would go with V. I felt that in a short time we'd reached total transparency in our relationship. It was refreshing, stunning, and—respectfully—familiar. V was secure in her individuality and the depth of our relationship on its own. So I was able to tell her, without scaring her, that she and Kaye had a lot of similarities. A lot. They could have been related.

I felt that I'd found one soul mate with Kaye, and another with V.

One day I was driving Lindsay back to Elon. It's a nice drive from Raleigh, taking a little over an hour. I always enjoyed these times with my daughters, just to hear what they were thinking and seeing. Lindsay raised a topic that surprised me.

"Dad, I know you're still seeing V. Do you love her?"

"Yes, Linds. I do love her."

"If you love her, you should marry her. You're too young not to have someone with you the rest of your life."

19

The Wedding

On most nights, V and I like to go to our balcony to look out at the New York City skyline. In TV language, it's our own post-game show. We'll sit there, talk through our days, and look ahead to what's next. On one summer night in 2013, it led to the most unusual party we've ever thrown.

Lindsay planted the seed in 2012 when she mentioned I should marry V. Then Lindsay got her own proposal. Her boyfriend, Ryan Kelly, surprised her with it in 2013. As we sat on the balcony, we decided that we should also do it soon. Why were we even waiting?

My daughters had grown much closer to V in the past three years. They'd seen the V I told them about and even more. The four of them also shared their own connection as strong women. After Kaye passed, I realized I'd tried to be there for my daughters as a mother and a father. But I could never be their mother. I tried to be there for them and still be me. V never tried to be their mother, either. But she'd developed three distinct relationships with them, for which they (and I) are eternally grateful.

My own mother, almost ninety, was also a fan of V's. V had a small-venue show in Lawrenceville, just outside downtown Pittsburgh. My mother and brothers went to the club to see it. I tried to give Mom some earplugs because I anticipated the music might get a little loud for her taste.

"Oh, Billy"—she swatted my hand away—"I don't need these things. I love her. I love her music. I want to hear the lyrics."

We definitely had everyone's blessing. It was time. We thought about 2014—the same year as Lindsay's wedding—so we had to check with her to see if it was all right. She responded with pure joy. V and I then decided we'd buy the rings and agreed one day, when she wasn't expecting it, I'd officially propose.

V and I enjoy walking through Central Park, admiring its architectural marvels. It has some beautiful archways, and I thought doing it under one of them would be special. I picked a Friday night, October 11, to propose. Somewhere. I thought it would be Central Park.

"Let's go for a walk," I said to V.

"Sure."

As we headed out, though, it was too windy for the perfect proposal in the park. I decided to adjust. I had the ring with me, so I could do it anywhere.

"Do you want to have dinner?" I asked.

She agreed again. Perfect. Near our place is a restaurant called the East Pole. We'd get a nice table, just the two of us, and I'd propose. As I thought about what I was going to say, a couple sat down right next to us.

It didn't feel right. On to the next plan.

"Let's go home after this, get a bottle of wine," I said.

Even when V said it was her friend's birthday and V planned to pop in to say hello, that didn't spoil a great plan in my head. As V was out, I'd get some candles, light them, and surprise her with the nice scene as she walked in. I lit all the candles and had everything perfectly set up. I got ready as I heard her coming and then . . .

Whoosh! The opened door, on a windy night, blew out the candles in an instant.

So V came into a dark room. "What are you doing?"

I remember smiling. "Oh, I was just going to ask you to marry me. Will you marry me?"

"Oh, hell yes. Absolutely."

Then we laughed. Then she cried.

We knew what we wanted, so it became our project and we planned it quickly. It would be in New York at the St. Regis Hotel. We wouldn't hold back in celebrating the love that we'd found. This would be a long weekend of joining two families and two cultures—sports and music—together.

When the week arrived, we basked in every moment. V has a great song, "Honest," in which she sings about those deeply connected (and vulnerable) moments of a relationship. It's when you know, for sure, that you're ready for total commitment, but you haven't yet articulated that and neither has the other person. She captured it beautifully in the lyrics:

WE STARTED SOMETHING AND I DON'T WANT TO STOP
BUT I DON'T WANT YOU FALLING FOR SOMEONE I'M NOT
SO IF I CAN BE HONEST, ALL I WANT IS TO BE LOVED
LOVED BY YOU

Exactly.

We were both there, and I felt that we'd been there for a while. We found we had the same interests. Music—music has always played a big part in everything that I've done. I love putting on an iPod and listening to music. And V loves all the different genres. It's interesting: She went from being this hard rocker to writing love songs. I went from being a fan of music to having a deeper appreciation for what goes into writing a song and producing it.

The day before the wedding, we had a rehearsal dinner at the St. Regis. We had a cocktail reception at our apartment on Friday night and then had a bus take us all down the street to the hotel. Once there, we gathered at a huge table. Anyone who was moved could stand and say a few words. The first one was Lindsay, in an incredibly welcoming gesture. V's father, Fred, in good Swiss tradition presented me with the family coat of arms—his way of saying that I was part of their clan. Her mother, Helena, was also welcoming and kind.

The next day, the wedding itself, told the story via the guests. I told V it was like the three rivers in Pittsburgh—the Allegheny, Ohio, and Monongahela—a convergence of all our rivers. Music. Sports. New Jersey. Pittsburgh. Raleigh. Friends from college. A lot of my CBS colleagues were there, along with Marty and NFL commissioner Roger Goodell. Chet Fuhrman, from my first Steelers coaching staff, was there as well. This time he didn't need to report if the room was tuned in or not. It was a great celebration. And among all the sports stars in attendance there were musicians, with multicolored hair, bold attire, unaffected by the sports celebrities in the room. Even our wedding cake told our story. It was topped with a football that had a long guitar neck, tuning posts and string trees included, protruding from it.

One of the funniest and most sincere moments was when a guest, clearly not a sports fan, sat next to Hall of Fame quarterback Dan Marino.

"So, what do you do?" the guest asked.

"I played football." Marino was a little surprised.

"Were you any good?"

That was an actual question. I'll never forget Marino's *Is-this-happening?* expression.

My mom attended, along with V's parents, Fred and Helena. George and Judy Richards were there, too, with George serving as my best man. My daughters, all married or soon to be, were genuinely happy for us. I quoted one of my favorite lines from *When Harry Met Sally*: "When you realize you want to spend the rest of your life with somebody, you want the rest of your life to start as soon as possible."

We had a deejay from Nashville whose specialty was spinning vinyl. He played a lot of classic rock and my go-to stuff from the '70s. I danced as freely as I had in college, a dance that V has dubbed The Bill.

With everyone booked at the hotel, the party went well into the next morning. For a quickly planned celebration, it touched on everything that we'd wanted. The next day, we left for a month-long honeymoon. I'd retired from the Steelers after the 2006 season and thought of traveling then. Eight years later, it was the itinerary of a lifetime:

Capri. Sorrento. Venice. Rome. Geneva. Bern, to spend time with family V had there. We finished the trip in Israel with more family. It was all phenomenal.

I came back refreshed and energized. I needed to be. I was well into my media career, and things were about to ramp up in the fall. After Lindsay's wedding in August, I got ready for the 2014 season. It was the first year CBS had *Thursday Night Football*, so I was part of that with JB and Deion Sanders. I also continued my *NFL Today* work on Sundays. It meant my Mondays were spent talking with Shawn Robbins, my producer for *Thursday Night Football*. Tuesdays,

I talked with Drew Kaliski, the producer for *NFL Today*. Wednesday was for traveling. Thursday was the game.

No, I wasn't "coaching busy." But I was media busy. And with the changes in my life, I wondered if that's who I was now. A former coach who was still inspired to talk about the game and strategy on TV . . . excited to talk with contacts around the league, and to condense football concepts into digestible bites for fans . . . excited by all of that, but not getting back into the lifestyle.

The sport had been good to me, and the life I'd gotten out of it was a blessing. I often told myself I'd answered all of the questions about myself with football. I'd worked with my hometown team, coached great players and men, won a lot of games, won a Super Bowl. I told myself I was at peace if nothing else happened.

But it wasn't true.

20

Operation Gold Jacket

My mother turned ninety-three in 2016. She was an example that you never have to stop growing, no matter what your age. The way she approached life was a lifelong reminder you should always be open to a pleasant surprise, because one is possible at any time.

I wasn't shocked that Mom loved V. I was a little surprised when she saw her perform in Lawrenceville—without the earplugs—in 2013. But there's no way I ever thought that Dorothy Cowher would turn into a V roadie in '16 and '17. And even bring a nursing-home friend along with her a couple of times. But that's exactly what happened. Mom saw V play twice at the Barn in Sewickley Heights, just outside Pittsburgh. She also traveled to V's hometown, Montclair, New Jersey, to see another show.

"I'm so happy for you, Billy," Mom said. "We really love V. And your father would have loved her, too."

In early 2019, before she reached her ninety-sixth birthday, my mother started to have some issues with her colon. I remember flying to Pittsburgh in April to see her. I thought this was a repeat of what I'd seen from my father nearly ten years earlier. She was told she needed to get out of bed to get her circulation going, but she wouldn't do it.

"I'll do it tomorrow," she'd say, and not do it then, either.

On the day that I was scheduled to leave town, I walked into her room. Once again, Mom was unpredictable. She was out of bed, sitting in her chair, alert as ever.

"Mom," I said excitedly, "you're out of bed."

She responded as if this were hardly new information. "Yes. But my hair still doesn't look right. I'll get it done next week."

I sat with my brothers, Dale and Doug, and we began telling old stories. Some of the familiar humorous ones came up, and the three of us sat there laughing away. We didn't notice our mother watching us closely, as she knew—and we didn't—that we were giving her the goodbye gift that she wanted: laughter.

As soon as I left town, I learned she'd refused to take her medicine and had stopped eating. Her final words to her nurse were "It was great to see my boys laughing again." After that she went to sleep and never woke up.

Ninety-five years old. If I can reach that age and have her peace of mind and wholeness, sign me up right now.

When she died in April 2019, my mother had witnessed all that I'd ever hoped she would. She'd been alive to see five small children who knew me as Gramps and V as VeeVee. She'd been there for my first game coaching the Steelers, the Super Bowl win, and the final game and win of my career.

I'd gotten used to saying that's all I wanted, but one more thing was out there. It was a spot in the Pro Football Hall of Fame in Canton, Ohio—located close enough to Crafton that Mom could have gone there and back as part of a day trip.

On December 19, 2019, V and I had just finished a workout when I checked my phone. It had some alerts and texts, congratulating me on becoming a 2020 Hall of Fame finalist. The Centennial Class to the Hall would include ten players and two coaches. I used my skepticism to hide how much I wanted to be in.

"Well, I wasn't always a media darling when I coached. I had some media run-ins every now and then. And they're the ones who are voting on this," I explained to V.

But this panel of voters wasn't composed of people who had covered me; it was people who had, in some cases, strategized *against* me, including Bill Belichick, Ozzie Newsome, Dick LeBeau, and Bill Polian.

I couldn't lie to myself: I wanted to make the Hall. These were the best players, coaches, and contributors in the history of football. It would be an honor for my name to be mentioned with theirs. I called my friend Pat Kirwan, a former NFL coach and executive, and asked him to let me know if or when he heard anything.

By now it was January 2020, with the vote to take place on a Thursday, January 9. I called Pat on Thursday and asked if he'd heard anything, and he said he hadn't. Two days later, Saturday the eleventh, V and I had our morning coffee together. No one had said anything to me.

"V, I don't think I'm getting in. I want you to know I'm at peace with it. These are football people making the decisions. If they deem someone else worthy of getting in, then I'm happy for that person."

I worked the Titans-Ravens AFC Divisional playoff game that night for CBS. Before each game, we have a production meeting. This is usually full of life—debate, jokes, chatter. But that night, JB, Boomer Esiason, Phil Simms, Nate Burleson, Drew Kaliski, and even Pat Kirwan didn't mention the Hall. Not a word about the vote. I knew I wasn't getting in then. These guys seemed as if they felt sorry for me.

I thought, *They're giving me that "respectful" space.*

Instead of talk about the Hall vote, I was given notice I'd be doing a segment with Phil from what we call "the back wall" in the studio. It's a different location, and I was told the big bosses wanted to experiment with how it looked on camera. David Berson and Sean McManus, the top executives, would be watching. I'd better be on my game.

As I started talking with Phil about Baltimore quarterback Lamar Jackson, the back studio door opened and I saw the six-nine David Baker walk in. When you see Baker, you know you're about to get into the Hall of Fame. I briefly closed my eyes. I couldn't believe this was happening. I'd already had closure on this, but now this was the dream—only on live television.

I looked past Baker and saw V and Meagan standing there. They'd arrived together, and both had tears in their eyes. We'd all come a long way as a family. It had been almost nine years since our safari, before the girls had been married. And I hadn't been married to V. It was hard to remember specifics of when that was because she was part of the family now.

My mother had been right to expect those surprises. Life is full of them. No one would have guessed V and Meagan would develop the kind of relationship that sometimes has Meagan and Kevin dancing onstage during a Queen V show.

This honor had so many great aspects, starting with CBS knowing the Cowhers well enough to understand no one in our family is capable of keeping a secret. If a surprise party or anything else is planned, don't tell me. I love seeing surprises but am incapable of staying quiet about them, and most of our family is the same way. Maybe that's why Jen Sabatelle, CBS's communications executive, waited for me to be safely out of the house and on the air before calling V, who then called Meagan.

It was also great to share the moment with all the people, on air and behind the scenes, who help produce our CBS content. I found out later that all week there'd been a CBS group email with "Operation Gold Jacket" as its subject. This stealth email had been passed around to get ideas on the best segments and times to bring in Baker.

I was stunned. When JB asked me to give a speech, I do know that words came out of my mouth. But I didn't know what I was saying. I turned to Nate during the break. "What did I just say? Did that make sense?"

"You were good, Coach."

All of that took place around 7:50 eastern time. When I checked my phone, the very first message came in at 7:51: "Congratulations, Coach. I'm so happy for you."

It was from Ben Roethlisberger. That speaks volumes about where we were. Through the years, he'd sent multiple messages saying he wished he'd played for me later in his career. He says he would have appreciated me more than he did in the first few years. I only coached him for three seasons. He's had a tremendous career, and Mike Tomlin's done a great job with him.

I also heard from Barry Foster. Early in my Pittsburgh career, we'd had tense moments and he didn't always agree with the things I told him to do. But he sent a text, and before that a beautiful handwritten letter, thanking me for all I tried to teach him. Those are the stories that make you smile. Yes, you want players to get it in the moment. But when they're done playing, they're men who are trying to live productive lives. And if they figure that out, it's more important than the game.

I glanced at my phone during the show, and the texts poured in. I'd look down and quickly back up. The texts would be at two hundred . . . then four hundred . . . then six hundred. It was surreal. You get into this game because you have a passion for playing it. Then you acquire some knowledge you want to share, which becomes coaching and leading. Along the way, you have an opportunity to shape lives. It's humbling. I knew it would take a while, but it was important for me to return each of those texts. Even if it would take a month to do it, I was going to return them. I wanted to thank everyone who had any role in my success. Many of those texts were from players who'd bought in and allowed themselves to be coached.

They allowed me to coach them at football, in theory, but I was also coaching what I thought worked. I was trying to communicate principles that can be applied in several areas of life. I've talked with my daughter Lauren about this. I love talking to her about leadership. People from all over the country have recruited her, and she's worked in London, Boston, New York, and Denver. She now heads a department with sixty-five to seventy people under her. As I tell her, what she does still has to come back to dealing with people.

That word *people* repeats regardless of the industry. One of the friends I've made recently, John Esposito, is the head of Warner Music in Nashville. He talks to me about managing artists, and I talk about managing players. He has Kenny Chesney and Blake Shelton; I've had Hines Ward and Troy Polamalu. We're all trying to figure out what the team is and the best way to inspire it.

For example, as a manager, you're not trying to change people, but you can't let them change you. Give them what they need to hear and not what they want. Be compassionate, understanding, and a good listener. Those things all work, whether it's in coaching, the arts, the tech world, or running a hospital. Whatever it may be, the same core values need to exist for you to have something flourish.

||||||||||||

Now that I'm officially in the Hall, I think of those people who have shaped me for this moment but can't be present for it. Kaye, Mr. Rooney, Marty, my mom and dad. They all understood the multiple things that took place along the way. They understood.

These were the people who gave me a sense of self-worth, meaning, and purpose. They knew where I'd come from and, in some cases, how unlikely it is for me to be here.

When I think of the Hall of Fame, there's one person I want to present me in Canton, Ohio. It's Art Rooney. I was thirty-four years old and a brash coach when I began my Steelers career. As I progressed as a coach there, I became better at the job, but I also became a better person, husband, and father. With the Steelers, it wasn't solely about wins and losses. It was also about growth. Being there for fifteen years, there's no question about the impact the Rooney family had on me. I've already told Art that he's the perfect man for the presenting job.

I also believe making the Hall has helped me face my insecurities. A lot of people who are successful are also highly insecure; I'm no exception. Do you know why? I realized that I had a fear of failure and losing. Of course I wanted to win, but the fear of losing was intense. When I didn't make the Hall, it was technically a loss, and it tapped into my fear of rejection and losing.

I didn't realize how much it mattered to me until I received the honor. Now I feel freer, and I don't find myself even subtly trying to prove that I belong or need validation. It's just the opposite. My days are spent in appreciation of the life I've been given.

Essentially, that's what keeps me standing at sunset. V will ask, "Why do you always want to go outside at the end of a day?"

It's a good question, and she's right: On most nights, I'll ask her to come with me to the balcony and look out at New York City. Why do I want to go out there every night? My answer might change, just as life does, but for now it's this:

At the end of a day, it's another day I'll never get back. I just want to be so thankful to have a chance . . . to be this kid from Crafton who's sitting on a balcony in New York City; to have friendships that inspire and educate me; to be someone who gave my energy to football as an eight-year-old kid and then, in turn, have it give so much more to me as an adult; to be a man who is surrounded by the unconditional love of his children, grandchildren, and wife.

In retrospect, I'm thankful for all the lessons I've received along the way.

God's never said, "Here's your life. You get a contract. It's loaded with everything you want." No, it doesn't work like that. You can't take the years you think you're going to get and chart them out. You take what you're given and try to fashion the best life you can out of it.

I'm a lucky guy. A blessed guy. So thankful for the path that God has put me on. Yet, I still know there's more. More to learn. More room to grow. More dreams to realize. More people to help.

I can't wait to get started.

Acknowledgments

At every stage of my life, I've been surrounded by people who have brought out the best in me. This book-writing process has led me to reflect on and acknowledge them all.

In some ways, writing this book has been similar to life itself. That is, you don't always plan to do something, but events unfold in such a way that opportunities present themselves.

A few things in the last couple of years made me think about writing: my 2019 induction into the Steelers' Hall of Honor, my 2020 election into the Pro Football Hall of Fame, and the pandemic. All of them, for distinct reasons, led to a period of pronounced introspection and reflection. I wanted to write a book that describes the game I love, but also acknowledges the people I love, the ones who helped me get into this position. I appreciate you all.

Thank you to my brothers, Dale and Doug, along with all my teachers, friends, and teammates at Carlynton High School. When I became head coach of the Steelers in 1992, my modest goal was to hang on to the job and not get fired before my twentieth high school reunion. Well, I made it. I hope I was able to make my school and town proud, because I was always proud to represent you.

I'm grateful for all my coaches and teammates at NC State. The area and the school changed my life. I became a better player and leader there, and it's also where I met Kaye.

While I wasn't drafted out of college, I was fortunate to play five NFL years in Cleveland and Philadelphia. I want to thank all the coaches and players in both cities. Playing in the NFL was a dream, and you all helped me reach it.

I was an assistant coach in two cities, Cleveland and Kansas City. Thanks to all the coaches who generously shared what they knew and, in turn, accelerated my development. I'm also thankful that I had dozens upon dozens of players who were eager to be coached, enthusiastic about football, and willing to sacrifice so we could win.

In Pittsburgh, I had the job of a lifetime for fifteen seasons. Thank you to everyone who's had any connection to the Steelers franchise: ownership, front office, coaches, players, support staff, and fans. There's not an organization quite like it in the NFL. Keep waving The Terrible Towel. The black and gold is with me, in me, forever.

It's hard to believe that I've worked at CBS nearly as long as I coached the Steelers. I appreciate everyone at the network. Thanks for creating an atmosphere in which coming to work is always fun.

My team at Octagon has me covered in all areas. It's a relief to know that I have a quick-thinking and committed group working with me at all times. Thanks for all that you do.

I'm appreciative of the hardworking staff at Atria Books. From the beginning of this journey, you've shown a genuine interest in telling and sharing my story, and I'm honored that your focus has remained on that throughout.

Finally, thank you to Michael Holley. Our collaboration was eye-opening. Your ability to take me down memory lane allowed me to reveal myself like I never have. You're a true friend; you're a true pro. I look forward to many more projects together.

Photo Credits

About the Authors

Bill Cowher coached the Pittsburgh Steelers from 1992 through 2006, winning Super Bowl XL. He's one of only two coaches in NFL history to lead his team to the playoffs in each of his first six seasons and, at the time, was the youngest coach to ever lead a team to the Super Bowl. Cowher currently is a cohost of CBS's *NFL Today*. In 2020, he was inducted into the Pro Football Hall of Fame. Cowher lives in New York with wife, Veronica. You can follow him on Twitter @CowherCBS.

Michael Holley is a six-time *New York Times* bestselling author and former *Boston Globe* columnist. He currently works for NBC Sports and cohosts the popular show *Brother from Another* on Peacock. Holley is a graduate of Point Park University in Pittsburgh and also is a professor of journalism at Boston University. He lives in Massachusetts. You can follow him on Twitter @MichaelSHolley.